Metaphor and Gender in Busi

CW00902878

Metaphor and Gender in Business Media Discourse

A Critical Cognitive Study

Veronika Koller

© Veronika Koller 2004

All rights reserved. No reproduction, copy or transmission of this publication may be made without written permission.

No paragraph of this publication may be reproduced, copied or transmitted save with written permission or in accordance with the provisions of the Copyright, Designs and Patents Act 1988, or under the terms of any licence permitting limited copying issued by the Copyright Licensing Agency, 90 Tottenham Court Road, London W1T 4LP.

Any person who does any unauthorized act in relation to this publication may be liable to criminal prosecution and civil claims for damages.

The author has asserted her right to be identified as the author of this work in accordance with the Copyright, Designs and Patents Act 1988.

First published in hardcover 2004

First published in paperback 2008 by
PALGRAVE MACMILLAN
Houndmills, Basingstoke, Hampshire RG21 6XS, and 175 Fifth Avenue, New York, N.Y. 10010
Companies and representatives throughout the world

PALGRAVE MACMILLAN is the global academic imprint of the Palgrave Macmillan division of St. Martin's Press, LLC and of Palgrave Macmillan Ltd. Macmillan® is a registered trademark in the United States, United Kingdom and other countries. Palgrave is registered trademark in the European Union and other countries.

ISBN-13: 978-1-4039-3291-4   hardback
ISBN-10: 1-4039-3291-3   hardback
ISBN-13: 978-0-230-21707-2   paperback
ISBN-10: 0-230-21707-9   paperback

This book is printed on paper suitable for recycling and made from fully managed and sustained forest sources. Logging, pulping and manufacturing processes are expected to conform to the environmental regulations of the country of origin.

A catalogue record for this book is available from the British Library.

Library of Congress Cataloging-in-Publication Data
Koller, Veronika, 1973–
    Metaphor and gender in business media discourse : a critical cognitive study / Veronika Koller.
        p. cm.
    Includes bibliographical references and index.
    ISBN 1-4039-3291-3 (cloth)   ISBN 0-230-21707-9 (pbk)
    1. Mass media and language.   2. Metaphor.   3. Language and languages – Sex differences.   4. Business – Language.   5. Discourse analysis.   I. Title.

P96.L34K65 2004
302.23'01'4 – dc22   2003065494

Printed and bound in Great Britain by
CPI Antony Rowe Ltd, Chippenham and Eastbourne

'As time and scars go by, one finally arrives at a book, some with twenty, some with seventy.'

(Eco, 1995, p. 52)

This book is dedicated to Bianca Rusu, for giving to me all the time in the world while leaving me unscarred.

Contents

List of Figures

List of Tables

Acknowledgements

'Portal combat' (pp. 98–100) reproduced from 17 January 2000 issue of *Business Week* by special permission, ©2000 the McGraw-Hill Companies, Inc. 'Store wars' (pp. 100–1) reproduced by kind permission of and ©The Economist Newspaper Limited, London (9 December 2000). 'A game of inches' (pp. 101–3) reproduced by kind permission of and ©2001 Time Inc. All rights reserved. 'Labelled as the devil of the consumer society' (pp. 103–4) reproduced by kind permission of and © The Financial Times (25 April 2001). 'The big grab' (pp. 153–5) reproduced from 24 January 2000 issue of *Business Week* by special permission, copyright ©2000 the McGraw-Hill Companies, Inc. 'How mergers go wrong' (pp. 155–7) reproduced by kind permission of and ©The Economist Newspaper Limited, London (22 July 2000). 'Gorilla in the midst' (pp. 157–8) reproduced by kind permission of and ©2000 Time Inc. All rights reserved. 'Dotcoms devoured' (pp. 158–60) reproduced by kind permission of and ©The Financial Times (23 October 2000).

List of Abbreviations

MA   Mergers and acquisitions
MS   Marketing and sales
BW   *Business Week*
EC   *Economist*
FO   *Fortune*
FT   *Financial Times*

Note: Sources in brackets (for example, MA EC 5) denote the corpus, the publication and the article as listed in the Appendix.

British words listed also include US variant spellings.

1
Introduction:
Masculinized Metaphors

> War metaphors played a great part in [the seminars]: by definition, we
> lived in a hostile environment and it was my task to bring forth in the
> participants that natural aggressiveness which can make them more
> committed, more efficient and thus eventually more productive.
>
> (Emmanuel, 2000, p. 10)

Even the most cursory glance at any business magazine or newspaper
will leave the reader stunned by the abundance of metaphoric language
to be found there. Just consider the following random sample:

> From hardball pricing tactics that have knocked rivals back on their
> heels to a capital-spending war chest that's the largest in telecom,
> he's determined to transform what was once just another sleepy
> phone company into the pacesetter for the industry.
>
> (Rosenbush, 2003)

> In this summer of corporate love, the unwanted embrace of Pechiney,
> a French aluminium company, by Alcan, its Canadian rival, could
> become a thorny romance. (*The Economist*, 2003, p. 58)

> Ready to get swallowed: We found three takeover targets that look
> appetizing. (Stires, 2003)

> MGM's withdrawal is the latest twist in the long-running battle over
> the future of Vivendi's assets. (Larsen, 2003)

So what exactly is going on in business media discourse? And, more
specifically, what constitutes the fascination that metaphor in business
media discourse holds for the critical researcher?

A great deal of that fascination is accounted for by the multi-functional nature of metaphor. First, there is its important textual function (see Goatly, 1997, pp. 163–4). As realizations of underlying conceptual metaphors, metaphoric expressions

> contribute to cohesion of the text while at the same time, the tightness and consistency of the argumentation which results from the structural logic provided by the metaphor ... contributes to such an essential textual feature as is coherence.   (White, 1997, p. 242)

As we shall see in the following chapters, metaphors are organized in chains across a text, involving other cognitive models such as frames and scripts. Such 'chains provide "connectivity" so that a simple statement ... tells us much more than is relayed by [the] words alone' (Augoustinos and Walker, 1995, p. 42). Moreover, metaphor also organizes the interpersonal relations between discourse participants, by virtue of being embedded in a 'communicative complex that surrounds and supports individual metaphors' (Eubanks, 2000, p. 8). By using particular metaphors, writers can therefore define a topic, argue for that conceptualization and persuade readers to share in their metaphor and thus relate to them. In short, metaphor is ancillary in constructing a particular view of reality. In doing so, it also serves an ideational function. This book is, in fact, based on a hypothesis focusing on that ideational function of metaphor. Yet the interpersonal function is obviously a vital issue in any analysis of the ideological work that metaphor does.

The three Hallidayan macro-functions of metaphor outlined above (Halliday, 1978) of course also feature in the print media. As for the textual function, it has been noted that 'there is an imperious necessity for newspaper language to display clarity and facilitate ... the readability of its text' (White, 1997, p. 242) and metaphor is indeed instrumental in achieving that end. As far as the relationship between journalists and readers is concerned, the former draw heavily on metaphor to get the latter's attention. In fact, this is one of the main functions of metaphor in media discourse, as the 'media have forced ... reporters ... to search out fresh and dramatic ways to keep their audience or readership attentive' (Malszecki, 1995, pp. 199–200). This is particularly true for metaphoric expressions of war, which emotionalize a subject by demarcating an 'enemy', and thus appeal to the reader (Küster, 1978, p. 74). Prince and Ferrari (1996, p. 230) note that, apart from serving as an attention-getter, metaphors in printed media texts also underscore the explanatory perspective of those texts, thus helping journalists to 'undergo a partially educationally-oriented task' *vis-à-vis* their readers (Prince and Ferrari, 1996, pp. 226–7). Enforced use of metaphoric language makes for the highly expressive, vivid and inventive style usually found in the printed media. Yet, while 'vividness is [undoubtedly] a virtue in newspaper writing . . . inventions are not entirely accidental' (Eubanks, 2000, p. 46). This is where the third function of metaphor – the ideational construction of reality – finds its reflection in media discourse. By favouring particular metaphors in discourse, journalists can reinforce, or even create, particular mental models in their readers' cognition.

The original rationale for writing this book was the perceived dominance of the WAR metaphor in business media discourse. The particularity of that metaphor resides in the fact that war is itself not a uniform domain, comprising as it does a blend of both physical violence and military strategy. Indeed, journalists draw on both aspects to a greater or lesser extent, yielding metaphoric expressions such as *bruising battle* (see Appendix for references: MS BW 7 and MS BW 24), *cutthroat killer* (MA FO 17) or *brutal Internet price war* (MA BW16) on the one hand, and *target group* (for example, MS FT 94), *maneuver* (for example, MA BW 19) and *strategic alliance* (for example, MA EC 33) on the other. Furthermore, the blend has a temporal sequence as, in the history of humankind, organized war originated from unsophisticated fighting. Thus Clausewitz (1952 [1832], p. 178) traces warfare back to medieval fistfights, while Lakoff and Johnson (1980, p. 62) go back even further in stating that 'we have institutionalized our [animal] fighting in a number of ways, one of them being war'. Indeed, the chapter on mergers and acquisitions discourse will show how the WAR or FIGHTING metaphor can become part of a wider metaphoric scenario of evolutionary struggle and Economic Darwinism, showing both specific [+HUMAN] and more general [+ANIMATE] features. According to Lakoff and Johnson, this sublimation of raw brutality into the 'art' of war accounts for the pervasiveness of the WAR metaphor in conceptualizing a number of social practices. With reference to the metaphor ARGUMENT IS WAR, they claim that

> even if you have never fought a fistfight in your life, much less a war, but have been arguing from the time you began to talk, you still conceive of arguments, and execute them, according to the ARGUMENT IS WAR metaphor because the metaphor is built into the conceptual system of the culture in which you live.
>
> (Lakoff and Johnson, 1980, pp. 63–4)

The above statement can easily be transferred to the BUSINESS IS WAR metaphor: the related conceptual model is entrenched in Western culture, and enforced usage of the metaphor will not only root it even more firmly but will also have an impact on the way business is being done. Nevertheless, the WAR model, although pervasive, is by no means the only one available, raising the issue of why it is used so predominantly. In Hallidayan terms, what is the ideational function it holds for its users? This function is mainly fulfilled by metaphor highlighting certain semantic components of the source domain and omitting others. For example, the expression *M&A veteran* (MA FO 15) foregrounds the component [+EXPERIENCED] while simultaneously backgrounding more problematic ones such as [+BRUTAL]. Along with this 'metaphoric filtering' (Walters-York, 1996, p. 57), control over metaphoric resources and selective metaphor usage can establish discursive power of definition and social power of exclusion – given, of course, that non-dominant groups in society grant that power to more dominant groups. To sum up the point in the words of Goatly (1997, p. 155),

> metaphor . . . is not a mere reflection of a pre-existing objective reality but a construction of reality, through a categorization entailing the selection of some features as critical and others as non-critical . . . metaphors can consciously be used to construct . . . reality.

Another discursive aspect of metaphoric expression is the fact that, by virtue of its non-literal nature, speakers can hide behind metaphoric language, claiming that they 'cannot be held responsible for the message' (Cameron and Low, 1999, p. 86). The metaphoric expressions then seem to be the unproblematic picture of reality, 'reveal[ing] some universal structure naturally inherent in the object of discussion' (Walters-York, 1996, p. 58). The term in question is thus 'naturalized' (Fairclough, 1995a, p. 35) – that is, stripped of its ideology by being rendered uncontested 'common sense'. This hedging aspect is particularly important in the case of the potentially problematic WAR metaphor: Which conceptual links between the two social spheres of war and business are highlighted and naturalized by the WAR metaphor, and why are these links metaphorized in the first place? The purpose of any critical study of metaphor is to make explicit such socially constructed implicit meanings and test them for their ideological content.

In view of the above considerations, this book is based on the following hypothesis: business media discourse is characterized by coherent metaphor clusters centring on the WAR metaphor, and this metaphor helps to masculinize both that discourse and related social practices. The claim that the WAR metaphor functions as a masculinization device is backed by, for example, Fleischmann (2001, p. 485), who states that 'to the extent that war is still a largely male enterprise, [the WAR] metaphor subtly reinforces [the social domain's] traditional gender bias'. Since war can be considered a 'quintessentially masculine activity and an essential test of manhood' (Wilson, 1992, p. 892),[1] its metaphoric usage helps to marginalize, if not eliminate, metaphoric femininity and, consequently, position actual women as an out-group in business. Accordingly, the metaphor's effect on dominant masculinity is to further activate masculine patterns of behaviour and to evoke latent desires for social formations characterized by male bonding (Küster, 1978, pp. 81–2). Enforced usage of the WAR metaphor, in both quantitative and qualitative terms, thus 'strengthens the individual's sense of maleness . . . and a predominantly male culture' (Wilson, 1992, p. 898). This strengthening is particularly significant in the male arena of corporate business, in which women still feature only very marginally.[2] Because of its ideological function, the WAR metaphor may very well help 'the top levels of business [to] provide a fairly convincing corporate display of masculinity' (Connell, 1995, p. 77).

The gendered ideological work metaphor does in the business media finds a reflection in readership figures: as detailed in Chapter 3, on method, a stunning 90 per cent of business magazine readers are in fact men. This fact again raises questions about the interpersonal function of metaphor: journalists do not only use particular metaphor selectively to conceptualize topics from a particular vantage point. In view of readership demographics, their interpersonal aim in doing so may be not so much to influence readers' cognition than to mirror the metaphoric models they perceive in their male readers. Apart from that, WAR metaphors are, for some corporate representatives, not only 'built into the conceptual system of the culture in which [they] live' (Lakoff and Johnson, 1980, p. 64) but also have a very vivid literal counterpart in military service. Indeed, executives are quoted by journalists as literalizing, and thus intensifying, the WAR metaphor by referring to their army experience (see, for example, MA FO 4).

In order to avoid spreading the topic too thin, various questions arising in the context of metaphor and gender in business media discourse had to be neglected. Thus this study will not address the issue of genre – that is, whether metaphor usage differs across various media-related text types such as commentary, cover story or interview. For want of reliable data, another point to be left untackled is the gendered use of metaphor – that is, whether metaphoric expressions are different according to the speaker's gender. Previous studies on this topic show different results, ranging from Eubanks' (2000) findings that 'no salient gender pattern emerged with respect to Trade Is War' (p. 162)[3] to Wilson's (1992) observation that 'metaphors used by women involved in the process [of implementing a new software] were quite different and not associated with war' (p. 897). Such vastly divergent results obviously call for further research. Another topic only mentioned in passing is the culture-specific differences between British and US journalists' use of metaphor. Finally, the empirical analysis will concentrate on linguistic realizations of metaphor only, leaving the vast field of multi-modal metaphor to future projects.

Yet, one issue that does play a part – and an important one at that – is that of media as secondary discourse: the particular role business media discourse plays in relation to corporate discourse is discussed in Chapter 2, on theory, and the qualitative analyses (sections 4.2 on page 78 and 5.2 on page 130) also include a discussion of the links between the two discourses. As for that last question, it should be kept in mind that

> social groupings are rarely hermetically sealed, and it may well be that metaphors used by other groups influence those used by the group being studied, and vice versa.   (Low, 1999, pp. 60–1)

The two spheres of corporate and business media discourse share a number of similarities, starting with the fact that both produce technical texts referring to one or several institutional–professional domain(s) (Engberg, 2003). Another resemblance is constituted by shared metaphors: media texts incorporate quotations from primary corporate discourse which corroborate the observation that 'military terminology has crept down to the level of popular managerial discourse' (Raghavan, 1990, p. 13). Finally, primary and secondary discourses are similar in the effect their metaphors have on text recipients: if 'corporate rhetoric [shapes] corporations and ultimately, the customers they serve' (Boyd, 1995, p. 4), metaphoric expressions in business media texts similarly influence readers' cognition.

This book is structured as follows: first, Chapter 2 employs the notion of social cognition to develop a framework that links the cognitive semantics approach to metaphor to a critical study of language and discourse. Chapter 3 introduces corpus-based quantitative analysis combined with qualitative text analysis drawing on functional grammar. Applying functional grammar to the study of metaphor reacts on the observation that 'linguists of . . . the functional Hallidayan tradition have found metaphor diffcult to integrate with their theories' (Goatly, 1997, p. 4), seeking to remedy that situation. These methods are then used empirically on media marketing texts on the one hand (Chapter 4) and media text on mergers and acquisitions on the other (Chapter 5). The analyses will be supplemented by a discussion of the socio-cognitive impact of the emergent metaphoric scenarios and of possible alternatives to those dominant models. Finally, the conclusion (Chapter 6) will address the question as to whether gender-neutral metaphors are a viable option in business media discourse at all.

In its mission statement, *Business Week*, one of the four publications in the corpora at hand, promises that it 'takes readers . . . inside the minds of CEOs and corporate boards' (*Business Week*, 2002c, para. 2). By unravelling the cognitive and ideological fabric of business media discourse, this book aims at taking its readers inside the minds of journalists working for business publications. As outlined above, the first step on that tour is a theory reconciling cognitive and critical studies of metaphor.

2
Theory: A Critical Cognitive Framework for Metaphor Research

> If genius, and hence learning, consists in connecting remote notions and finding similarity in dissimilar things, then metaphor, which is the keenest and most peculiar among the tropes, is the only one capable of producing wonder, out of which pleasure is born ... metaphor, carrying our mind on wings from one kind to another, makes us discern in a single word more than one object.
>
> (Eco, 1994, pp. 85–6)

This chapter will lay the foundation for the subsequent empirical analyses by presenting an integrated theoretical paradigm that combines cognitive theories of metaphor with critical approaches to language and discourse. Such an approach seems desirable as, up to now, integration of the two areas has been only marginal, to say the least. Metaphor has not been much of an issue in Critical Discourse Analysis (CDA) so far, nor have many researchers in cognitive metaphor drawn on the framework of CDA in their work. In view of this situation, metaphor research still has much to gain from incorporating a CDA perspective and thus focusing more on socio-cultural and ideological functions of metaphor. And in contrast, critical approaches to language can be considerably enriched by also taking cognitive aspects into account. One area that is particularly amenable to such an integrated approach is the issue of metaphor and gender in business media discourse.

In order to establish the theory, this chapter will outline briefly both classical cognitive metaphor theory in the tradition of Lakoff and Johnson (1980) as well as recent approaches such as the theory of conceptual blending and neural theories of language. In this context, the focus will be on blending theory, as it lends itself very well to research on metaphor in discourse. Neural theories of language, on the other hand, signify a paradigm shift that can be countered by combining elements of cognitive metaphor theory, especially blending, with a critical approach to language. To this end, the main tenets of CDA and the Hallidayan tradition it is based upon will also be discussed, including a view of journalism as secondary discourse.

Finally, the two strands are combined in an approach that views discourse participants as drawing on a pool of complex metaphors to negotiate social identities and relations through text. Text is here seen as being rooted in both discourse practice and (metaphoric) cognitive models. Which metaphors come to be used in a text is thus determined by, and constitutive of, which metaphors are anchored in the related discourse and in social cognition. The overarching aim of critical metaphor research is, then, to disclose the vested interests influencing the choice of metaphor in text.

The first part of the discussion will show that, in its early days, cognitive metaphor theory was not at all incompatible with such a critical outlook on metaphor.

2.1 Classical cognitive metaphor theory

In a nutshell, the classical cognitive view on metaphor holds that metaphor is a conceptual phenomenon that is realized at the surface level of language. It can be thought of as a mapping of features from a source to a target domain. This mapping is ubiquitous, unidirectional, systematic, invariable and grounded in physical and socio-cultural experience (Lakoff and Johnson, 1980). To distinguish the conceptual and linguistic aspects of metaphor, metaphoric concepts are represented graphically by small capitals throughout this book – for example, MARKETING IS ATTACKING. By contrast, their linguistic realizations are referred to as 'metaphoric expressions' and represented by italics – for example, *the French [supermarket chain] withdrew from Germany in 1996 after a brief foray* (MS EC 5). A bi-level view of metaphor holds that metaphoric expressions witnessed in actual texts are just different realizations of productive underlying metaphors. Accordingly, the above concept (MARKETING IS ATTACKING) also yields the following expressions:

ABN-Amro . . . will this week launch credit cards in Taiwan.

(MS FT 92)

[Oracle] *has launched a two-pronged assault to make its name a household word.* (MS EC 34)

backed by a local TV-ad blitz . . . the . . . beverage blew off the shelves.

(MS BW 18)

According to Lakoff and Johnson (1980, p. 9), it is not only surface-level metaphoric expressions that are systematically related. Different sub-metaphors may be part of a broader conceptual system as well and 'jointly provide a coherent understanding of the concept as a whole' (Lakoff and Johnson, 1980, p. 89). Thus, MARKETING IS ATTACKING ties in with COMPETITORS ARE ENEMIES (*The . . . company has . . . no greater rival than Siebel Systems* [MS FO 36]) and ADVERTISING IS A WEAPON (*people can soon expect to be bombarded with telephone commercials* [MS FT 87]).[1] Here, the common link is MARKETING IS WAR. There is, moreover, a related yet distinct metaphor, namely MARKETING IS A SPORTS COMPETITION, as evidenced by expressions such as

upstarts have scored with younger consumers.   (MS BW 18)

Tesco [is] *positioning itself as a consumer champion.*   (MS FT 91)

Already, three front-runners have emerged. At the head of the pack is Yahoo.   (MS BW 7)

As we shall see, such related metaphoric mappings can also bring about clustering.

Single sub-metaphors have a coherent structure in their own right, but also show coherence with other sub-metaphors at the same level, yielding a structured concept. To elaborate on the above example, MARKETING IS WAR emphasizes the aspect of both fighting and strategy. MARKETING IS A SPORTS COMPETITION rather focuses on the competitive aspects, and MARKETING IS A GAME conveys the idea of playfulness in competition. Within a metaphor, very much the same highlighting and hiding mechanisms can be observed. Thus the dominant metaphor MARKETING IS WAR does not account for non-aggressive aspects of the target domain of marketing such as persuasion of would-be customers or co-operation with other suppliers. The reverse is also true: any given metaphor will only be productive for certain parts of its source domain. It is an astonishing fact that while in MARKETING IS WAR (or more generally still, BUSINESS IS WAR), only selected aspects of the target domain are highlighted, almost all of the aspects of the source domain are indeed realized. This indicates the extreme productivity of this dominant metaphor. Moreover, it shows that even the more taboo characteristics of the source domain are acceptable in business discourse (as in, for example, '*there could be a lot of blood spilt in banging together the two organisations*' [MA FT 32]).[2]

The process of mapping fixed correspondences is constrained by the so-called Invariance Principle, which denotes that 'mappings preserve . . . the cognitive topology . . . of the source domain, in a way consistent with the inherent structure of the target domain' (Lakoff, 1993, p. 215). This notion entails the target domain in fact being inviolable, thus limiting the potential number of mappings.

As for how metaphors actually come into being – that is, how they are grounded – Lakoff and Johnson (1980) maintain that metaphors 'have a basis in our physical and cultural experience' (p. 14). Those two realms of experience are, in fact, often inextricable, 'since the choice of one physical basis from among many possible ones has to do with cultural coherence' (p. 19). While Lakoff and Johnson's (1980) seminal work on metaphor still foregrounds its social grounding and effects, later developments rather focus on the embodied aspect of metaphor generation. Before looking at the so-called neural theory of metaphor, however, the recent framework of blending will be introduced.

2.2 Blending and neural theories of metaphor

Like metaphoric mapping, blending processes are ubiquitous – even more so since they are not restricted to metaphor but constitute 'a fundamental aspect of all human experience' (Coulson and Oakley, 2000, p. 182). Blending theory sets out to account for 'blending as an online-process' (Grady *et al.*, 1999, para. 64) applied to individual, often novel metaphoric expressions. Blending theory's main deviation from mapping as used in classical cognitive metaphor theory resides in the fact that it assumes four spaces instead of the two of source and target domain. Blending processes typically involve two (or more) input spaces as well as a generic space showing basic characteristics common to the input spaces, and a blended space partially drawing on the input spaces and showing an emergent structure. To illustrate this, consider an expression such as [Hypobank's] *management was scared of being gobbled up by Deutsche Bank* (MA EC 27). Here, two input spaces, namely the FEEDING and the TAKE-OVER scenario, are connected into a blend.[3] Attributing elements from one space to elements from other spaces, however, is only partial, with 'additional structure [becoming] available through default and pragmatic procedures' (Turner and Fauconnier, 1995, para. 3). The generic space connecting the two input spaces would in this case feature a basic scenario of one entity incorporating another, and extinguishing the latter's existence in the process. A blend is therefore more than the sum of two input spaces, since its structure is completed by information stored in long-term memory.

Blending theory does not propagate the invariance hypothesis. Instead, it takes a rather differentiated stance on the relative importance of the source and target input spaces. In the example from mergers and acquisitions discourse above, the source input space of FEEDING provided the frame to organize the blend. This shows that, in metaphoric processes, 'input spaces do not have equal status as topics' (Grady *et al.*, 1999, para. 55): in composing the blend, the source domain tends to have more prominence (Turner and Fauconnier, 1995, para. 61). Thus the source input space of the MARKETING IS WAR metaphor provides expressions like the following:

Newspapers and magazines also face the technology assault.
(MS FO 1)

the company's high customer-acquisition costs after its $150m advertising blitz. (MS EC 40)

Pfizer's salesmanship is about more than . . . ads bombarding the airwaves.
(MS EC 13)

Blending theory, too, endorses the idea that only particular features from the input spaces are drawn upon to compose the blend. This does not only hold true at the formal linguistic but at the conceptual level as well, since 'the target material yields to the source material, which is explicitly represented in the blend' (Grady *et al.*, 1999, para. 50). However, this 'asymmetric topicality' (ibid., para. 56) is reversed in the process of inference from blend to target input space, resulting in an overriding target domain as the ultimate purpose of blending. It should thus be clear that the multi-directionality of blending processes does not represent a return to the bi-directionality advocated by interaction theory (Black, 1962; 1977/1993) and subsequently refuted by, for example, Lakoff and Turner (1989, pp. 131–2).

An important feature of blending processes is their status as 'a compression tool par excellence' (Fauconnier and Turner, 2002, p. 114). By compression, so-called vital relations (ibid., p. 92) including identity, time, space, cause–effect, change and part–whole, can be compacted (ibid., pp. 93–101). For the purposes of the argument, it should be kept in mind that compression can be 'syncopated'. In syncopation, such relations are activated only partially during the blending process, thus serving a highlighting function (ibid., pp. 114, 325). An example would be the following:

> War metaphors come easily to the decorated Vietnam veteran. After
> all, [he] says . . . 'I know what it feels like to get your butt shot off'.
>
> (MS BW 15)

Here the relations of time (Vietnam War and 1996), space (Vietnam and
the USA) as well as cause–effect (a certain leadership style as caused by
the war experience) have been compressed. Similarly, identity and
change (from soldier to CEO) have been compressed into metaphoric
uniqueness (CEO as soldier). Moreover, the compression is syncopated
as only particular elements of the soldier-in-the-Vietnam-War input
space are drawn upon (being under attack as opposed to being the
attacker himself). While this short example accounts for the cognitive
principles bringing about metaphoric blends, the question of what
might influence those principles and what possible purposes the
ensuing metaphoric blends serve obviously looms large. Some answers
will be provided in the following section.

As for the issue of how metaphoric blending processes are grounded,
Fauconnier and Turner (2002) allow for the above-mentioned vital
relations, the basis of compression in blending, to be 'rooted in [both]
fundamental human neurobiology and shared social experience'
(p. xiii). However, we shall see below that the social aspect is rather backgrounded in the analysis of concrete examples.

For the time being, Table 2.1 summarizes the differences and similarities between classical cognitive metaphor theory on the one hand and
blending theory on the other.

As for the double nature of metaphor being both embodied and socio-
culturally determined, it can be observed that, in their more recent
work, Lakoff and Johnson (1999) favour the embodiment model of
explanation at the expense of the socio-cultural one:

> Reason and conceptual structure are shaped by our bodies, brains,
> and modes of functioning in the world. [They] are therefore not tran-
> scendent, that is, not utterly independent of the body.   (p. 128)

Having thus outlined the basic assumptions of their research, they go
on to distinguish between primary and complex metaphors. Primary
metaphors 'link our subjective experiences and judgments to our sensorimotor experience' (ibid., p. 128). This acquisition process takes place
during the so-called conflation phase in early childhood (Johnson,
1999), in which subjective and sensorimotor experiences are not yet

Table 2.1   Comparison of classical cognitive metaphor theory and blending theory

	Classical cognitive metaphor theory	Blending theory
Scope	Mapping processes are applied to metaphor and metonymy	Blending processes are applied to metaphor and metonymy, counterfactuals, irony, grammar, etc.
Focus	Theory investigates conventional, entrenched conceptual metaphors	Theory investigates online processing of particular, novel cases
Characteristics	Mapping processes involve two domains	Blending processes involve multiple spaces
	Mapping processes are ubiquitous	Blending processes are ubiquitous
	Mapping processes are unidirectional	Blending processes are multidirectional
	Mapping processes are systematic	Blending processes are systematic
	Mapping processes are invariable: target domain structure overrides	Blending processes are integral and asymmetrical, inference is from blend to target
	Mapping processes are grounded physically and socio-culturally	Blending processes are grounded physically and socio-culturally
Schematic process		

differentiated. Connections established during that phase continue to be active in later phases of life. Complex metaphor, on the other hand, is formed by conceptual blending (Lakoff and Johnson, 1999, p. 46). It should be noted that primary metaphors can blend into complex ones (Coulson and Oakley, 2000, para. 23). Lakoff and Johnson's neural theory of language emphasizes the neurobiological determinants of cognition, maintaining that 'the cognitive effects at the top level [of cognition] are achieved by the neurobiology at the bottom level' (ibid., p. 570). The theory hence accounts for the acquisition of concepts of spatial relations and the links between motor control and abstract reasoning (ibid., p. 572). However, Lakoff and Johnson caution that neural processes do not necessarily have to be used to reason metaphorically; they only provide a possible means of doing so.

Originally developed to falsify objectivist correspondence theories of truth (and metaphor) by contrasting it with embodied truth (and metaphor), Lakoff and Johnson's recent theory also sets itself in opposition to 'at least the most extreme postmodern views' (1999, p. 331) and their perceived claim that, for example, values are arbitrarily constructed. If metaphors are experientially grounded (that is, embodied), then 'such extreme forms of social constructivism are wrong' (1999, p. 331). The following section will show that some critical approaches to language could indeed be balanced by an additional cognitive angle.

2.3 Critical approaches to language

Halliday (1978), on whose work both Critical Linguistics and Critical Discourse Analysis (CDA) are founded, regards language as being in a dialectic relation to society: 'Language is controlled by the social structure, and the social structure is maintained and transmitted through language' (ibid., p. 89). Hence, text becomes 'defined as actualized meaning potential' (ibid., p. 109), representing a string of motivated choices from the potential of the linguistic system.

In this context, language shows three macro-functions: first, in its ideational function, language represents and constructs socio-cultural reality.[4] Second, in its interpersonal function, language constitutes social relations and identities. Finally, in its textual function, language structures texts and the relationships between texts as well as their verbal co-text and non-verbal context of situation and culture (Halliday and Hasan, 1985, p. 23). The three linguistic macro-functions work together, making each instance of language use multi-functional. Consequently, metaphoric expressions as a specific feature of language serve all three functions (Goatly, 1997, pp. 148–67), with the ideological aspect of metaphor incorporating both the ideational and the interpersonal function (ibid., p. 155).

The three macro-functions of language are mirrored in the extralinguistic context of situation, consisting of field (the activity as part of which language occurs), tenor (the participants involved in the activity and the relationships between them), and mode (the role of language in the activity, including the form linguistic interaction takes and the effects it achieves) (Halliday, 1978, pp. 62, 110). Both the wider context of culture as well as the more narrowly defined context of situation are in a mutually constitutive relationship to text. Further, the three aspects of the context of situation are related systematically to the three macro-functions of language, with field, tenor and mode determining the ideational, interpersonal and textual function of language, respectively (Halliday, 1978, p. 117).

The following example and its brief analysis illustrate the basic Hallidayan framework:

> *Tom Bearden* [host]: Microsoft publicly calls this a battle for survival. Literally, tens of billions of dollars hang in the balance. Steve Ballmer is executive vice president of worldwide sales of Microsoft.
>
> *Steve Ballmer*, Microsoft: Everything that our company is, is at stake to us – plus everything that we might hope for in terms of future growth – because these technologies are at the core of whether what we've done so far moves forward.
>
> *Tom Bearden*: Life or death.
>
> *Steve Ballmer*: You've got it.
>
> *Tom Bearden*: What could possibly threaten the survival of the world's largest software company? It's because this is more than just a fight over a single piece of software – this is a standards battle – much like a shootout between VHS and Betamax over control of the format of home videotape. What's at stake is nothing less than control of the computer desktop of the future.
>
> ('Cyber Wars', 1996, paras. 14–16)

The activity (field) is a TV news show about competition in the Internet software industry. The host provides background information about the issue, interviews guests in the studio and comments on inserted video clips of statements by industry representatives. Language is one of the three modes of communication in the activity, the other two being visuals and, to a lesser extent, music. The ideational function is constructing the issue of the competition on Internet technology from a particular perspective. This ideological vantage point is already betrayed in the programme's metaphoric title ('Cyber Wars') and sub-sequent realizations of the WAR metaphor (*battle for survival, life or death, threaten the survival, fight, standards battle, shootout*).[5] This particular con-ceptualization of the issue is influenced by the context of culture, here the US market economy, which is run mostly by men and relies heavily on technological progress. The participants involved (tenor) are the host, his guests, industry representatives and the viewers as an anonymous group. While the host interacts directly with his guests, the industry representatives' statements are inserted into the programme from other origins such as product presentations and so on. The interpersonal function is realized in positioning the host as the dominant figure, with the industry representatives as supplementary characters in the expert role. The viewers' role involves no direct exchange with the other participants; they receive the text and thereby reconstruct its meaning. These roles are shaped by the context of cultural practice (producing, broadcasting and watching a news programme). Concerning the mode, the host uses language to structure, inform, explain and comment. The mode is extremely complex, also because the news show is available on the Internet both as a transcript including stills from the show and as an audio file. The visual component is largely lost in both cases. As for the textual function, the structure of the text with its turns between host and guests (direct interaction), host and industry representatives (interaction through recontextualization) and host and viewers (unilateral communication) is to a large extent determined by the genre of the news show.

Elaborating on the Hallidayan notion of text as a string of motivated choices, Kress (1989) notes that 'language may be used to challenge, to subvert . . . , and to alter distributions of power' (p. 52). On the other hand, language can also be employed as 'an instrument for consolidating . . . concepts and relationships in the area of power' (Fowler, 1985, p. 61). In terms of metaphoric expressions, both statements mesh with Lakoff and Johnson's (1980) notion of metaphor choice as motivated by its highlighting and hiding function (p. 163). Seen as such, it can help to achieve hegemonic ends. The concept of hegemony, dating back to Gramsci, supplements the 'theory of state-as-force' (Gramsci, 2000, p. 195), which secures power by means of violence. In a hegemonic setting, existing power asymmetries between dominant and less dominant groups are instead based on the consent of the marginalized group. To manufacture consent, 'a certain compromise equilibrium should be formed' (ibid., p. 211), meaning that the dominant group grants the dominated group some advantages – never enough, however, to threaten the existing order. Power is thus secured by co-opting delegates of the marginalized, potentially subversive group so that the asymmetry appears to be 'supported by the consent of the majority' (ibid., p. 261). Cox (1993, p. 63) uses a powerful metaphoric expression to describe the nature of hegemony: 'Hegemony is like a pillow: it absorbs blows and sooner or later the would-be assailant will find it comfortable to rest upon'. In the media, struggle over hegemonic representations can be witnessed in debates about textual features, including metaphoric expressions (Finney, 1998).

Hegemony is also a central concept in CDA. While hegemony at the socio-cultural level is still seen as being played out at the level of text, Critical Discourse Analysis, as the name suggests, introduces (and indeed focuses on) discourse as the interface between text and context. Fairclough (1996, p. 71) uses 'discourse' 'to refer to any spoken or written language use conceived as social practice'.[6] Similarly, discourse can also be conceived of as a complex event (van Dijk, 1985, p. 4). By contrast, an ' "order of discourse" [is] the overall configuration of discourse practices of a society or one of its institutions' (Chouliaraki and Fairclough, 1999, p. 58). The structured set of discursive practices which discourse represents is linked to a social field such as media or education. Actors in the social field are characterized by Bourdieu's habitus or set of 'inculcated, structured, durable, generative and transposable' dispositions acquired under particular social conditions (1991, p. 12), and, in addition, their mental models, all of which form their discursive equipment. In what follows, 'discourse' will be used to mean the totality of interrelated texts, both written and spoken, which are produced about a particular domain, for example, marketing and sales. A discourse originates in a discourse domain – equal to the social field quoted above – and is structured by the order of discourse prevailing in that domain.

Discourse is linked to genre in so far as there are 'preferred conjunctions of discourses and genres, and prohibitions on other conjunctions' (Kress, 1989, p. 20). Mixing discourses and genres is also restricted by taboos (for example, including jokes in a funeral speech, or secretaries making more than the most marginal comments at boardroom meetings). An example of how discourses and genres do not mix freely is the discourse of marketing. Heavily determined by the socio-economic formation of a free market economy, it finds its expressions in genres such as the various forms of advertising, product presentations and leaflets, to name but a few. In the case of media texts on marketing, however, different genres, such as feature, analysis, interview and editorial, prevail.[7] Genres in turn determine the linguistic features of texts. As an example, metaphoric expressions of war do not feature to the same extent in all genres of business discourse (advertisements, for example, show only limited evidence of the WAR metaphor). With discourses determining genres, and genres determining language-in-text, 'discourse finds its [ultimate] expression in text' (Kress, 1985, p. 27).

Discourse as expressed in actual text is often marked by hybridity; indeed, 'hybridity is an irreducible characteristic of complex modern discourse' (Chouliaraki and Fairclough, 1999, p. 59). This is because negotiating common definitions of situations against the backdrop of the lifeworld (Habermas, 1981) becomes increasingly difficult in post-traditional societies. Increasing rationalization and problematization of the lifeworld leads to a growing need for negotiation and interpretation, and ultimately to a higher risk of dissent. Such dissent can then manifest itself in hybrid discourses and, ultimately, in hybrid cognitive models. Semantic heterogeneity of that kind could, among other devices, be indicated by metaphor clusters. An example would be the expression *she did some serious housekeeping and bolstered the morale of the troops* (*The Economist*, 2001, para. 7), which combines the diametrically opposed domains of war and housekeeping within the comparatively small unit of the sentence. Such clustering indicates a fluctuating, dissenting discourse; it is apparently no longer self-explanatory how women in business should be conceptualized metaphorically.

The more hybrid a text, the less homogeneous the group that produces and/or receives it:

How texts are produced and interpreted, and therefore how genres and discourses are drawn upon and combined, depends upon the nature of the social context. Thus a relatively stable social domain and set of social relations and identities would [manifest] itself in texts which are relatively semantically homogeneous.

(Fairclough, 1992, p. 213)

While hybridity can vary according to social contexts such as a group's degree of homogeneity, it should be kept in mind that 'hybridity as such is inherent in all social uses of language' (Chouliaraki and Fairclough, 1999, p. 13). Such pervasiveness is caused by the inherently intertextual nature of all discourse. As the news programme example showed, intertextuality often works by recontextualization, hiding particular meaning potentials and highlighting others (Chouliaraki and Fairclough, 1999, p. 119). In this function, intertextual recontextualization is parallel to metaphor, which also highlights and hides meanings by blending them into new contexts. The concept of intertextuality can also be expanded to include interdiscursivity, and complex metaphors indicate such interdiscursivity as their different input spaces are linked to different discourses.

The news programme example mentioned above further exemplified that the boundaries between particular discourses and genres are not entirely fixed. This leaves text producers some creative leeway. In the news show, texts from the genre of product presentation were transplanted and thus recontextualized in a TV feature. The very dominant linguistic feature of metaphoric expressions of war in the ensuing text indicates a mixing of discourses as the metaphor's two input spaces are linked to the different discourses of business and war, respectively. The creative and, theoretically, subversive activity of the text producer forming hybrid genres and texts is mirrored in the recipient's cognitive 'ability to think critically outside existing ideological discourses and representations' (Augoustinos and Walker, 1995, p. 9), as shown by their ideological activity of constructing alternative readings. Meaning itself is then just a product of the recipients' interaction with the text (Hodge and Kress, 1993, pp. 174–5).

Yet such readings are by no means unrestricted. First, any recipient 'is discursively equipped prior to the encounter with the text' (Fowler, 1987, p. 7) and will bring his or her habitus to the reading. Beyond that, the habitus is also inculcated in cognition, which again influences discourse. Also, a text 'constructs its ideal reader by providing a certain ' "reading position" from which the text seems unproblematic' (Kress, 1989, p. 36). These constraints help to push the recipient to process a text as 'more or less congruent with the ideology which informs the text' (Fowler, 1987, p. 7). Moreover, readers are determined by the access they have to different texts, genres and discourses, rendering discourse 'not only a *means* in the enactment of power, ... but at the same time itself a power *resource*' (van Dijk, 1997, p. 20; original emphasis). This explains why increasing intertextuality and hybridity do not necessarily translate into enlarged discursive resources. Power and control active in particular contexts restrict hybridity by enabling text producers to mix some texts, genres and discourses, but not others (Chouliaraki and Fairclough, 1999, p. 119).

By constructing readers and their social relations from a particular point of view, discourse functions as a vehicle for ideology. Beyond that, it also helps to naturalize ideology 'by making what is social seem natural' (Kress, 1989, p. 10). Metaphor can support such naturalization by identification processes of the 'A is B' type, establishing a particular view of an issue as naturalized common sense. Although A is B is by no means the only form metaphors can take, it can nevertheless occasionally be found in metaphoric expressions. Examples of such reifications of the BUSINESS IS WAR metaphor are the following:

[Change in marketing conditions] *means war!*

(Perez, 1997, para. 1)

Microsoft vs. AOL: now it's war.

(MS FO 20)

'[Globalized marketing] *is war,'* declares Rolf Kunisch, *chief executive of the Hamburg-based cosmetics company.*

(MS BW 6)

Examples are scarce, though, probably because there are subtler means of naturalizing ideology (for example, agent deletion and ergative processes, non-nominal metaphoric expressions, deictic construction of in-groups and out-groups, and so on).

Dominant discourses integrate the domain they are linked to by providing a concept of that domain and more or less excluding others. Given this ideologically vested nature of discourse as it manifests itself in texts of particular genres and their (linguistic) features, the agenda of Critical Linguistics has been defined as 'defamiliarisation or consciousness-raising' (Fowler, 1987, p. 5). Accordingly, any critical research into metaphor seeks to convey how dominant metaphors come into being, how they are reified in discourse, and what agendas are met by using them.

Borrowing from Halliday, CDA identifies discourses as meaning potential. Halliday's concept of field, tenor and mode as determining the ideational, interpersonal and textual functions of language interacts with the three dimensions of text, discourse practice and sociocultural practice (Fairclough, 1995a, p. 98). Text is to be understood as an instance of written or spoken language use (or use of any other semiotic system) of indeterminate length and needs to be studied in relation to the conditions of its production, distribution and reception. According to the claim that recipients actively construct a text's meaning, reception coincides with interpretation. Production, distribution and reception of a text together represent the situation in which the text occurs. Althusser's (1970 [1971], pp. 127–30) observation that production also needs to reproduce its conditions and the conditions of consumption in order to be sustainable, can be applied to discourse practice as well: text producers interested in preserving existing practices will also look to reproduce means of production, distribution and reception of text. Discourse practice is in turn positioned in a mutually constitutive relationship with more broadly defined socio-cultural practices. The dimension of socio-cultural practice can be sub-divided into societal, institutional and situational levels. Although the situational level lends itself most easily to notions of field, tenor and mode, the outer circles

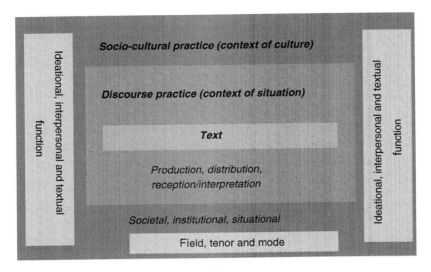

Figure 2.1 Three-level framework of CDA
Source: Adapted from Fairclough, 1995a, p. 98.

of institutional and societal socio-cultural practice can be understood in terms of those Hallidayan notions as well. By virtue of all three levels being embedded in and (re)producing each other (Bourdieu, 1991, p. 2), field, tenor and mode are indeed pervasive aspects of this framework. Their interrelationships are already formulated in Halliday's (1978) claim that not only field and tenor are socially structured, but also mode (p. 113). Consequently, the three macro-functions – that is, the ideational, interpersonal and textual – also permeate the structure. The integrated three-level framework of CDA is represented graphically in Figure 2.1.

To illustrate the concept with an example, consider the meeting of a company's marketing department. The meeting (situational level) happens within a corporate structure (institutional level), which is in turn determined by the particular economic structure of a free market economy (societal level). The meeting will probably include written and spoken forms of multimodal text representing certain genres, such as reports in the form of computer-animated presentations, as well as discussion. These texts will show particular grammatical features (for example, progressive aspect and medial transitivity, as in 'their market share is reducing'), collocations to express central concepts ('market leader', 'market share', 'market segment'), and metaphoric expressions (*Aggressive in terms that we fight in the market place for . . . clients*).[8] Some texts are prepared, distributed and received before the meeting (for example, in the form of an email on product development), while other texts are distributed and received at the meeting itself (for example, spontaneous contributions to a discussion). Field, tenor and mode, as well as the functions they determine, show at the societal level in the sense that the provision and consumption of goods and services (field) are carried out by people in the roles of entrepreneurs, employees and consumers (tenor). At this level, language is positioned, for example, at the interface of provision and consumption – that is, meeting market-ing purposes such as personal selling to persuade prospects or polls to determine demand (mode). At the institutional level, we again find a hierarchically organized structure including employees, middle man-agement and directors (tenor), who are engaged in 'running the busi-ness' (field), and making use of corporate communication to do so (mode). At the level of discourse practice, there is the activity of text production, distribution and reception (field) as carried out by the members of the marketing department (tenor). Status comes into play when considering that the executives with more responsibility and power are likely to produce and distribute texts, while lower-level employees are at the receiving end of text. At the discourse practice level, language is the centre around which activities emerge and par-ticipants act (mode). Finally, at the text level, texts serve to construct cognitive representations of, and beliefs about, social practices (field), relations and identities (tenor), with the help of particular linguistic fea-tures (mode). Applied to the example of a marketing department's meeting, sales figures could, within a certain range, be represented as either more favourable or more detrimental to one's own company: the former representation could serve to motivate and appraise the sales staff and downgrade the competition, while the latter would upgrade the competition and thus threaten the sales staff into working harder. Therefore we can see that because the three levels of socio-cultural prac-tice, discourse practice and text are embedded within each other, ideational, interpersonal and textual functions – as determined by field, tenor and mode – cut across all dimensions in this framework. In addi-tion, personal and social cognition are intertwined with discourse as central cognitive models are over-represented in discourse. Such dis-cursive prominence will in turn lead to these models being anchored even more firmly in cognition.

Finally, it should be noted that some discourses are to a large extent defined by the commentary on them. In a Foucauldian framework, commentary is an internal constraint on discourse, constituting a secondary text that acts as a lens through which the primary one is reified and modified at the same time (Foucault, 1972, p. 221). One form of commentary is journalism: the secondary discourse domain of the business media can be associated with a limited number of publications, which largely converge in their ideological outlook on the primary domain of business. Primary discourses especially are defined by the commentary on them when access to them is extremely restricted: examples are cabinet or boardroom meetings, about which the public is exclusively informed through the media. The fact that corporate discourse is not public is obviously a major power resource for its participants: communication between the inner circle of the corporate elite and more or less peripheral constituencies (employees, shareholders, customers, the general public) is controlled through channels such as appraisal sessions, annual reports, sales letters and, last but not least, magazine articles or interviews.

As for the latter channel, it is important to note that the relationship between primary corporate discourse and secondary business media discourse is by no means one-sided. True, corporate elites redouble their economic and political power by having preferential access to journalists and being able to control the setting (for example, press briefings), participants (for example, only journalists accredited by the corporation), turn allocation and sequencing (for example, declining to take more questions) and topics (see van Dijk, 1996, p. 89 for these and other criteria of access). However, some participants, namely a privileged group of journalists, can themselves become what Foucault (1972) calls 'fellowships of discourse', close communities whose role is to preserve, reproduce and distribute discourse in such a way as not to lose their own symbolic power (p. 225). They are hegemonic groups in the sense of Gramsci, an in-group influencing discourse practice. Journalists may (re)produce the technical jargon of the primary corporate discourse domain through lexical choice and, in this sense, both the primary corporate and the secondary media discourse on business are good examples that 'one of the most important functions of an expert language is exclusion' (Cohn, 1987, p. 149). Still, journalists are not entirely at the mercy of corporate communication policies. Depending on their relative power, they can decide whom to quote, and in what context. Then again, they may be restricted even in this decision as the resources to which they have access have already been funnelled to reflect the view of the original text producers (Jacobs, 1999). The media can thus – more or less involuntarily – help in 'managing the public image of [corporate] elites' (van Dijk, 1997, p. 23).

The third group of participants – the readers of magazine and newspaper articles – is even further removed from primary corporate discourse. While business journalists at least have access to the version provided for them, readers see corporate discourse through the additional lens of the media. Reception of such indirectly produced texts is obviously less easy to control by corporations. Yet, pre-selected information presented in a collaborative way may to some extent anticipate the reception of media texts. In any case, readers are positioned mainly as consumers and their power is restricted to meaning construction in reading, and 'modest forms of counter-power' (van Dijk, 1993, p. 256) such as letters to the editor or phone-in programmes. As a result, media communication is monologic rather than dialogic (Fairclough, 1995b, p. 40). Primary and secondary discourse are related in so far as journalists rearrange those parts of the corporate discourse to which they have access, omitting or only presupposing information and meanings, backgrounding or foregrounding content according to their own ideological vantage point (Fairclough, 1995b, p. 106). Also, the metaphoric expressions abounding in business publications can exclude readers who do not share the underlying concepts and can thus establish out-groups. Yet writers' success in persuading readers to share their viewpoint will obviously not only rely on the form of recontextualization or the linguistic features employed, but also on the authority the recipients ascribe to a particular magazine or programme (van Dijk, 1993, p. 268).

The examination above of relations between corporate and media discourse rounds off the discussion of cognitive metaphor theory and critical approaches to language. We shall now see how the two can – and indeed, need to – be combined into a comprehensive theoretical paradigm.

2.4 An integrated approach

The present theoretical approach to metaphor, which takes both its socio-cultural and its cognitive function into account, was triggered by the marginal integration of cognitive semantics and critical language study.[9] Ironically, a focus on the socio-cultural repercussions of metaphor was very much present in the early days of cognitive metaphor theory, corroborating Eubanks' (2000) observation that the 'connection between the cognitive and the cultural is the greatest strength of cognitive metaphor theory' (p. 25). Thus Lakoff and Johnson (1980) observe that

> metaphors ... highlight and make coherent certain aspects of our experience ... metaphors may create realities for us, especially social realities. A metaphor may thus be a guide for future action ... this will, in turn, reinforce the power of the metaphor to make experience coherent. In this sense metaphors can be self-fulfilling prophecies. (p. 156)

The above quotation does nothing short of applying one of the central claims of CDA to metaphor: as discourse is embedded in socio-cultural practice, it constructs this context from a particular perspective and is in turn constructed by it. The same holds true for the instantiations of discourse in texts and the specific genres and linguistic features they draw upon – for example, metaphoric expressions. Lakoff and Johnson (1980) take a rather critical position in the sense that they do not readily subscribe to a purely physical explanation of metaphor. Although, in particular, spatial concepts derive from physical interaction with the environment, the authors hold that even '"direct physical experience" ... takes place within a vast background of cultural presuppositions' (p. 57). Selective representation along those lines constitutes the persuasive power of metaphor (Lakoff and Turner, 1989, p. 63). Further, Lakoff and Johnson state that selective representation is motivated by intentions, in that 'people in power get to impose their metaphors' (ibid., p. 157). If we consider discourse and, by extension, metaphor as being constitutive of socio-cultural relations, one of the clearest manifestations of power is the power to control discourse, and hence cognition – for example, by 'a coherent network of [metaphoric] entailments that highlight some features of reality and hide others' (ibid., p. 157). Thus Lakoff and Johnson are in fact very close to Critical Linguistics, which was developed around the time of *Metaphors We Live By* (1980).

Since then, however, critical views on socio-cultural aspects of metaphor seem to have waned significantly in cognitive semantics. Lakoff (1987, p. 12) repeats his and Johnson's earlier claim that

> the properties of certain categories are a consequence of the nature of human biological capacities and of the experience of functioning in a physical and social environment.

He thus opposes the 'myth of objectivism' (Lakoff and Johnson, 1980, p. 195), and its notion of absolute inherent truth and meaning, by setting out an experientialist strategy (Lakoff, 1987, pp. 266–8). Such experientialist realism, as it is also called,

> characterizes meaning in terms of embodiment, that is, in terms of our collective biological capacities and our physical and social experiences as beings functioning in our environment.
>
> (ibid., p. 267)

While Lakoff in the two quotations above still takes the social factor into account, his subsequent case study of the metaphoric concept of anger stresses its embodied nature by quoting research on the human nervous system (ibid., pp. 406–8). Although the notion of metaphor as being at least socio-culturally grounded never quite disappears, it seems to be pushed to the background. This development continues in more recent cognitive accounts of metaphor. While Lakoff and Johnson still elaborate on the reasons why metaphors are used for selective representation (1980, pp. 156–63), Grady *et al.*, (1999, para. 33) only state that

> what started out . . . as some individual's . . . conceptual achievement has become a shared, entrenched conceptualization, presumably because the blend proved successful for some purpose.

Yet, what exactly that purpose might be is not included in their summary of cognitive metaphor theory's agenda (1999, para. 72).[10] While blending theory is an enormous enrichment of cognitive metaphor theory, investigating the origins and structures of metaphor, but not the effects and purposes of metaphor usage, is only half the story. The same holds true for neurobiological approaches to metaphor, as evidenced in Lakoff and Johnson (1999). Although neural theories of metaphor are certainly tremendous achievements in so far as they explain origin and structure of primary metaphors, and hence much of the human conceptual system (Grady, 1997), they run the risk of reductionism when applied to the blending and use of complex metaphors. Although the liberty to use primary metaphors may indeed be severely restricted by physical factors (Lakoff and Johnson, 1999, pp. 47, 128), it seems doubtful whether even complex metaphoric concepts are merely inevitable entailments of embodied primary metaphors. Rather, socio-cultural constraints on blending complex metaphors should be taken into account as well.[11] Another crucial question is that of how much freedom text producers have when it comes to metaphor *usage*. Lakoff and Johnson (1999) do not tackle this question either. In general, the focus in Lakoff and Johnson's later work signals a broader paradigm shift towards the natural sciences and away from the critical approach of their earlier framework. The potential for ideological critique held by cognitive metaphor theory (Jäkel, 1997, p. 39 n.) is thus not realized.

We could see that, in accordance with a 1970's academic paradigm, Lakoff and Johnson's earlier account of the social and political effects of, and motivation for, metaphor in fact reflects some tenets of Critical Linguistics. The influence was not unidirectional, however, as Critical Linguistics to some extent included metaphor in its research as well. This was done most notably by Kress, who defines metaphor as 'a potent factor in ideological contention, a means to bring an area into one rather than another ideological domain' (1989, p. 70). Further still, Kress (1989) also states that

> metaphorical activity occurs at sites of difference, in struggles over power, . . . whenever an attempt is made to assimilate an event into one ideological system rather than another.   (p. 71)

This statement is elaborated on in the above claim that any metaphoric expression drawing on complex metaphor is itself indicative of a hybrid discourse. Finally, Kress (1989) is among the few to acknowledge that metaphor is ubiquitous and essential in both linguistic and cognitive activity (p. 72).

Still, Kress's account of metaphor represents an exception rather than the rule, rendering the relationship between cognitive and critical metaphor study 'an area that warrants much greater exploration' (Eubanks, 2000, p. 25). Although Lakoff and Johnson (1980) sketched how metaphor might lend itself to a critical study, metaphor has featured only marginally in critical approaches to language. More important still, the cognitive nature of metaphor has all too often gone, if not unnoticed, then at least unmentioned. Fowler's (1987, p. 11) stance on metaphor is a case in point. In a proposal to enrich Critical Linguistics in an interdisciplinary way, he suggests drawing on schema theory developed in cognitive psychology, on the notion of prototypes originating in cognitive semantics and on metaphor as an object of research in literary criticism. It is hard to see why, given the immediate context of cognitive semantics, metaphor is confined to literary criticism – the more so as Fowler only shortly afterwards (1987, p. 12) observes that metaphors betray 'general and normative paradigms used as referential bases [in discourse]'.

As for metaphor in CDA, Fairclough (1995a, p. 74) mirrors Lakoff and

Johnson's (1980) claim about metaphor's 'central role in the construction of social and political reality' (p. 159) when citing metaphor as a feature of 'language and discourse [which] may be ideologically invested'. As metaphor can be attached to ideology, the 'relationship between alternative metaphors . . . is of particular interest' (Fairclough, 1989, p. 119). This statement is very much in line with Kress's (1989) notion of metaphor as an indicator of discursive and, by extension, socio-cultural struggle. Consequently, dominant metaphors construct domains 'in a way which helps to marginalize other constructions from the perspective of oppositional groups' (Fairclough, 1995b, pp. 71–2). The BUSINESS IS WAR metaphor is an almost classic example: its predominance in both primary and secondary business discourse leads to its perpetuation in intertextual chains, making it hard for proponents of alternative metaphors such as MARKETS ARE CONVERSATIONS (Searls and Weinberger, 2000) to root their metaphors firmly in business discourse. In a cognitive perspective, alternative metaphors are at a further disadvantage as they are schema-inconsistent and thus less likely to be processed and reproduced (Augoustinos and Walker, 1995, p. 44). Fairclough's (1992) observation that 'metaphor is used . . . as a vehicle for achieving reclassification' (1992, p. 207) could include cognitive reclassification at the discourse level. Yet, the announcement to focus on 'relatively superficial linguistic features of vocabulary and metaphor' (1995b, p. 70) in an instance of text analysis seems to indicate that Fairclough, too, emphasizes the linguistic realization of metaphor rather than its cognitive force.

Thus we can see that theoretical integration of metaphor into critical approaches to discourse, and vice versa, is quite marginal and often incomplete. Nevertheless, headway has been made in empirical analyses of metaphor in medical, political and economics discourse. While some of the research is more cognitively orientated (Henderson, 1994; Read *et al.*, 1990; White, 1997), other work focuses on the ideological and socio-cultural function of metaphor (Akioye, 1994; Browne and Quinn, 1999; Howe, 1988; Montgomery *et al.*, 1989; Wilson, 1992). Still other contributions employ the cognitive theory of metaphor to unravel ideological implications (Boers, 2000; Chilton, 1987; Chilton and Ilyin, 1993; Chilton and Lakoff, 1995; Lakoff, 1992; Nelson, 1995). It is this last approach that can be enriched by a framework in which the ideological function of metaphor is seen as both a cognitive and a social phenomenon.

Such a model combines elements of both cognitive semantics and CDA. Taking up the notion that primary metaphors are embodied during the conflation phase (Johnson, 1999) acknowledges van Dijk's (1997, p. 10) demand that

> in the analysis of discourse as action, we need to assume some level of . . . basic actions, below which linguistic and mental activity is no longer intentional but more or less automatic.

The notion of embodied primary metaphors contradicts radical constructivist claims (such as Fairclough's) that 'any aspect of experience can be represented in terms of any number of metaphors' (Fairclough, 1989, p. 119). Such a view seems unsuitable when researching metaphor, as it would preclude the possibility of primary metaphors and subsequently complex metaphoric blends altogether. One of metaphor's main functions is to explain the abstract in terms of the concrete. If, however, the concrete is seen as being constructed, too, we would end up in a metaphoric chain without any beginning. This is what Hodge and Kress (1993) seem to propose when saying that

> there is no 'pure' act of perception, no seeing without thinking. We all interpret the flux of experience through means of interpretative schemata, initial expectations about the world, and priorities of interest.   (p. 5)

However, such perceptual funnelling brought about by cognitive and socio-cultural constraints presupposes pre-existing schemata – that is, 'mental structure[s] which contain general expectations and knowledge of the world' (Augoustinos and Walker, 1995, p. 32), and which can act as filters in the first place. This filtering process is undoubtedly very prominent as a secondary mechanism once those cognitive schemata and ideological interests have taken hold, and certainly does influence the blending and usage of complex metaphors. Yet, it does not account for the formation of primary metaphors, which form the basis for later metaphoric conceptualizations.

Further, complex metaphors are gained by blending primary ones. In this, they prove to be a special case of

> schema development [which] proceeds from an initial learning of a number of independent and unintegrated components to a single and integrated schematic unit with strong associative links between the components. These associative links become strengthened through experience and use.[12]
>
> (Augoustinos and Walker, 1995, p. 52)

The pool of complex metaphors thus achieved is the cognitive counterpart to a more discourse-orientated 'interpretative repertoire' (Potter and Wetherell, 1987) and as such a resource that text producers can draw upon. This pool can be enlarged by adding new complex metaphors. Moreover, the ones already in it can be recombined in secondary and further blending processes. This recombination can also take the form of blending previously neglected semantic components. The notion that 'input spaces are themselves often blends, often with an elaborate conceptual history' (Turner and Fauconnier, 1995, para. 21) is exemplified by the BUSINESS IS WAR metaphor.[13] Not only does it represent a blend with two asymmetric input spaces, namely the originally embodied concept of FIGHT and its sophistication as STRATEGY.[14] In a second step, the WAR blend is moreover blended with the BUSINESS space, itself a highly complex blend.

However, just as discourses, genres and texts cannot be mixed freely, the blending of primary into complex metaphors, or any subsequent combinations of complex metaphors obtained through blending is by no means free of constraints either. And just as discourse participants have only restricted access to discourses and texts, text producers do not have unlimited access to their pool of complex metaphors. Restrictions on these processes of blending, recombining and selecting are captured by the concept of social cognition.[15] (For overviews of that branch of social psychology, see Augoustinos and Walker, 1995; Fiske and Taylor 1991 as well as Kunda, 1999.) Starting from the assumption that hegemonic power often takes the form of controlling people's minds, social cognition here refers to the mental models structuring ideologies. Such models are acquired and (re)produced through social practices such as discourses (van Dijk, 1993, pp. 254, 257) and interact with the personal cognition of group members. Cognitively structured ideologies provide group cohesion by defining membership in a group as well as its tasks/activities, goals, norms/values, position and resources (van Dijk, 1995, pp. 19–21, 32). More often than not, these different schemata are structured metaphorically. For example, membership, with its entailing notion of in-groups and out-groups, is conceptualized by means of the CONTAINER metaphor (see Hodge *et al.*, 1979 for examples such as *the people that fall outside the line*). Both tasks/activities and goals can be represented as trajectories (*business school graduates . . . have been heading for dotcoms* [MA FT 42]), while position may be defined by a number of different spatial metaphors (*two of the world's drug titans are facing off in a war for dominance* [MS FO 6]). The resources schema is ambiguous as it can conceptualize both literal (that is, natural) resources as well as metaphoric ones (that is, cultural resources such as access to discourse and influence on discourse practices, or symbolic resources such as authority). Metaphoric resources are then conceptualized in the form of CONTAINER metaphors (*the banks that own Tradepoint have it in their power to make it . . . profitable* [MA FT 9]). Norms/values ties in with Lakoff and Johnson's (1999, pp. 290–334) analysis of moral concepts as based on a relatively small set of embodied primary metaphors (healthy, pure, light, balanced and so on). While any moral concept or set of norms/values may be the result of blending such primary metaphors, what is regarded as morally sound can obviously differ vastly from culture to culture, and even from group to group. Such group schemata are reflected in, and reproduced through, discourse and text. By learning a group's language, even members of a very different group can to some extent adopt its cognitive schemata, as demonstrated by Cohn's (1987, p. 54) account of a pacifist feminist learning to speak, and consequently to think, like male defence intellectuals.[16]

The claim that choice of metaphor reveals a vested interest in elevating or downgrading a person or group and, as can be inferred, in manipulating recipients, in fact ties in with Lakoff and Johnson's (1980; pp. 10–13) view that the very systematicity of metaphor helps to highlight some aspects of a concept while hiding others. With reference to the topic at hand, the dominant usage of the conceptual metaphor DOING BUSINESS IS WAGING WAR by journalists indeed helps to shape mental models of business. Alternative metaphors such as MARKETING IS CREATING AND DEVELOPING RELATIONSHIPS or NEGOTIATING A MERGER IS DANCING could therefore make a vast difference indeed. Just consider the striking contrast between *Smirnoff Ice could be a potent weapon* (MS BW 18) on the one hand and [the service they offer] *is like their baby* (MS BW 2) on the other. Nor is using a well-established metaphor a trivial matter. Following the view that metaphor influences perception, using a well-established dominant metaphor helps to cement accepted models that are usually in the interest of a dominant group. The WAR metaphor proves this point: since war has long been, and still is to a large extent, a male activity, the metaphoric view of business as war is highly masculinized and, when used in discourse, helps maintain business as a male-dominated domain, thus building relations between members of an in-group while at the same time excluding members of the respective out-group.

Groups are also made coherent by ideology controlling their members' actions, including their discursive actions as text producers and recipients (van Dijk, 1995, pp. 21, 32). Thus participants in the discourse domain of business will have particular cognitive models of, say, their group's tasks/activities and goals. These models may be structured metaphorically in terms of war. While this metaphoric structure can ultimately be traced back to primary metaphors informed by a force schema (Talmy, 1988), the purpose of blending the WAR metaphor with the business space is ideologically motivated. While the force schema rests on a universal experience, the ensuing concept of fight is already highly gendered – that is, masculinized (Enloe, 1983, p. 12). Thus WAR metaphors draw on task/activity concepts of men as a group. As noted above, the propagation of WAR metaphors in business discourse provides this discourse with a masculinized conceptual structuring and serves to establish women as an out-group. (Note that, in this process, business-women's ascribed gender roles are combined with their achieved occupational roles.) Exposure to a discourse thus characterized will (re)produce the discourse participants' mental models of their task/activities and goals. The ideal reader would share the concept either prior to his or her reception of the text, or come to share it while processing the text – if it blends with previous concepts, that is. Thus readers who, because of their cognitive, discursive and social make-up, already conceptualize much of their world in terms of, say, sports, are more likely to blend those concepts with the WAR metaphor. By contrast, a person conceptualizing his or her world in terms of dancing or talking is likely to feel alienated by abounding evidence of the WAR metaphor. The former reader would then be part of the in-group, while the latter would soon find himself (or, rather, *her*self) confined to an out-group. Moreover, group schemata will influence the participants' actions, increasing the likelihood of them reproducing the WAR metaphor in text production. In the secondary domain of journalism, this could mean that

> reporters bring [particular metaphoric models] to bear in interpreting events and source texts, models which [they] try to convey to audiences in the way they write.   (Fairclough, 1995b, p. 30)

In a circular fashion, these texts will serve as the starting point for new intertextual chains, each reifying and conventionalizing the WAR metaphor. Given the particular production practices in media discourse, conventionalized metaphors are also more likely to be used in 'quickly produced newspaper prose' (Eubanks, 2000, p. 44). The sample analyses will show the *Financial Times* to be a case in point.

It should also be noted that the cognitive inculcation of social practices continues to have its effects even when those practices are no longer enacted. Thus war keeps functioning as constitutive of male identity even in prolonged periods of peace (Schmölzer, 1996, p. 164). Similarly, employing the WAR metaphor is not conditioned by having any literal experience of war, because WAR metaphors are part of a culture's pool of complex metaphors (Lakoff and Johnson, 1980, pp. 62–4). Depending on the socio-cultural conditions, particular metaphors can thus gain hegemonic status.

The WAR metaphor is a special case as it also serves to sustain hegemonic masculinity. It was Connell (1987, 1995) who applied Gramsci's notion of hegemony to gender relations. Since hegemonic masculinity 'is always constructed in relation to various subordinated masculinities as well as in relation to women' (Connell, 1987, p. 183) it is those two groups with which a consensus has to be achieved.[17] This can be accomplished by a combined naturalization of patriarchal gender constructs and the promise of benefits. Connell maintains that 'the forms of femininity and masculinity constituted at [the societal] level are stylized and impoverished', mere social stereotypes (see p. 41). As hegemony is always negotiable,

> those men who have a stake in hegemonic masculinity must constantly reassert their symbolic opposition to femininity in order to confirm their own sense of masculinity. (Johnson, 1997, p. 22)

One way of doing so is by employing the WAR metaphor, and one way of doing so most effectively is by applying the WAR metaphor to business, as both military and corporate elites are highly masculinized. Accordingly, Connell (1998) identifies multinational corporate executives as representatives of hegemonic masculinity in late capitalism. He sets out to define a global gender order as 'the structure of relationships that interconnect the gender regimes of institutions, and the gender orders of local society, on a world scale' (ibid., p. 7). Accordingly, global markets are just one site of such a global gender order and the global hegemonic masculinity that accompanies it. The same holds true for multinational corporations, which 'in the great majority of cases are culturally masculinized and controlled by men' (ibid., p. 8). Globalizing institutions and the masculinities embedded in them leads to the emergence of a global hegemonic masculinity. In late capitalism, the most influential institution to be globalized is the corporation, leading to the ascent of a hegemonic transnational business masculinity . . . marked by increasing egocentrism, very conditional loyalties . . . and a declining sense of responsibility for others.   (ibid., p. 16)

It is this new form of hegemonic masculinity that has all but replaced the 'rigid, control-oriented masculinity of the military' (ibid., p. 17). The global executive has become a virtual 'ersatz soldier' who has backgrounded the military as a constituent of male identity.[18] Given those parallels between soldiers and executives, it comes as no surprise that the connections between these two models of hegemonic masculinity should be reflected in discourse and cognition as well.

One of the most obvious reflections is the presence of WAR metaphors in business discourse. Through blending the war with the business input space, WAR metaphor helps to convey and implement a combination of the two most powerful images of hegemonic masculinity. Out-group members are likely to adapt this central metaphor to themselves in the hope of becoming part of the dominant discourse, and thus the power elite. In this case, women as members of a negatively evaluated group would try *de facto* to leave their ascribed role through their linguistic behaviour, although 'the markers of the original group membership persist' (Augoustinos and Walker, 1995, p. 114). Indeed, self-descriptions of corporate women do occasionally betray the same, if not more extreme, machismo running riot (Koller, 2004).

Given the seemingly endless cyclical process of hegemony sketched above, the question arises as to how far individuals can resist cognitive (and hence discursive) control, especially from text producers endowed with much symbolic capital – like, for example, a business journal considered to be 'leading' in its field. One corrective can be personal cognition, which is constituted by individual values, ideologies, attitudes and knowledge deriving from specific biographical experience. This personal cognition can reflect and reproduce, but also contrast or even subvert, social cognition. For example, if the ideology embraced by a business journal depicts a company's aggressive acquisition policy in terms of metaphoric expressions of war in a positively connoted context, an individual recipient's personal cognition may still make him or her reject such a belligerent approach. If that person is found to employ metaphoric expressions of war, it is likely that the metaphor is ascribed to others to discredit their position rather than being claimed by the person (Eubanks, 2000, pp. 27–8).

Another factor influencing the strength of social cognition is discourse access – for example, in the form of access to a variety of business publications representing similar corporate behaviour by drawing on different (metaphoric) models. However, discourse participants may find themselves in a situation in which they do not have access to either alternative discourses or 'the mental resources to oppose . . . persuasive messages' (van Dijk, 1996, p. 85). Such a situation will then lead to the emergence of preferred models. If social cognition controls mental models through discourse, widely shared preferred (that is, hegemonic) models lend cohesion to a group's beliefs and thus help to predict group members' actions. Further, such ideological mental models also have a social function in that they support existing power relations, which are often asymmetric in nature. As outlined above, power is best secured by naturalizing the very ideology it rests upon – that is, by eliminating internal contradictions in models. In this context, it is worthwhile looking at the notion of Idealized Cognitive Models (ICMs) (Lakoff, 1987). It is according to them that prototypes (that is, most representative members of a category) are distinguished (Rosch, 1975, 1978). So-called prototype effects arise when there is asymmetry between more- and less-representative members, with the latter being on the mostly fuzzy boundaries of a category and thus deviating from the ICM. But even members clearly located within the category can be differentiated. Thus we find typical cases, ideal cases and social stereotypes. Typical cases help to 'draw inferences about category members in the absence of any special contextual information' (Lakoff and Johnson, 1999, p. 19). As categorization, being a largely theory-driven process, is based on pre-existing assumptions,[19] a category member, unless marked for some untypical feature, will be taken to show the typical traits of the unmarked default value (Lakoff, 1987, pp. 61, 116). Such inference works from centre to periphery (ibid., 1987, pp. 86–7) – that is, characteristics of prototypical members are transferred to less typical members and so on, according to a scale of typicality. Seen as such, prototypes are an important conceptual structuring device. Ratings of the extent of prototypicality, however, are obviously culture-specific (White, 1998, p. 35). To illustrate, categories of soldiers in many cultures show male soldiers as prototypes. Further, soldiers are also conceptualized as being aggressive. Consequently, unless a soldier is marked explicitly as female, even untypical (for example, soft-spoken and peace-loving) soldiers are presupposed to be male. In addition to typical cases, ICMs also inform ideal cases. To elaborate on the example, the ideal Western soldier would be brave and courageous (features such as patriotism or belief in authority might also come into play). Finally, an ideal case can develop into a social stereotype, a schema which comes to represent different social categories as a whole (Lakoff, 1987, pp. 85–6). The three types work accordingly for dynamic prototype scenarios.

All three types – typical cases, ideal cases and social stereotypes – may inform the input space (I_1) of a metaphoric blend. If the second input space (I_2) shows characteristics which are peripheral to the category represented by I_1, the more typical characteristics of I_1 will be projected on to I_2 in the blend. This modification of I_2 is reinforced by the fact that, although characteristics of the source input space tend to be more salient (Eubanks, 2000, p. 76), inferences are still drawn from the blend back to the target input space. A metaphoric expression such as *foot soldiers such as Ms Knapp* (*Economist* 1999, p. 64), for example, thus serves to masculinize the portrayed executive and hence to co-opt her hegemonically into a dominant paradigm. Such examples show how metaphors drawing on prototypes do ideological work. In this context, the description of prototypes as 'neural structure that permits us to do some sort of inferential . . . task relative to a category' (Lakoff and Johnson, 1999, p. 19) only serves to make ideology all the more powerful, as it can also be inculcated neurobiologically. The focus of this book, however, is on the reasons why some models and subsequent metaphoric blends are favoured over others in discourse, and what effects this has on cognition, discourse and socio-cultural practice.

In accordance with the claim that 'it is . . . metaphors rather than statements which determine most of our . . . convictions' (Rorty, 1979, p. 12), metaphor is particularly salient in the context of social cognition. Metaphoric expressions as instantiations of underlying conceptual metaphors are a valuable starting point to study cognitive and ideological determinants of discourse. Thanks to the ubiquity of conceptual metaphors, they account for much of the cognitive construction of social relations. What is more, their function of highlighting and hiding particular semantic features makes it possible to trace ideologically vested choices in blending processes using complex metaphors. Metaphor thus not only proves to be an interface between the cognitive structure underlying a discourse on the one hand, and the ideology permeating it on the other. In addition, metaphor, as it is realized in surface-level metaphoric expressions, also links discourse and its manifestation in text. It follows that any discourse is structured cognitively by the metaphors prevailing in the respective discourse domain. On the micro-level, texts are linguistically/semiotically structured by the metaphoric expressions deriving from those prevailing metaphors. As such, metaphoric expressions may help to reify cognitive models governing discourse, and underlying metaphors may partly determine the surface structure of text. From such a perspective, one can only analyze metaphor when 'at the same time analyzing the discourses that catalyze it and shape each metaphoric utterance and the patterns these utterances form' (Eubanks, 2000, p. 4).

It is two aspects of metaphor in particular that deserve to be highlighted, namely syncopation and clustering.[20] While syncopation is a frequent feature of any blending process, metaphoric blends are syncopated by definition: metaphor always draws only on a particular set of semantic features in its formation, omitting all but a few central characteristics of the input spaces.[21] The question is, for what exactly are those characteristics central. In the context of social cognition, they serve ultimately to reproduce or subvert existing social relations. In the BUSINESS IS WAR metaphor, for example, discourse participants interested in maintaining the WAR metaphor to foster solidarity among an in-group are likely to draw mainly on the positively connoted aspects of the WAR domain, such as courage, victory and glory. One strategy for groups seeking to subvert the dominant metaphor, on the other hand, could be to focus on the more gruesome aspects of the WAR domain. In the case of in-group members incorporating the more taboo characteristics into the blend, this is often done in the form of denoting what 'we' shall do to 'them' (*'on any given day, we can beat Morgan Stanley'* [MA BW 23]).

Other ways of subverting a dominant metaphor would be to reject it altogether and propose an alternative one (MARKETS ARE CONVERSATIONS instead of MARKETS ARE BATTLEFIELDS), to modify the target input space (COMPETITION IS WAR instead of the broader MARKETING IS WAR) or to elaborate on the whole metaphor in terms of either its static frame (EMERGING MARKETS ARE NEW FRONTLINES) or dynamic script (INTRODUCING A PRODUCT IS LAUNCHING A WEAPON) (Chilton and Ilyin, 1993, pp. 12–13).

Yet another subversion strategy is hybridization. It has already been outlined how discourses and genres can be mixed to achieve hybrid and 'parodic-ironic' effects (Bakhtin, 1986, p. 80). Further, any complex metaphor was seen as itself indicating a hybrid discourse, blending as it does two distinct domains and their discourses with them. Metaphor thus hybridizes two discourses in the form of a blend (see Figure 2.2).

Apart from such metaphoric hybridization on the interdiscursive level, metaphoric shifts may also occur within the boundaries of a discourse. This is made possible by complex metaphors being recombined to enlarge the pool of cognitive resources. Wider cognitive resources obviously lead also to broadened linguistic resources, which in turn bring about hybrid genres and texts. Intertextual hybridity can, for

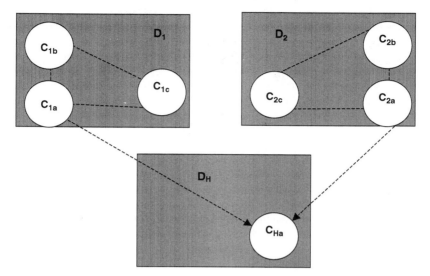

Figure 2.2 Metaphoric hybridization at the level of discourse
Note: D = discourse; C = complex metaphor; C/D_H = hybrid form.

example, be realized in hybrid metaphoric expressions reflecting hybrid conceptual metaphors. (As was pointed out above, recontextualization also brings about hybrid forms; however, the focus here is on hybridization achieved through metaphor.) The upshot is a very complex web of both internal and cross-boundary metaphoric mixing, active at the level not only of discourse, but also of genre and text (see Figure 2.3).

In fact, the complexity is such that 'one cannot always predict which features of a specific text . . . will have which effects on the mind of specific recipients' (van Dijk, 2001, p. 358). Figures 2.2 and 2.3 illustrate that, theoretically, there are no constraints on what can be mixed. However, we have seen that, in practice, mixing is often restrained by ideology manifested in cognition as well as in discourses and the genres and text features they favour. In the ensuing hybrid forms, metaphors can be found in clusters. In extreme cases, clusters can turn into clashes. Clashes in metaphoric expressions are often referred to as 'mixed metaphors' and chided as rhetorical blunders (an example would be *amid a rash of corporate weddings, AOL Europe still plays the field* [Boudette, 2000]). While there may be idiosyncratic cases coherent only in a producer's personal cognition, it seems likely that most metaphor clusters

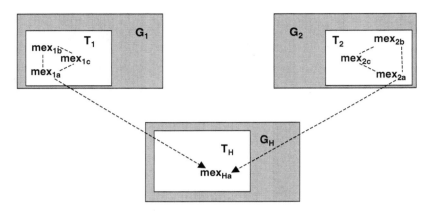

Figure 2.3   Metaphoric hybridization at the level of genre and text

Note: G = genre; T = text; C = complex metaphor; mex = metaphoric expression; G/T/C/mex$_H$ = hybrid form.

are informed by social cognition. (A similar point is made by Emanatian (2000), who holds that the target concepts of metaphor clusters are related in a corresponding cultural model.) Thus, clusters such as WAR, SPORTS and GAME metaphors in marketing discourse or FIGHTING, MATING and FEEDING metaphors in mergers and acquisitions discourse are brought about by cognitively- and socially-structured ideologies. In the first case, the ideological purpose can be identified as excluding female discourse participants by not only drawing on one masculinized domain (WAR) but reinforcing it by combining it into a cluster with another equally masculinized one (SPORTS). The GAME metaphor, a blend of competition and playfulness, serves the dual function of both reinforcing and attenuating the WAR metaphor. The second cluster is slightly more complex as it draws on conceptual parallels between three seemingly unrelated domains. Still, these can be subsumed under the heading of an EVOLUTIONARY STRUGGLE metaphor and we shall see that clustering of those domains ultimately serves to establish a coherent conceptual system that functions to position women as out-group members.

Developing Richards' notion of tension in metaphor (1936/2001, p. 84), one could say that the further a metaphor's input spaces are removed from each other, the more tension the entailing hybrid discourse will show. In a critical cognitive perspective, increased heterogeneity additionally signals struggle about conceptualizations. However, while clusters certainly indicate hybridity, not every co-occurrence of different metaphors necessarily signals conflicting discourses and struggle. Different metaphors can show complex coherences and thus reinforce a particular concept. An example is ORGANISM metaphors (and, by extension, either GARDENING or DOCTORING metaphors), which show features of physical brutality rather than nurturing, and thus support aspects of the WAR metaphor (*Ford has slashed Mazda's payroll by 7% . . . and taken an ax to its subsidiaries* [MA BW 21]). Even if metaphor clusters are not linked conceptually but represent real alternatives they need by no means be counter-discursive. It is questionable, for example, whether 'women . . . using metaphors from cooking, birthing, and sewing along with those from war' (Tannen, 1994, p. 121) do not rather reproduce stereotypes and thus help to sustain an asymmetric gender paradigm. After all, 'the idea that females are inherently nurturing and loving . . . fits depressingly well into the military ideology about the role and purpose of women' (Chapkis, 1988, p. 107). This, of course, begs the question of whether there can be ungendered metaphors at all, an issue that will be re-addressed in the Conclusion. As pointed out before, however, change in the cognitive models is brought about in discourse – for example, by metaphoric hybridization and clustering – yet it also influences future text production and comprehension. By making 'current conceptualizations undergo transformations' (Kittay, 1987, p. 4), metaphoric processes thus serve an important function in spreading ideology.

By virtue of ideology's double – social and cognitive – function, it can be considered

> the 'interface' between the cognitive representations and processes underlying discourse and action, on the one hand, and the societal position and interests of social groups, on the other hand.
>
> (van Dijk, 1995, p. 18)

Any account of discourse and its features – for example, metaphor – therefore needs to integrate the two functions.[22] Contrary to the view of 'discourse idealism' (Chouliaraki and Fairclough, 1999, p. 28), social life is not a product of discourse but rather a product of cognition, which is in turn reflected in discourse. It follows that the study of discourse alone, albeit indispensable to a critical approach, will not suffice to explain fully the workings of ideology. On the other hand, looking at the cognitive aspects of ideology as conveyed in discourse should not result in disregard for its social functions. A balanced framework will account for ideology *'also, but not exclusively*, in terms of mental representations and eventually in terms of the neurobiological structures of the brain' (van Dijk, 1998, p. 22; original emphasis). Both the cognitive and the social functions of ideology indeed deserve equal attention, as neither of them is more material or objective (Lakoff and Johnson, 1980, p. 59; van Dijk, 1998, p. 22). Similarly, the scope of such a framework should not only account for the micro-structures of social cognition but also look at how such social cognition influences discourse practices and hence wider socio-cultural shifts (Fairclough, 1995b, p. 29). It is the aim of this book to contribute to such an integrated account of ideology. By drawing on blending theory, the focus on the dual structure of metaphor that has been prevailing since Aristotle (Eubanks, 2000, pp. 14–15) is replaced by an emphasis on interrelated metaphoric networks. In addition, a framework incorporating social cognition locates metaphor at the interface between the cognitive and the social, and explores its origins in – and effects on – both. In short, such an approach acknowledges that 'conceptual metaphor is a shared cognitive, cultural resource' (Eubanks, 2000, p. 21).

To sum up, primary metaphors are embodied and blended into complex metaphors, which may be recombined through further blending processes (hybridization and clustering) and semantic re-accentuation (for example, syncopation). Each individual has a dynamic pool of shifting complex metaphors and concomitant metaphoric expressions at his or her disposal. However, access to that pool and possible recombinations within it are restrained by the interplay of social and personal cognition. Cognition informs ideology in the form of (metaphoric) mental models which are drawn on in discourse production. Through discourse and text production, particular metaphors can rise to hegemonic prominence to establish, reify or challenge social relations. As such, metaphoric expressions in discourse have repercussions on conceptual metaphors at the cognitive level (Boers, 2000, p. 139). In this cyclical process, ideology as manifested in metaphor is inculcated both socially and cognitively, with metaphor functioning to convey 'suggestive illustration' (Beneke, 1988, p. 204). So it may well be true that because of their neurobiological make-up, individuals have only limited 'control over how [they] conceptualize situations and reasons about them' (Lakoff and Johnson, 1999, p. 556). However, the cognitive restraints on their freedom are not the result of some quasi-automatic process set in motion during the conflation phase. Rather, social cognition in the form of ideology is at work at every stage after the formation of primary metaphors.

This, in short, is the basic theoretical framework. Let us now see how such a theory translates into method.

3
Method: Quantitative and Qualitative Analyses of Metaphor

> I wade through the filth of mighty metaphors, meta, meta, meta by
> metre.   (Einstürzende Neubauten, 1993)

The method section translates the above integrated theoretical framework into a tripartite research paradigm. This combines computer-assisted quantitative analysis with qualitative investigations along the lines of functional grammar in the Hallidayan tradition. Quantitative corpus analysis is here regarded as a valuable starting point, granting a sound empirical basis to subsequent claims about the metaphoric features of the cognition and discourse prevailing in a particular domain. Although quantitative results alone do not provide for sufficient insights, they can, if recontextualized, support qualitative analyses of particular texts (see Koller and Mautner, forthcoming). To integrate those two fundamental methodologies, the present work has been based on machine-readable data. Let us first look at the corpora and then at the two steps in the analysis.

The two text corpora this practical approach to metaphor study is based on are collections of magazine and newspaper articles on marketing and sales on the one hand, and mergers and acquisitions (M&A) on the other. Those corpora as a whole will be subjected to quantitative analysis, whereas qualitative analysis will be used on selected texts from them. Those analyses then give rise to a strategy for discussing the ideological impacts of metaphor on both discourse and cognition. Generally speaking, the focus of this study is metaphor in the language use of groups, allowing for assumptions about the related conceptual system. As spelt out in the previous chapter, language use is not regarded as a mere derivative of the conceptual system but rather conceived of

Table 3.1   Data on publications in marketing and sales corpus

Publication	Type of publication	Date range	Number of articles/% of corpus	Number of words/%	Average article length (no. of words)
BW	Weekly magazine (USA)	1996–2001	34 16.19%	40,946 25.66%	1204
EC	Weekly magazine (UK)	1997–2001	42 20.00%	39,205 24.57%	933
FO	Bi-weekly magazine (USA)	1998–2001	36 17.14%	38,907 24.38%	1081
FT	Daily newspaper (UK)	1997–2001	98 46.67%	40,518 25.39%	413
Total			**210 (100%)**	**159,576 (100%)**	

as being in a mutually constitutive relation to it, with ideology as the interface between them.

The two electronic text corpora mentioned above were specifically compiled for the project. As such, they are machine-readable, consisting of texts published between 1996 and 2001, taken from four different business publications (*Business Week, The Economist, Fortune, Financial Times*). Each corpus contains approximately 160,000 words (see Tables 3.1 and 3.2). The fact that the corpora include three magazines and a daily newspaper (*Financial Times*) accounts for a marked difference in average article length, as newspapers as a format are characterized by short news items usually absent from magazines. Accordingly, the *Financial Times* shows the shortest articles by far. To make up for this bias, a larger number of articles were included so that each publication contributes roughly a quarter of all words to the corpora.

One of the key particularities of business – and, in fact, any special-interest – media discourse resides in the fact that the people journalists write about are overwhelmingly the readers themselves. It therefore seems useful to provide some insight into the demographics of that readership. The subscriber profile of *Business Week*, which was estab-

Table 3.2 Data on publications in mergers and acquisitions corpus

Publication	Type of publication	Date range	Number of articles/% of corpus	Number of words/%	Average article length (no. of words)
BW	Weekly magazine (USA)	1999–2000	29 17.68%	42,022 25.57%	1456
EC	Weekly magazine (UK)	1998–2000	49 29.88%	41,363 25.17%	844
FO	Bi-weekly magazine (USA)	1996–2000	22 13.41%	40,765 24.81%	1853
FT	Daily newspaper (UK)	1997–2000	64 39.02%	40,168 24.46%	628
Total			**164 (100%)**	**164,318 (100%)**	

lished in 1929 and had a worldwide circulation of 1,155,785 copies in 2000 (*Business Week*, 2002b), shows an astounding 90 per cent of the readership to be male, with just over three-quarters (76 per cent) being in the 25–54 age bracket. In terms of education and profession, 86 per cent hold a university degree and 63 per cent have a top management position. The latter fact in particular explains the readers' average household income of $207,000 in 1999 (*Business Week*, 2002a).

The worldwide circulation of *The Economist*, established in Britain in 1843, amounted to 838,080 copies in the first half of 2002. The readership is again almost exclusively male, with women accounting for only a meagre 9 per cent. The majority of readers (52 per cent) are aged between 35 and 54 years of age, and another 33 per cent are older than 55. Similar to the *Business Week* readership, 93 per cent of *Economist* readers are university graduates, which translates into an average household income of $186,000 (*The Economist*, 2002). *The Economist* differs from the other publications in the corpora – with the possible exception of the *Financial Times* – in that it does not put its focus on finance and economics alone, but devotes half of the magazine to political issues. More important for current purposes, it is unique in yet another respect: it is the only one of the four publications to elaborate on its style of writing in the form of a style guide. Apart from the general statement that '*The Economist* believes in plain language' (*The Economist*, n.d. a, para. 8), it more specifically advises writers to 'use all metaphors, dead or alive, sparingly' (*The Economist*, n.d. b, para. 3). As far as metaphor frequency in the marketing and sales corpus is concerned, the anonymous journalists writing for the magazine seem to take this recommendation to heart: as can be seen from Table A.1 (p. 191), 17.16 per cent of all metaphoric expressions occur in *The Economist*, which indeed represents the lowest figure among the publications contained in the corpus. However, this does not hold true for the mergers and acquisitions texts: here, *The Economist* ranks second, with 29.59 per cent.[1] *The Economist* publisher's aim of metaphoric scarcity does not square with researchers' and readers' perception of its style either. While the former rather regard it as 'journalistic writing designed to exploit . . . metaphor to its fullest in order to capture . . . attention' (Henderson, 2000, p. 169), the latter note that 'colourful comparisons always were irresistible to *The Economist*' (Merry, 2000, p. 4). The following sample analyses will show that *The Economist* is indeed a rich source for metaphor research.

The third publication to be included in the corpora, the US magazine *Fortune*, was founded in 1930. In the first half of 2002, circulation figures stood at 103,032. Again, its readership was 90 per cent male in 1997 (the most recent data available), with a median age of 45.9 years. In terms of education, 84 per cent of international readers are university graduates with an average household income of $280,400 (Time Inc. *Fortune*®, 1998, pp. 5–6).[2]

Finally, the British newspaper *Financial Times* (FT), first published in 1888, recorded a worldwide circulation of 486,463 copies in the first half of 2002. The reader profile shows that the average age of the FT reader is 48; and 38 per cent are board-level directors. Consequently, their personal income averages £104,000 ($164,250). While, unfortunately, no figures were available for average household income, gender or education, there is no reason to believe that these differ vastly from those of the other publications.[3]

Before outlining how the data were extracted from the two corpora built from the publications, attention should be given to a number of caveats. First, culture-specific aspects of metaphor usage arising from the British or US origin of the texts were not dealt with systematically. This is despite the fact that, with some metaphoric expressions, cultural phenomena could well be drawn upon for interpretation – for example, the strikingly higher number of metaphoric expressions from the domain of KINGSHIP in the US magazine *Fortune* (see Table A.6 in the Appendix) and its slightly exotic and hence distancing and attenuating effect. While the difference between publications from different cultural backgrounds will be discussed in cases where it seems very pronounced, such discussion is limited to individual findings. Similarly, the corpora are not systematically analyzed for different genres either, to avoid 'trading off resolution for scope' (Seidel, 1991, p. 112). Suffice it to say that the highest percentage in both corpora – between two-thirds and three-quarters – is accounted for by general articles, followed by reports and surveys in both cases, making up just over 10 per cent. At the other end of the scale, interviews and book reviews hardly feature at all.

Finally, the hardest decision concerning a possible research question was related to the issue of authorship and gender. The corpora had originally been tagged for the authors' gender, as this parameter suggests itself to any researcher interested in the ideological aspect of metaphor. When analysing the data on gender and authorship yielded by a computer-based search of the relevant tags, however, findings were ambiguous. For example, marketing texts in *Business Week* are overwhelmingly written by women, while the situation is reversed in *Fortune*. Also, there seems to be a slight male bias in authorship of M&A texts, which, however, is accounted for exclusively by the *Financial Times*. More importantly, there are considerable obstacles in the way of a serious study of how gender influences metaphor usage in the data. First, there is the high percentage of anonymous articles (30 per cent in the marketing and sales corpus, and 39.63 per cent in the mergers and acquisitions corpus). These high percentages are mainly accounted for by *The Economist*, the editorial policy of which is to put content before people (*The Economist*, n.d. a, para. 5). In addition, the total of 246 articles marked for authorship together matches only 173 different authors, raising questions of idiosyncratic rather than gender-specific metaphor usage. In view of such hurdles, the gender of the authors was eventually not taken into account. Yet the question remains an intriguing one and future research may well start out from a different set of data clearly marked for the text producers' gender.

After the decision to exclude systematic analysis of culture-specific phenomena, genre issues and the authors' gender, the question remained of how to ascertain clusters of dominant metaphors as well as alternative metaphors in the two corpora. (Clusters are defined as a set of metaphoric expressions that tend to co-occur frequently in any given discourse – for example, *hostile takeover* and *corporate marriage* co-occurring as instantiations of the FIGHTING and the MATING metaphor, respectively, in texts on mergers and acquisitions.) The first step in answering the above question was to define a lexical field that captures 35 lemmas each from three clustering domains, amounting to 105 lemmas for both marketing and sales as well as mergers and acquisitions.[4] Accordingly, the lexical field for the alternative domain also contains 35 lemmas. In the case of marketing and sales, the dominant clusters are WAR, SPORTS and GAMES, with ROMANCE serving as an alternative. For mergers and acquisitions (M&A), the lexical field is that of evolutionary struggle, containing types from the domains of FIGHTING, MATING and FEEDING, while DANCING functions as the example of an alternative metaphor. As the domains differ vastly in terms of their relevance for, and frequency of occurrence in, business media discourse, it was, for example, harder to decide on lemmas from the domain of dancing than it was for the domain of war. Nevertheless, all lexical fields eventually contained the same number of lemmas, so that they could be compared on the same basis. It should be noted that, while there is a field 'war' and 'romance' for marketing and sales, which matches 'fighting' and 'mating' in M&A discourse, the two fields do not fully converge in either case. Rather, all the three fields identified for M&A discourse are subsumed under an umbrella EVOLUTIONARY STRUGGLE metaphor. Apart from that, the lexical field of war/fighting in each case includes five flexible lemmas which, drawing on previous knowledge of marketing and sales as well as M&A media texts, were identified as typical of the respective discourse domains. These 'wildcards' are *blitz*, *campaign*, *cut-throat*, *field* and *launch* for marketing and sales, and *defence*, *hostility*, *raid*, *victim* and *vulnerability* in the case of M&A. Moreover, the two fields of romance/mating differ in three instances: whereas the 'romance' field in the case of marketing and sales discourse is extended into the more general domain of private relationships by incorporating *family*, *friend* and *heart*, the respective field for M&A discourse includes *maiden*, *rape* and *relationship* (for a further elaboration on the reasons for these differences, see sections 4.1.1 and 5.1.1).

While the selection process cannot be fully operationalized, the way towards the eight lexical fields (three fields plus one alternative field for each discourse) should at least be sketched. As mentioned above, previous knowledge of the two discourses and, in the case of possible alternative metaphors, anecdotal evidence from individual media texts, served as the starting point. After jotting down relevant lemmas collected from individual articles, thesauri and glossaries on the respective topics helped to corroborate the lemmas' membership of the respective source domain (Ammer, 1999; Ballroomdancers.com, 1997; CBS, n.d. a and b; First Base Sports, 2001; 'Gambling Glossary', n.d.; Hickok,

1999–2002; Jones, 1994; Kanzen, 2000–2002; Sommer and Weiss, 1996; Sydney Storm, 1998; US Department of Defense, 1988; Wilkinson, 1993). For fields such as that of dancing, which proved to be difficult to arrive at, those thesauri and glossaries also provided additional lemmas not ascertained by anecdotal evidence. The resulting fields of 35 lemmas each were then checked for word class distribution. It soon became clear that the orginal aim of including an equal number of nouns, verbs and adjectives/adverbs in each field could not be met. This is partly because, with some lemmas, a particular word class seemed to be outside the metaphoric spectrum, corroborating Low's (1988) observation that sometimes

> where two words exist which are . . . semantically related but of a different grammatical class, one may have a metaphorical use which is not extended to the other. (p. 131)

Hence, the lexical fields of romance/mating include *consummation* or *to consummate*, since these collocate with *marriage* (external reference data from the Bank of English), but not the adjective *consummate*. Another example is *suitor* as opposed to *to sue*. However, the fields were in some cases calibrated and revised to lessen the nominal bias that emerged. What is more, this imbalance is adjusted by calculating relative rather than absolute frequencies for word classes. As a final remark on word classes, it should be noted that prepositions have been omitted from the lexical fields. Although they undoubtedly play a crucial role for spatial metaphors (for example, *entry into the traditional ad market* [MS FO 15]), 'their noun/verb colligates are too general to yield any imagery or to make manifest any specific schemata' (Goatly, 1997, p. 91). Given this overly general nature of prepositions and the fact that this study does not focus on spatial metaphors, prepositions were disregarded. Adjectives/adverbs, however, were included, notwithstanding the fact that they, unless in predicative position, mainly occur in relation to nouns or verbs. Yet, not being mere function words, they evoke metaphoric models more readily than do prepositions. On a general note, looking at word class distribution in metaphor research heeds Kittay's (1987) demand that 'we must consider the unit of metaphor to be independent of any grammatical unit' (p. 24).

Another issue concerns so-called 'dead' metaphors, here defined as expressions where their origin is opaque to language users, who no longer recognize them as being metaphoric. While instances such as *campaign* – being derived from Latin *campus* or (battle)field – certainly function as metaphors in the diachronic system of the language, it is arguable whether they can still be regarded as having a metaphoric effect in the synchronic system, and hence in language use. To determine this question, one has to look at whether the blending process that gave rise to the expression is still transparent to text producers and recipients in the discourse community at hand and/or whether those discourse participants still perceive a contrast between literal and metaphoric senses (Gibbs and Steen, 2002). While this study does not include field research in metaphor processing, a look at the core meanings given in small dictionaries still serves as an indicator of how encroached a metaphoric meaning really is. Taking the case of *campaign*, the *Collins Cobuild Dictionary* (1995), the *Concise Oxford Dictionary* (1995) and the *Longman Dictionary of Contemporary English* (LDCE) (1995) all list the metaphoric meaning first, making it the predominant one ('Campaign', 1995 a–c). However, the picture is more complex in the case of *launch*. All three dictionaries list the nautical, military and business meaning of the lemma, with the third always being given last. However, the LDCE alone grants first-entry status to the military meaning ('Launch', 1995). In view of the fact that the metaphoric meaning of *target* is encroached in both the present corpora and the two reference corpora (that is, used exclusively or, in the case of the Bank of English and the British National Corpus, predominantly), it comes as a surprise that all three dictionaries in fact prioritize the sense of 'something at which someone is aiming a weapon' ('Target', 1995).

From the above, it can be seen that, on a scale of transparency, terms such as *campaign* and *launch* are rather located, if not at the extreme end of complete opaqueness, then certainly heading that way. Still, the question of how they came to be used in business discourse in the first place is a crucial one. After all, the very dominant presence of such terms from the military domain in business discourse is by no means a coincidence. While the lexemes in question are certainly not employed consciously by all text producers in every single instance, their presence is still significant as it ties in perfectly with that of other lemmas from the war domain that are perceived as being more metaphoric – for example, *blitz* or *battle*. To discard some technical metaphors (that is, those restricted to a particular discourse domain) because of their ambiguous status in the synchronic system would therefore impoverish the data.[5]

The contents of the fields finally decided on are sketched in Tables 4.1–4.4 (see pp. 66, 67, 69, 70) and Tables 5.1 and 5.2 (see pp. 116, 120). A complete list of all lemmas can also be found in Appendix Tables A.1

and A.2; and A.4 and A.5. With the lexical fields thus established, each corpus was searched for the 105 lemmas they comprise, accounting for spelling variants (for example, *home run versus home-run* or *homerun*, *maneuver versus. manoeuvre*) in doing so. Although the search was lemma-based, the various emerging lexemes were taken into account as well, because 'if only the base form is studied, some metaphorical uses may be missed' (Deignan, 1999, p. 189). While the search itself was enabled by the concordancing program of the WordSmith Tools 3.0 suite, the data obviously require manual reworking to filter out non-metaphoric instances and irrelevant metaphoric occurrences.[6] Irrelevant metaphoric occurrences are those that do not represent realizations of the conceptual metaphors identified – for example, *embrace* from the domain of MATING in M&A discourse, which does occur in the corpus as the collocation *to embrace the idea* (MA BW 12), but not as a metaphor for corporate mergers. The same holds true for all surface-level realizations of the metaphor ARGUMENT IS WAR, as in, for example, *she shot back* (MA BW 17, MA FO 17 and 21) or *he attacked reports . . . as 'simply not true'* (MA FT 30). While ARGUMENT IS WAR is certainly ancillary in creating a discourse marked for its belligerence, the metaphor does not really square with the present focal point of interest, namely the BUSINESS IS WAR metaphor. After such exceptions had been cleared, the procedure outlined above yielded the following results:

- absolute frequencies of metaphoric expressions and metaphor density in the two corpora, with the latter being arrived at by calculating an average per 1000 words
- in the case of metaphor clusters, relative frequency of metaphoric expressions across the three domains and
- relative frequency of metaphoric expressions across word classes and domains.

In their simplest form,

> counting techniques can offer a means to survey the whole corpus of data and to gain a sense of the flavour of the data.
>
> (Silverman, 1993, p. 163)

Beyond that, the above findings not only show how many of the 35 types from the lexical fields are in fact realized, but also how frequently the respective types occur. This type–token ratio differs vastly, in fact, with, for example, *launch* showing 127 occurrences (ratio 0.008) as opposed to *defeat*, with only one occurrence or a ratio of 100 (both examples occur in the marketing and sales corpus). Such numbers go some way to indicate how active the underlying mental models, or parts of them, in fact are. In addition, quantitative results serve as a starting point to discuss how relevant discourse participants consider those models to be for particular ends. Further, the results tell which conceptual metaphor from a cluster is most dominant in quantitative terms. This dominant metaphor is then hypothesized to be cognitively supported by other metaphors in the cluster. Again, such a dominant metaphor could be both especially vivid as a mental model, and particularly relevant to the higher-level socio-cultural ends of the text producer. In addition, the quantitative evidence is broken down into word classes to see whether a particular metaphoric type may be based on a prominent nominal-static, verbal-dynamic or adjectival-descriptive model. Deduction of such models is then taken as a first indication of the schemata prevailing in the group to which the metaphor producer belongs (van Dijk, 1998). Alternatively, the models could also reflect on the group schemata to which the writer refers; that is, business people. As can be seen from the reader profiles of the four publications, the group written about is largely convergent with the group written *for*; readers are obviously meant to recognize themselves in the journals and papers.

Despite the above insights being gained by quantitative investigation, tackling semantic issues by means of corpus analysis is anything but straightforward. For a start, as metaphor generation programs are not readily available to end users, corpus research into metaphor necessarily has to begin with attested linguistic expressions (Jäkel, 1997, p. 145). While this corpus-based approach is in line with *post-hoc* research focusing on metaphor in text and interaction (Cameron and Low, 1999, p. 79), any concordance program obviously only shows the more-or-less decontextualized chunk of text the researcher has been looking for. In the case at hand, this chunk shows one token of the 35 types of each lexical field, with five words to the right and five to the left of the search word or node. Although the fields are comprehensive, they are obviously not exhaustive, and some potential metaphoric expressions may well be missed and can only be retrieved by looking at longer stretches of text. Moreover, identifying what counts as an instance of metaphoric usage and deciding on the underlying conceptual metaphor can all too easily run the risk of subjectivism. Granted, some metaphoric expressions can be identified quite easily as they only occur in semi-fixed collocational phrases (for example *launch a campaign, target audience*; see

Deignan, 1999, p. 197),[7] or because their very occurrence in a text with a particular topic suggests metaphorical usage (for example, members of the lexical field of dancing in a corpus on corporate restructuring). Still, metaphor identification will, to some extent at least, always rely on 'informed intuition' (Deignan, 1999, p. 180). Such subjectivity may be further reinforced by the researcher's sensitivity to metaphors in general, and his or her familiarity with certain discourse domains in particular (Low, 1999, pp. 50–1). To counter random inference of underlying conceptual metaphors, Low (1999, p. 64) proposes a checklist that can be adapted and fleshed out with examples:

- Are conventional metaphors extended creatively? (For example, *shotgun courtship* [*The Economist*, 2000a] instead of the collocation *shotgun wedding* found in the Bank of English sample corpus used as reference.)[8]
- Are other people's conventional metaphors extended creatively as well? (Example: *'We're the infantry on the beach,'* says [E*Trade's CEO] *. . . It's unclear whether these initiatives will keep E*Trade ahead of the advancing troops* [MS BW 15].)
- Do text producers make it explicit that they conceive of a topic in the form of a particular metaphor? (Example: *'I view you like an equity investment'* [MA FO 17].)
- Do text producers discuss which semantic features are transferred? (Example: *Like football and trench warfare,* [trying to gain market share in the consumer products market] *is a contest of sweat, mud, and inches* [MS FO 4].)
- Do text producers challenge others whose use of phrases differs with regard to semantic or metaphoric overtones? (Example: *Should investors fear indigestion? 'We don't digest* [corporate cultures]; *we integrate them,' says CFO Muller* [MA FO 2].)

The above points represent valuable help in deducing conceptual metaphor from surface-level metaphoric expressions, and thus filter out idiosyncratic metaphor usage that is not part of the conceptual map informing the discourse. However, it is obvious that a single researcher cannot, within a reasonable time frame, apply them to each of the 1,597 occurrences of metaphoric expressions in the two corpora. Even checking the 66 instances of alternative metaphors against them will prove to be very time-consuming indeed. Hence, the above criteria will only be applied to those metaphoric expressions in the sample texts that are not accounted for by the lexical fields and thus need testing.

From the above it can be seen that computer-generated results require quite extensive manual reworking. Still, metaphor research can indeed gain from corpus analysis. One benefit is the latter's potential to reveal the use of metaphoric expressions across word classes, an issue neglected all too often in cognitive linguistic theory focusing on NOUN A IS NOUN B-type metaphors. Given the hypothesis that prevailing word classes point to the nature of underlying cognitive models, it is indeed vital to

> discriminate between types of metaphor embodying specific config-
> urations of metaphor features [and to this end] corpus research is
> crucial. (Steen, 1999, p. 81)

Moreover, if metaphor is regarded as a phenomenon of *social* cognition, it has to be ascertained whether a particular metaphor is really shared intertextually between a number of text producers. By analysing texts from various sources compiled into a whole, corpus linguistics can be helpful in deciding which metaphors are likely to be discourse charac-teristics, and which are rather idiosyncratic. In addition to such quali-tative benefits, it is one of the hallmarks of corpus analysis that it allows for the investigation of large amounts of data, thus broadening the empirical basis for testing hypotheses. Seen as such, corpus linguistics can accommodate the often-voiced criticism that cognitive metaphor research following Lakoff and Johnson 'relies on idealized cases, dis-connected from the context of actual use in natural discourse' (Quinn, 1991, p. 91).

Still, to avoid isolating the results and thus focus on lexical metaphors at the expense of phrasal and higher-level ones, the attested metaphoric tokens were, in a second step, linked back to their textual environment. Recontextualization at the paragraph level can be done with the help of the WordSmith Tools 3.0 concordancer itself, as the program not only provides the immediate co-text of up to 25 words left and right of the search word, but can also display maximized co-text of approximately 400 words for single concordance lines. In doing so, the researcher can heed Hodge and Kress's (1993) demand that

> the minimal unit for analysis is not a single form or text in isolation,
> but a reading of a sequence in context, containing prior or later forms
> in text. (p. 181)

However, more complex metaphoric chains within and across texts, which convey the structure of the underlying conceptual map, are still not easily detected and processed this way. The texts were therefore manually tagged for the attested metaphoric expressions derived from the different lexical fields, and a second search was run for those tags to see where a high density of metaphor clusters occurs. Next, one text showing such density was taken from each of the four publications, resulting in a sample of four texts for each discourse – a total of eight texts singled out for qualitative analysis.

The following questions can be answered by such an analysis: first, where in the text does clustering occur and does it serve the same function in different positions? Similar actions were employed in the case of alternative metaphors, the only exception being that a single metaphor's position, rather than a cluster's, was analysed. If one regards journalistic texts as being implicitly argumentative, metaphor clusters or alternative metaphors in a text's introduction might indicate an ideational, defining function ('setting the agenda'); clustering or the occurrence of single non-dominant metaphors in the middle could serve interpersonal, argumentative ends; and, finally, clustering or instances of single alternative metaphors towards the end of a text may have another interpersonal, namely persuasive, function ('driving a point home'). It would then be interesting to see if particular metaphors are linked to particular functions, and thus dominate the cluster in specific parts of the text. A variation on this is the question whether alternative metaphors are employed in particular slots for particular purposes. In any case, such a connection would point to a rather dynamic metaphoric cluster model, which can be accentuated differently in the process of text production and reception. Alternatively, dominant and alternative models could interact to achieve different ends as a text is being produced or processed. Should one function prevail in the texts, inferences could be drawn for the respective discourse as a whole as being characterized by, for example, persuasion rather than explanation. This would, in turn, reveal the text producer's and recipient's primary role in the discourse, and the relations between them.

Again, the WordSmith Tools concordancing program can help to find out where in the text the clusters or single metaphors are to be found. Its dispersion plot function provides a graphic representation of how the metaphoric tags that have been searched for are spread across the whole text. Comparing the graphs for all three metaphors in the cluster yielded a specific picture of where clusters occurred, and which metaphors were predominant in the various occurrences. In a second step, these cluster graphs were also compared to the ones for alternative metaphors. Beyond that, the computer-generated results were related back to the actual texts to see what role the specific metaphors had within, or in relation to, the respective clusters.

One question with regard to possible roles and functions is whether the metaphoric expressions in question represent quotations from primary business discourse participants – that is, business people – or whether they constitute original products of the secondary discourse of business journalists. This issue ties in with the query regarding whether the metaphor is ascribed to an out-group or claimed by an in-group (Eubanks, 2000). Obviously, the in-group can either be journalists ascribing the metaphor to business people by quoting them on it, or business people themselves ascribing the metaphor to other participants in the primary discourse, or to journalists. Furthermore, there is the question of whether metaphor producers feel the need to attenuate the more taboo aspects of the WAR metaphor, or whether they use it in an unbridled fashion. Attenuating may be present in the form of textual clues, particularly hedging markers (*like, sort of*). Other means of atten-uation are morphological devices (suffixes such as *-ly, -ish*), or typo-graphic indicators such as inverted commas (Prince and Ferrari, 1996, pp. 221, 223). Ironically, explicit lexical markers indicating a metaphor (*metaphorically speaking*) may serve to spoil its effect (Goatly, 1997, p. 174). On the other hard, lexical markers explicitly refuting a metaphoric reading – for example, *literally*, can paradoxically enhance metaphor (*Major League Baseball's embattled marketing chief . . . is getting kicked out of his office – literally* [MS BW 21]; see Goatly (1997), pp. 173–4). A final means by which producers can attenuate potentially problematical models such as the WAR metaphor is by drawing on its historical rather than contemporary aspect – for example, referring to a metaphorical *sword* rather than a *tank* (Eubanks, 2000, p. 47). The issue of whether metaphors stem from primary or secondary discourse, whether they are ascribed or claimed, and whether or not they are attenuated is vital, as it helps to reveal in-group schemata.

Going beyond mere frequency, a final question in this context is whether metaphors constitute metaphoric chains, again either within or, in the case of alternative metaphors, in relation to, the cluster. This question is as much about the textual function of metaphor as a device used to achieve text cohesion (Goatly, 1997, p. 166) as it is about the relevance and vividness of the respective metaphors within or outside the cluster. The most relevant and vivid metaphors can attain the status of a motif (Steen, 1999, p. 95), possibly not only in a particular sample text but also in a whole discourse (the collocation *hostile takeover* being a case in point). In addition, relations between the cluster metaphors and between cluster and alternative metaphors can also be investigated, such as metaphors extending, elaborating, exemplifying, generalizing or questioning each other (Kyratzis, 1997). Moreover, metaphoric expressions can also flatly negate or simply echo each other. Within the cluster, the questioning function in particular indicates a model characterized by cognitive heterogeneity, whereas a cluster combining different metaphors that elaborate on each other points to a more homogeneous model. This would then allow for a discussion of how hybrid, in fact, is the discourse conveying such a model. As far as the relationship between metaphor clusters and non-dominant metaphors is concerned, it is particularly intriguing to see whether alternative metaphors do indeed, as one might expect, question dominant metaphors, or whether they do not rather extend and thus covertly support them. Again, this will tell us something about the level of hybridity and struggle in the discourse at hand. Moreover, the functions within metaphoric chains can also corroborate assumptions about whether the underlying metaphoric models are – as hypothesized on the basis of the quantitative data – static, dynamic or descriptive, conveying particular group schemata.

Both the questions of the roles and functions of the attested metaphoric expressions and of metaphoric chains across the texts are addressed using a functional grammar framework (Beaugrande, 1997). It seemed reasonable to employ functional grammar because the quantitative analysis of word classes soon revealed that a purely formal approach is inadequate. This can be seen from the fact that the attested dominance of nominal expressions is to some extent relativized by the phenomenon of hidden adjectivity. Thus both compound nouns (for example, *target group*) as well as participles (for example, *bruising*) show an adjectival function. And participles are also being nominalized – for example, *bruising* in the idiom *cruising for a bruising* (reference data from the British National Corpus). The formal approach thus has to be complemented by a functional paradigm, an observation that dates back to the early days of critical language studies and has now developed into something of a tradition in that field (Fairclough, 1989, pp. 13–14). As with critical approaches to language, the taxonomy sketched in Table 3.3 has its roots in Halliday's (1994) seminal work.

Table 3.3 requires some clarification to link this specific methodological part to the theory it is based upon. First, polarity refers to the presence or absence of negation in an utterance (negative/positive polarity),

Table 3.3 Aspect

Polarity	Tense/Aspect	Transitivity	Status/Mood
negative We don't digest them, …	**past** trademarks benefited society (MS FT 91)	**active** the new entity … survives anti-trust scrutiny (MA EC 21)	**declarative** retail salespeople work on site (MS FT 86)
positive …we integrate them (MA FO 2)	**present** buyers get the widest choice of products (MA FT 57)	**passive** Pickens was threatened by proxy fights (MA FO 17)	**performative** war has been declared between the two …companies (MS EC 37)
	future Who will be left standing once the dust has cleared? (MS FO 33)	**reflexive** firms are allowed to shield themselves from competition (MS EC 41)	**conditional** If you get into bed with a company like [that], you will get squashed (MA EC 26)
	predecessive The two met … after Malone had moved through jobs at Bell Labs (MA FO 8)	**reciprocal** companies seem unable to resist … picking each other up (MA EC 15)	**contrafactual** If Warner had not done all that, J. P. Morgan would surely have been easy meat in a takeover battle (MA BW 23)
	progressive Online brokers [are] building up their brands (MS BW 10)	**medial** [those] business models …will not survive (MS BW 31)	**optative** If only you could shut the whole thing down for a while (MA FO 21)

Belief/Mood	Attitude	Trajectory/ Manner of action	Perspective
certain [They] would surely have been easy meat (MA BW 23)	**ameliorative** [it] had succeeded in building up brand name value (MS FT 27)	**inchoative** companies are beginning to believe this . . . could be the cure (MS FO 18)	**narrative** [He] stepped in as CEO when Kevin Kalkhoven retired (MA FO 2)
necessary Both companies badly need to win ground here (MS FO 4)	**pejorative** many organisations . . . do not have . . . the volume to warrant attention (MS FT 86)	**completive** Both have been watching this week's events with interest (MA EC 8)	**descriptive** competition is such that we have reached . . . product parity (MS FT 91)
obligatory He has to nurture his luxury marques (MS EC 17)	**diminutive** a shrunken Tiger was concluding [its] worst year (MA BW 27)	**tentative** local rivals are trying to ignite nationalist passions (MS BW 7)	**expository/explanatory** Britons pay more because they have been persuaded by skilful advertising (MS FT 91)
possible A full-blown shootout could well follow (MA BW 4)	**augmentative** All his hawking has increased . . . interest in the game (MS BW 21)	**intensive** Goldman needs to woo retail customers in a big way (MA BW 12)	**instructional** then you have to . . . keep the initial excitement going (MA EC 26)
	successive novel therapies used to enjoy years on the market before competitors arrived (MA BW 1)		**imperative** Don't mess with Darla (MA FO 17)
			interrogative Should investors fear indigestion? (MA FO 2)
			exclamatory 'What a huge waste of energy' (MS FO 32)

Table 3.3 (Continued)

Belief/Mood	Attitude	Trajectory/ Manner of action	Perspective
capable *The new company will be able to attack Asia (MA BW 16)* **permissible** *his company allows retailers to keep a share of the revenues (MS EC 10)* **impossible** *pharmaceuticals cannot be distributed across the Internet (MA EC 41)* **incapable** *weak food brands that they cannot easily sell or kill (MA EC 19)* **impermissible** *the viewer's enjoyment ... must not be affected by advertising (MS FT 69)*		**durative** *[He] will keep running the game from Milwaukee (MS BW 21)* **punctative** *local bankers immediately began offering customers cut-rate mortgages (MS BW 29)* **frequentive** *GI kept slipping its deadlines (MA FO 8)*	**argumentative** *you can rest assured you are being pulled down this path (MS FO 14)*

Source: Adapted from Beaugrande, 1997, p. 198.

with negation as the more marked choice. This can, depending on what is negated, be associated with either an ameliorative or a pejorative attitude. Second, tense/aspect is a somewhat ambiguous concept. In order to avoid confusion, it should be noted that the term 'aspect' is used here both as an umbrella term for the categories in Table 3.3 (the title of which stems from Beaugrande, 1997) as well as in a narrower sense – that is, referring to the grammaticalized marker for a type of activity denoted by a verb or verb phrase ('Aspect', 2003; 'Aspekt', 2002). In this latter meaning, aspect forms part of a triad of aspect, tense and mood. Thus, while the first three entries under the category of tense/aspect – past, present and future – embody tense, the remaining three – predecessive, progressive and successive – rather represent aspect. The third classical grammatical category to describe verbs – mood – is realized in both status and belief in Table 3.3. As such, mood forms a link between the two categories as it embodies the 'attitude on the part of the speaker towards the factual content of the utterance' ('Mood', 2003). Apart from reflecting mood, the status category also ties in with the notion of speech acts (Austin, 1962/1999; Cole and Morgan, 1975), in particular their illocutionary force: although dubbed 'performative', the concept in fact reflects the illocutionary force of a declarative speech act, such as opening a meeting. Further, imperative status may be realized in directive speech acts such as commanding.

Aspect, discussed above in connection with tense, is also closely linked to manner of action; in fact, manner of action – appearing under the heading of 'trajectory' in Beaugrande's (1997) taxonomy – determines aspect. (For example, verbs denoting a state cannot form progressives: *I am knowing ['Aktionsart', 2002].)

As for perspective, it ties in well with all three functions of metaphoric expressions in text: while their textual function in providing cohesion is related to argumentative perspective, their interpersonal function in organizing the subject positions of, and relations between, text producer and recipient are linked to expository and instructional perspective. Further, the ideational function of metaphoric expressions in constructing a topic from a particular vantage point is mirrored in the descriptive sub-division of perspective. Also, different perspectives are theorized to tie in with the location of metaphoric expressions in text, as elaborated upon earlier in this chapter (see p. 55).

Finally, the notion of transitivity has proved to be a very fruitful concept for critical approaches to language. An example is the following:

other companies, thought to include Oxford Biomedica, are understood to have had informal discussions with Peptide in the past but
are not believed to be in talks at present.   (MA FT 60)

By veiling the agent, and thus the ultimate responsibility for the process,
transitivity is very often ideologically loaded. This is true not only for
passive but also for medial transitivity. In obscuring agents, medial and
passive transitivity resemble nominalization, an instance of Hallidayan
grammatical metaphor (Halliday and Hasan, 1985, p. 19). Passivization
and nominalization, albeit not always equally important for critical
analysis, both 'permit deletion of . . . agency and modality' (Fowler,
1985, p. 69).

Although critical linguists agree on employing a functional approach,
the question as to what extent they should do so is less obvious. Despite
Fowler's (1987) belief that 'critical linguists get a very high mileage out
of a small selection of linguistic concepts such as transitivity and nom-
inalisation' (p. 8), it seems reasonable to draw, if not on all, then on
more than just one or two of the categories listed above to analyse the
co-text of a particular metaphoric expression in the sample texts. Thus,
tense/aspect, status/mood and belief/mood, trajectory/manner of action
as well as perspective will be of particular relevance. Tense/aspect and
trajectory/manner of action are regarded as important as they promise
to provide insights into how dynamic or static the model in fact is that
is assumed to underlie the attested metaphoric expression.

In a nutshell, the study at hand focuses on process types and participants in processes as well as on which kinds of aspect (in the broad
sense) are conceptualized metaphorically. Observing and describing
metaphor on the level of language by means of the above taxonomy
will allow for analysis of the group schemata prevailing for participants
in secondary business discourse (that is, journalists and their audiences).
Another object of analysis is the relationships between discourse participants, comprising both the relationships between text producers and
recipients in secondary discourse and, to a lesser extent, their relationships with participants of primary discourse (that is, business people).
These relationships are seen as being conveyed by the text producers'
specific usage of metaphor clusters and alternative metaphors.

While the quantitative analysis is meant to yield initial results about
the productivity of particular metaphors and their prominence and
perceived relevance in the discourses at hand, recontextualizing the
attested frequencies in sample texts paves the way for assumptions
about what underlying conceptual models influence those discourses.

The findings from this qualitative part of the empirical study will be presented in graphic form, showing how the interplay among the metaphoric blends in the clusters, as well as the relationships between them and alternative metaphors, may form complex cognitive models (see Figures 4.1 on p. 106 and 5.1 on p. 162). The graphic representation follows, albeit somewhat loosely, Abric's (1984) notion of representations as containing interdependent elements organized around a core, with hierarchy decreasing as the distance from that core increases. Those conceptual models extend the local systematicity that metaphor chains lend to the sample texts, since they show the emergent metaphoric systematicity at the level of discourse (Cameron, 1999, p. 16).

This concise discussion of results will be followed by a more macroscopic look at both the discourse and the socio-economic practice the conceptual models help to (re)produce or subvert. In short, the present methodology combines the framework proposed by CDA (see Figure 2.1) and the three-level analysis of ideology and discourse as described by van Dijk (1995, p. 20). Both methodologies include descriptive text analysis of a wide variety of features (Fairclough, 1995b, pp. 202–3; van Dijk, 1993, pp. 273–7). The method and perspective applied here (that is, electronic corpus analysis and functional grammar) accounts for both quantitative text description as well as qualitative text analysis. As for the discourse level of analysis, Fairclough focuses on an interpretative analysis of how discourse practice – that is, production, distribution and reception/interpretation of texts – is enacted. In contrast, van Dijk stresses the need for analysis along the lines of personal and social cognition to assess the values, ideologies, attitudes and types of knowledge that inform a text. Both theorists find common ground again in broadening the scope to the explanation of socio-cultural practice, including identities and relationships in groups on the situational, institutional and societal level. The aim of summarizing results in the form of conceptual models, and discussing the impact of such cognition on text, discourse and socio-economic practice is to verify the claim that only an integrated 'study of . . . cognitive and social dimensions . . . enables us to fully understand the relations between discourse and society' (van Dijk, 1997, p. 35).

The next chapter will show how the method outlined in this section can be applied to concrete empirical data.

4
Business Media on Marketing: Metaphors of War, Sports and Games

> [The marketing people's] war vocabulary betrays them: they talk about *campaigns, targets, strategies, impact.* They plan *objectives*, a *first wave*, a *second wave*. They are afraid of *cannibalization,* refuse to have themselves *vampirized* . . . These are the soldiers about to fight WWIII.
>
> (Beigbeder, 2000, p. 32; emphasis as original)

This first empirical chapter will provide an analysis of the dominant cluster of WAR, SPORTS and GAMES metaphors to be found in media discourse on marketing and sales. Additionally, alternative metaphors will also be investigated, most notably the ROMANCE metaphor as emerging in the sub-discourse of Relationship Marketing (Sheth and Parvatiyar, 2000), and its interaction with the prevailing metaphor cluster. From the initial quantitative analysis of the corpus, based on pre-defined lexical fields, it will be seen that the WAR metaphor is the most frequent one in the corpus, followed by SPORTS and, lagging far behind, the GAMES metaphor. Alternative metaphors are even less frequent. Further, the quantitative analysis also reveals that metaphoric expressions in the corpus show a nominal bias across all three cluster metaphors. This analysis will be complemented by a more in-depth qualitative analysis drawing on four sample texts. There, the dominance of the WAR/SPORTS cluster is further corroborated, as the metaphors are observed to occur in salient textual positions and to be conceptually supported by the GAMES metaphor. Similarly, the qualitative analysis of sample texts provides further evidence of the weak standing of alternative metaphors. After this twofold analysis, the chapter will close by sketching the possible conceptual model underlying contemporary marketing discourse, and by discussing its socio-cognitive impact on, and origins in, the broader social formation in which this discourse is embedded. This discussion will focus on how the masculinized nature of the dominant metaphor cluster helps to reify marketing as a male-defined social practice. First, however, let us turn to quantitative findings, starting with the lexical fields they are based upon.

4.1 Quantitative analysis

4.1.1 Lexical fields

Identified according to the procedure outlined in Chapter 3, the lemmas in Tables 4.1–4.4 are spread across the three word classes of nouns, verbs and adjectives/adverbs, and incorporate relations of antonymy, hyperonymy, synonymy and metonymy. An example of hyperonymy from Table 4.3 is *game, to gamble*, which yields *casino*. This in turn shows *roulette* as a hyponym, which then functions as a hyperonym for *chip*. Metonymy is present in Table 4.1's *soldiers* versus *troops* or *army*, whereas antonymy shows in the *surrender–victory* contrast. Finally, synonymy is present in *attack* and *assault*.

According to the blended nature of war itself – combining archaic physical fight with more sophisticated strategy, the first lexical field contains items relating to physical violence (*blood, to bleed, bloody; bruise, to bruise; cut-throat; killer, to kill*) as well as those stemming from military science (*to beleaguer; campaign, to campaign; launch, to launch; target/targeting, to target; manoeuvre, to manoeuvre*, including examples in US spelling).[1] The whole field is shown in Table 4.1.

The field contains 35 lemmas or headwords, which can be split up into 81 lexemes (for example, the lemma *battle* comprises the lexemes *battle, battlefield, battleground, to battle*). Of these lexemes, a majority of 45, or 55.56 per cent, are nouns, while 25, or 30.86 per cent, are verbs, and only eleven, or 13.58 per cent, are adjectives. As word-class distribution is skewed, the quantitative findings will have to be interpreted in relative rather than absolute terms. The same holds true for the second field in the cluster, sports (see Table 4.2).

In this second field, the 35 lemmas comprise 62 different lexemes. While nouns again feature most prominently (50 per cent), the relationship between them and adjectives (19.35 per cent) is slightly more balanced than in the lexical field of war. Verbs show almost the same figures as in Table 4.1 (30.64 per cent). As can be seen, the types of sports drawn upon to compose the lexical field include the ones most popular in the Western world – that is, football, basketball and baseball – as those are most likely to be used metaphorically.[2] Apart from these contact sports, additional lexical items were taken from car and horse racing

Table 4.1 Lexical field 'war'

Noun	Verb	Adjective/adverb
armour, arms, army	to arm	–
assault	to assault	–
attack	to attack	–
–	to backfire	–
battle, (battle)field, battleground	to battle	embattled
–	to beleaguer	–
blitz	to blitz	–
blood	to bleed	bloody
bomb, bombshell	to bomb, to bombard	–
bruise	to bruise	–
brutality	–	brutal
campaign, campaigner	to campaign	–
casualty	–	–
combat	to combat	combative
conqueror, conquest	to conquer	–
–	–	cut-throat
defeat	to defeat	–
enemy	–	inimical
–	–	fierce
fight, fighter	to fight	–
front	–	–
killer, killing	to kill	–
launch	to launch	pre-launch, post-launch
manoeuvre	to manoeuvre	–
shot, shotgun	to shoot	–
soldier	–	soldierly
surrender	to surrender	–
survival, survivor	to survive	–
target	to target	–
trench	to entrench, to retrench	–
troops	–	–
veteran	–	–
victory	–	victorious
war, warfare, warrior	–	warlike, warring
weapon, weaponry	–	–

(*pack, pole position, race, turf*), while tennis terms play only a minor role (*grand slam, volley*). Because of its lack of widespread popularity, the type of sport closest to war – that is, boxing – is missing from both the lexical field and, as a metaphoric expression, from the corpus. However, anecdotal evidence, including illustrations in business magazines, suggests that related concepts are occasionally drawn upon in business discourse,

Table 4.2 Lexical field 'sports'

Noun	Verb	Adjective/adverb
ball	–	–
–	–	breathless
catch	to catch	–
champion	to champion	–
coach	to coach	–
–	to dribble	–
fairness	–	fair, unfair
–	–	fast
field	to field	–
foul	to foul	foul
game	–	–
goal	–	–
grand slam	–	–
–	to guard	–
–	–	head-to-head
jump	to jump	–
kick	to kick	–
league	–	–
match[3]	–	–
pack	–	–
pass	to pass	–
play, player	to play, to outplay	–
pole position	–	–
punch	to punch	–
race	to race	racy
red card, yellow card	–	–
run, runner	to run	runaway
score	to score	–
shot[4]	to shoot	–
speed	to speed	speedy
throw	to throw	–
time-out	–	–
–	to tire	tired, tireless, tiresome
turf	–	–
volley	–	–

as in the following example: ' "We've got WorldCom on the mat. Now it's time to kick them," boasts one sales rep' (Haddad and Foust, 2002, p. 41).

The observation that sports, especially contact and/or team sports, function as a sublimation of war shows in the overlap between the two lexical fields, as reflected in frequent polysemy (Küster, 1978, p. 82). Among the 'pervasive, colourful metaphors of war used for . . . sport'

(Malszecki, 1995, p. 8), the military terminology of football coverage is most prominent (Jansen and Sabo, 1994, p. 3). Further, there is the technical metaphor *shot, to shoot* (see n. 3) as well as the item *field*, which can refer to either a battlefield or a playing field. Less obviously, *champion* also ties in with war terminology, as it is related etymologically to *campaign*, both of which derive from the Latin word for 'field', *campus*. Originally, the champion was the last gladiator to persist in the arena or field (Malszecki, 1995, p. 12). While this etymology is hardly of any synchronic importance, it nevertheless reveals the conceptual links between war and sports leading to diachronic semantic change: war and sports do indeed form a conceptual model defined by the 'compression of opposites in [an] extreme state of excitement' (ibid., p. 91). As can be seen from the third lexical field (see Table 4.3), this model is enlarged further by the domain of games.

The lexical field in Table 4.3 comprises 51 lexemes and is the one most biased for nouns, which account for 64.7 per cent. In contrast, only just over a quarter (27.45 per cent) of all lexemes are verbal ones. Adjectives, of which there are four (7.84 per cent), lag far behind, once more necessitating a discussion of relative rather than absolute frequencies.

While the field of sports shows a number of similarities with that of war, the domain of games is in turn related to sports. This is most clearly conveyed by the fact that the two lexical fields share one top-level item, namely the lemmas *play* and *game*. However, in terms of lexemes, *to gamble* and *playful* have been added, the latter focusing on the fun rather than the contest aspect of games. The third common lexical unit, *ball*, appears here as roulette equipment, rather than as a hyperonym for different ball games, a sub-field too close to sports to be included. The conceptual links between sports and games are obviously quite tight, so tight, in fact, that Eubanks (2000, pp. 51–4) discusses the TRADE IS A GAME metaphor as one showing 'considerable variation . . . , including most prominently metaphors of cards, chess, and football' (ibid., p. 53). Despite the apparent cognitive proximity of the two, sports and games are still differentiated in Tables 4.2 and 4.3. After all, sports rather foreground the competitive contest aspect whereas games highlight a collaborative fun aspect. Yet, 'game metaphors have a hologramic quality' (Eubanks, 2000, p. 128) in that they can either be attenuated to display the notion of peaceful leisure activity or intensified to approximate the WAR metaphor. An example of a belligerent game is chess, 'itself a war metaphor' (ibid., p. 41).[5] Finally, the lexeme *rip-off, to rip off* also betrays the idea of physical aggressiveness, if not violence, and thus itself constitutes a metaphoric expression.

Table 4.3 Lexical field 'games'

Noun	Verb	Adjective/adverb
ace	–	–
ball	–	–
bankroll	to bankroll	–
bet	to bet	–
blank	–	–
card	–	–
casino	–	–
cheat	to cheat	–
–	–	checkmate
chess	–	–
chip	–	–
–	to deal	–
die	to dice	–
–	to double down	–
draw	to draw	–
endgame	–	–
gambit	–	–
game	to gamble	–
hand	–	–
jackpot	–	–
joker	–	–
lottery	–	–
luck	–	lucky
opening	–	–
pawn	–	–
piker	–	–
play, player	to play, to outplay	playful
poker	to poker	pokerfaced
raffle	to raffle	–
rip-off	to rip off	–
roulette	–	–
–	to shuffle	–
stakes	–	–
trump	to trump	–
winning streak, losing streak	–	–

Summing up, we can see that the war–sports–games cluster is obviously very tightly-knit. A seemingly quite different field, namely that of romance, will conclude this presentation of the lexical fields (see Table 4.4). This last field comprises possible alternative metaphoric expressions in media discourse on marketing.

Table 4.4 Lexical field 'romance'

Noun	Verb	Adjective/adverb
affair	–	–
affection	–	affectionate
altar	–	–
arms	–	–
bed, bedfellow	–	–
bride, bridegroom	–	bridal
consummation	to consummate	–
courtship	to court	courtly
dalliance	to dally	–
desire	to desire	desirable
divorce	to divorce	–
embrace	to embrace	–
–	–	faithful
family	–	–
fiancé, fiancée	–	–
flirt	to flirt	flirtatious, flirty
friend, friendship	–	friendly
heart	–	–
honeymoon	–	–
husband	–	–
infatuation	–	infatuated
kiss	to kiss	–
love, lover	to love	lovable
lust	to lust	lustful
marriage	to marry	–
mate	to mate	–
nuptials	–	nuptial
passion	–	passionate
romance	–	romantic
sex	–	sexual, sexy
spouse	–	–
suitor	–	–
wedding	to wed	–
wife	–	–
wooer	to woo	–

The field represented in Table 4.4 is unique in that, among its 68 word forms, adjectives show a higher percentage than verbs (23.35 per cent as opposed to only 20.59 per cent), making them rank second behind nouns (55.88 per cent). As the possible alternative metaphor in marketing and sales was chosen with regard to the framework of Relationship Marketing, the field also features the lexemes *family* and *friend/friendship, friendly*, although these denote non-romantic private relationships. Still, the label 'romance' was retained to represent the majority of lemmas. It is striking that a number of lexemes – such as *dalliance, to dally; courtship, to court, courtly; nuptials, nuptial* and *wooer, to woo* – are in fact marked as old-fashioned. Anticipating the findings of Table A.3 (see p. 98), quite a few of these are actually realized metaphorically, indicating that the ROMANCE metaphor is sometimes attenuated or used humourously by drawing on historical rather than contemporary expressions of love and relationships.

Having thus established the basis for corpus-driven analysis, let us now see how the quantitative findings corroborate the central position of the WAR metaphor.

4.1.2 Absolute and relative frequencies

This sub-section will detail the absolute frequencies of metaphoric expression in the marketing and sales corpus and, following from these figures, its overall metaphor density. Further, the metaphor cluster will be broken down into relative frequencies. Relative frequency is also at stake when it comes to identifying the spread of metaphoric expression across word classes. As for the metaphor cluster, this final analysis will be specified further by crossing it with figures for the word class frequencies of the three metaphors. It will be seen that the lexical field 'war' shows the highest number of items realized, and that the WAR metaphor is indeed quantitatively most prominent in all four publications. As far as word classes are concerned, results convey that verbal forms of the metaphors investigated are over-represented when compared to word-class distribution in the lexical fields, although nominal forms are most frequent overall. Those quantitative results will allow for first assumptions on the nature of the underlying conceptual map in terms of its structure (static versus dynamic, homogeneous versus hybrid). Moreover, it is inferred that the dominant metaphor cluster is perceived as being particularly relevant by discourse participants.

From Tables A.1 and A.2 (pp. 191 and 194) it can be seen that 845 metaphoric expressions have been found in the corpus, equalling a metaphor density of an average 5.3 metaphoric expressions per 1,000 words. Apart from that, the first most obvious finding is that the lexical field 'war' is the one from which most lemmas are realized as metaphoric expressions. Of the overall 35 lemmas, as many as 94.28 per cent are indeed used metaphorically. Lemmas from the field of 'sports' are second, with 25 out of 35 (71.43 per cent) occurring metaphorically.

Finally, the field of 'games' shows 18 items (51.43 per cent) in metaphoric expressions and thus ranks third. This order is also reflected in how much the three metaphors contribute to the 845 attested metaphoric expressions in the marketing and sales corpus.[6] While the WAR metaphor accounts for more than two-thirds (69.59 per cent), the SPORTS metaphor represents a quarter (25.6 per cent), with the GAMES metaphor amounting to a mere 13.25 per cent. A final, related indicator of these vast differences is the respective type-token ratios, which, based on the metaphoric types actually realized, are 0.056 for the WAR metaphor, 0.116 for the SPORTS metaphor, and 0.161 for the GAMES metaphor: the more lemmas selected from a particular lexical field, the greater the variety of the related conceptual metaphor in the corpus.

However, while expressions based on the WAR metaphor are varied, the most frequent ones are also rather conventionalized: the three top slots are occupied by the lemmas *campaign*, *launch* and *target*. Together, they show 368 tokens and thus make up over 40 per cent of all the 845 metaphoric expressions in the corpus as a whole, and nearly two-thirds of all metaphoric expressions of WAR.[7] As corroborated by both the 100-million-word British National Corpus (BNC) as well the 450-million-word Bank of English (BoE), *campaign* and *launch*, the two most frequent types, collocate with each other, a fact which explains their similar frequencies. As for the third most frequent type, *target*, a look at the single concordance lines conveys that its metaphoric meaning is found exclusively in the corpus. This conventionalization is not restricted to marketing discourse, however, as reflected in the two reference corpora: in a random sample of 100 lines, there were only seven instances of a literal *target* in the BNC and only sixteen in the BoE.[8]

To sum up, the conceptual metaphor MARKETING IS WAR is highly entrenched, as seen from the number of metaphoric expressions it generates in the corpus. Although it gives rise to very conventionalized expressions such as *Coca-Cola is to launch a global advertising campaign this weekend* (MS FT 51) or *firms are having to target potential customers more precisely* (MS EC 18), there are also a number of relatively unconventional or even new expressions – for example, *by being first* [to go public], '*you get blood on your spear . . . ,*' *he says* (MS BW 15), or even *Dell's efficiency jihad* (Park and Burrows, 2001, para. 9). Another case in point is the notion of *guerrilla marketing* (MS EC 15), which is less prototypical than expressions metaphorizing fights between armies (Eubanks, 2000, p. 60).[9] It is those less entrenched metaphoric expressions which convey the underlying metaphor's productivity (Clausner and Croft, 1997). When it comes to productivity, the two other metaphors in the cluster, SPORTS and GAMES, pale in comparison. Further, the lexical fields have shown that the concept of war also permeates the other two domains, but not vice versa, corroborating Desmond's (1997) observation that 'war . . . can embrace and subsume other topics with little reciprocal effect' (p. 341). In the qualitative analysis, we shall see that despite tight conceptual links between war, sports and games, the latter two more often serve to support rather than to attenuate the former. For the time being, it should be noted that the greater productivity of the WAR metaphor reduces the other two metaphors in the cluster to an ancillary status.

Still, the question remains *why* text producers draw so heavily on the WAR metaphor, making it almost paradigmatic for media discourse on marketing. The obvious answer relates to the gendered – that is, masculinized – nature of war, and hence the WAR metaphor. One of the consequences of the fact that 'cultural conceptions of war specifically exclude the "feminine"' (Desmond, 1997, p. 338) is that their widespread use in marketing discourse in the form of metaphoric expressions helps to maintain marketing as a male arena. Seen as such, the abundant metaphoric expressions of WAR in the corpus serve their producers' – probably largely unconscious – aim to reify a masculine discourse community. The sheer numbers indicate that

> conceptions of warfare have traditionally acted to maintain the dominance of male over female interests in society and . . . marketing has largely aided and abetted this process.   (ibid.)

Moreover, high frequency and hence dominance of the WAR metaphor as used for those particular ends does not only have an impact on the nature of a specific discourse, but also on the socio-cognitive models underlying that discourse: by being prominent in discourse, the metaphor is also reified and anchored cognitively, in turn influencing marketing as a practice. Still, the quantitative analysis alone does not suffice to theorize about such effects; it will take the analysis of how the metaphor employed to corroborate the above inferences. However, before that, a look at word class distribution will shed some more light on the possible nature of any basic conceptual model.

As stated in section 4.1.1, all lexical fields show a more-or-less prominent nominal bias. To see if a particular word class is over- or underrepresented, the results given in Table A.2 (see p. 194) are compared to the percentages of word classes in the three lexical fields.

Even a cursory glance at Table 4.5 reveals that, compared to their per-

Table 4.5 Relative frequencies of word classes in marketing and sales cluster,[10] numbers and percentages

Lexical field	METAPHOR	Noun		Verb		Adjective/adverb		Totals	
		Lexical field	Metaphorical expressions	Lexical field	Metaphorical expressions	Lexical field	Metaphorical expressions	Lexical field	Metaphorical expressions
War	WAR	45	351	25	221	11	16	81	588
		55.56%	59.69%	30.86%	37.59%	13.58%	2.72%	100%	100%
Sports	SPORTS	31	99	19	80	12	37	62	216
		50.00%	45.83%	30.64%	37.04%	19.35%	17.13%	100%	100%
Games	GAMES	33	77	14	33	4	4	51	114
		64.70%	67.54%	27.45%	28.95%	7.84%	3.51%	100%	100%
Totals		109	527	58	334	27	57	194	918
		56.18%	57.41%	29.90%	36.38%	13.92%	6.2%	100%	100%

Note: The absolute number of nouns/verbs/adj in lexical fields and metaphoric expression have been added horizontally, yielding the totals in the two right-hand columns, lines 1, 3 and 5. The individual figures have further been added vertically, yielding the totals in the bottom line. As for percentages, the totals in columns 9 and 10, lines 2, 4, 6 and 8 represent 100%, and percentages in columns 3–8, lines 2, 4, 6 and 8 the proportions thereof.

centages in all three lexical fields (Tables 4.1–4.3), both nouns and verbs are over-represented when used metaphorically. In contrast, adjectives/adverbs are remarkably under-represented, being on the whole more than twice as frequent in the lexical fields as in metaphoric usage. When looking at the separate metaphors, the same tendencies show in intensified form in the case of the WAR metaphor. Although this seems to contradict the view of war as a process rather than as a state,[11] it should be noted that the strong nominal bias is largely accounted for by the most frequent and highly conventionalized lemma, *campaign*. Another search word showing notably more nominal than adjectival forms is *war* itself. A broader picture of the word forms *war* and *warfare* reveals that they most often show up as an object affected by some process – that is, as a disposed entity (*these companies have a better chance of surviving the online price wars* [MS BW 31]). An equal number of occurrences is accounted for by *war/-fare* in predicative function (for example, *AOL vs. Microsoft: Now It's War* [MS FO 20]), an extremely static way of using the word forms. *War* further features as both the first or the second part of a compound noun (*war zone* [MS BW 15], *branding wars* [MS FT 20]). Perhaps the most remarkable fact is that the forms *war/-fare* occur only once in an enactive process (*with price wars breaking out in this category daily* [MS BW 31]). This anticipatory qualitative glimpse of the functions of two particular lexemes suggests WAR to be a rather static concept. Yet, more in-depth qualitative analysis will to some degree relativize the role of word classes by revealing the key importance of metaphoric expressions combined with grammatical functions in constructing dynamic or static scenarios.

While the GAMES metaphor mirrors the overall trend of nominal and verbal over-representation, the SPORTS metaphor in fact shows a slight under-representation of nominal forms and, more importantly, a percentage of adjectives/adverbs (17.13 per cent) that is far above the average for the three clusters. As the latter phenomenon is largely accounted for by the fairly general lemmas *fast* and *fair*, the verb-heavy course is more interesting to look at. It is set by the lemmas that were split up into a nominal and a verbal form, namely *catch, to catch; jump, to jump; kick-off, to kick off; play/player, to play; punch, to punch; race, to race; run/runner, to run; score, to score; speed, to speed; throw, to throw*. Of these ten lemmas, only two – *punch* and *race* – show more nominal than verbal forms. It is quite remarkable in this context that *play* shows almost as many verbal as nominal forms (17, compared to 19), despite a search for two different nominal lexemes (*play/player*) but only one verbal form (*to play*). This tendency of verbal metaphoric expressions outnumbering nominal ones makes the SPORTS metaphor a rather dynamic one, in accordance with its movement-centred nature. Given the choice of metaphoric models as reflecting both the in-group schema embraced by journalists and the group schemata journalists perceive to be held by marketing people, the quantitative evidence of word class assignment makes these models rather contradictory, combining a static WAR and a more dynamic SPORTS metaphor. Once again, recontextualization will show that the relations between the two differently structured metaphors, and their combination with grammatical features, precludes an overly static scenario.

Before addressing that issue, however, let us look at the frequency patterns of the alternative ROMANCE metaphor (see Table A.3 on p. 198). First, it is notably less frequent than even the least frequent cluster metaphor. Where the GAMES metaphor showed at least 112 occurrences, the ROMANCE metaphor has only 46 instantiations. Similarly, of the 35 lexical units in the field, only 15, or 42.86 per cent, are used in metaphoric expressions, accounting for a type–token ratio of 0.3. Being an alternative metaphor, the ROMANCE metaphor is obviously not particularly entrenched in secondary marketing discourse. Nor is it particularly productive in the sense of motivating novel metaphoric expressions: both the most frequent lemmas and those less often realized betray only very conventional expressions along the lines of *it has attracted those Nike lovers* (MS FO 19) or *sexy the storage business may not be* (MS EC 37). As a feature of media discourse on marketing, the ROMANCE metaphor is hence not entrenched, and consequently not productive either, and journalists obviously do not ascribe any great importance to this alternative metaphor. As the notions of romance and war are – at least on the surface – diametrically opposed, it should come as no surprise that their respective frequency patterns in discourse are reciprocally proportional. What the two have in common is that both are certainly highly gendered, in fact sustaining a fairly strict gender dichotomy. Their relative strength or weakness in quantitative terms therefore mirrors the demographic structure of the publications' overwhelmingly male readership, indicating the magazines' and newspaper's orientation towards their audience.

In terms of their spread over word classes, the alternative metaphoric expressions show a behaviour very similar to that of the cluster metaphors: verbal forms are over-represented, while adjectival ones are under-represented when compared to their percentage in the lexical fields. The original lexical field was remarkable in being the only one to include a higher percentage of adjectives than verbs. Yet, this structure does not translate into a similar pattern for metaphoric usage. Quite the contrary, in fact – while there are more than twice as many verbal metaphoric expressions than there are verbal forms in the lexical field, the percentage of adjectives and adverbs plummets to single-digit levels in metaphoric usage (6.52 per cent as opposed to 23.53 per cent). Although nouns are the single most prominent group among the metaphoric expressions in general, the ROMANCE metaphor shows a tendency to favour verbal realizations such as *banks are wooing affluent customers* (MS BW 22) or *he had been courting* [the organization] *for several months* (MS FO 6). This strong emphasis on verbs at the expense of adjectives is yet another example of the sparseness of adjectival metaphors.

To sum up the quantitative results, it can be seen that in media discourse on marketing and sales, the WAR metaphor is most frequent and most entrenched, and that the related lexical field shows the highest number of lexemes to be realized metaphorically. Within the cluster, it is followed by the SPORTS metaphor and, ranking third, the GAMES metaphor, making it dominant and, as we shall see in section 4.2, supported by the other two metaphors. The obvious explanation as to why journalists focus on the WAR metaphor so much lies in its masculinized nature: emphasis on that metaphor characterizes marketing discourse as a male arena and thus reifies the power of male readers. In addition, emphasis on the metaphor matches the cognitive schemata likely to be held by those readers. While the three concepts in the cluster are closely related – as indicated by overlaps in both lexical fields and metaphoric usage – they nevertheless show different patterns when it comes to word classes. Although nominal metaphoric expressions are the most frequent realizations of all three metaphors, relative word class frequencies differ with regard to the three metaphors, with a noun-heavy WAR and a relatively verb-heavy SPORTS metaphor. It is an interesting finding that, on the whole, the nominal bias of the lexical fields should transfer to the attested metaphoric expressions. While it is certainly possible that underlying conceptual metaphors 'may be more common [as verb metaphors] than nominal metaphors' (Cameron, 1999, p. 15), things are quite different when it comes to the surface-level realization of metaphor. Here, nominal metaphoric expressions dominate. This fact is in line with Goatly's (1997) claim that nominal metaphoric expressions 'are either more recognizable as [metaphoric expressions] or yield richer interpretations than [metaphoric expressions] from other word-classes' (p. 83). As nouns refer to things, they are 'referring expressions in the strictest sense' (ibid., p. 83). According to Goatly, things as referenda furthermore evoke whole bundles of semantic components, thus making for more vivid images, a claim corroborated by findings for business media discourse. The following qualitative analysis will reconsider these frequency and distribution patterns.

4.2 Qualitative analysis of sample texts

The following analysis draws on four sample texts, one from each publication in the corpus. The articles are reproduced at the end of this section (see p. 98), with the *Business Week* (BW) text being provided in unabridged form to illustrate significant absences of metaphor from stretches of text. The other three articles feature in the form of metaphor-rich excerpts. It should be noted that the fourth sample, MS FT 91, is rather unrepresentative of the *Financial Times* (FT) sub-corpus in that its length far exceeds the average length of *Financial Times* articles in the corpus. The reason for this particularity lies in the fact that the text constitutes a background feature rather than the short news item that is so characteristic of a daily paper, but yields little in terms of metaphor. Further, the *Financial Times* article also shows by far the lowest metaphor density – 6.13/1,000 words, compared to the *Business Week* text's 20.6/1,000. In terms of content, the *Financial Times* sample again differs from the others by dealing with a different topic in marketing: instead of describing the competition between two or more companies in a particular market, the author sets out to discuss the importance of brands in more general terms, choosing the strained relations between a brand owner and a retailer as his example.

In all articles reproduced, metaphoric realizations of lexemes from the lexical fields have been coded to provide a better overview of where and how often they occur: bold type is used for metaphoric expressions drawing on the WAR metaphor, bold italics for SPORTS and bold underlining for GAMES, with alternative expressions deriving from the ROMANCE metaphor given in simple italics. Wherever a word is preceded by an asterisk, it belongs to the respective domain but was not included in the lexical field. The texts selected all show high frequency as well as clustering of the metaphors in question. Further, all four texts originally included graphs and illustrations, which do not feature in their text-only reproduction.[12] Another shared characteristic is the demographic similarity of target readerships. Finally, participants to the text (journalists and readers) as well as the purpose of their interaction (that is, conveying and obtaining information as well as, on the part of the text producers, carrying a particular view on the topic at hand) are comparable for all four texts.

The following analysis will show that the four texts also share a number of features as far as metaphor usage is concerned. First, the WAR metaphor is most prominent in all four articles. Its related lexical field not only shows the highest number of items realized metaphorically, but the metaphor also accounts for most of the attested metaphoric expressions in the articles. Ranking second, we can find the SPORTS metaphor, with the GAMES metaphor being realized only infrequently – or, as in the case of *The Economist* – not at all. What is more, the blurred boundaries between the SPORTS and the GAMES metaphors also often have the two collapse into one and the same metaphoric expression. Because of this, clustering mainly refers to the WAR and SPORTS metaphors co-occurring in the texts. Second, all texts show spatial categorization in varying degrees – that is, each article constructs markets as spaces with particular characteristics in which marketers move in a particular fashion. Such metaphoric movement usually means either exerting antagonistic force or showing fast, goal-orientated parallel movement, and, less often, uncoordinated fast movement or non-aggressive positioning. It should be noted that aggression is not only directed against other market participants – it is directed just as often against the market itself. Third, metaphoric expressions are organized as chains across each of the four texts, with their links mostly elaborating on, and thus reifying, each other. Questioning, or even negating, occurs less frequently. Also, those metaphoric chains are in each article interrupted by stretches of texts that are devoid of the metaphors searched for. These parts of the articles provide factual information and have been cut from *The Economist* (EC), *Fortune* (FO) and *Financial Times* (FT) samples. Fourth, all articles convey intensification and/or attenuation, and most also literalization, of the respective metaphors, albeit to different degrees. Finally, all samples show an intricate relationship between the discourse of business people on the one hand and journalists on the other, with the former's metaphor usage being largely echoed by the latter.

Although the texts share a structure of metaphoric clusters and chains, the fillers for these slots differ from one article to the next. While the WAR metaphor serves as a bracket for the *Business Week* and *The Economist* articles, with the SPORTS metaphor tending to occur in the middle, the situation is almost reversed in the *Fortune* sample. The *Financial Times* shows a different pattern altogether: here, we find initial clustering only. Moreover, all texts show the SPORTS metaphor as the second most dominant one, tying in closely with the central WAR metaphor. However, the authors elaborate the metaphor differently, narrowing it down to racing as a form of the above-mentioned fast parallel movement towards a goal (*Business Week*), or to football as a struggle over space (*Fortune*). In addition, while the ROMANCE metaphor as an alternative is scarce, journalists do bring in metaphors from outside the dominant cluster, albeit not the same ones in each case. Thus, whereas both *Business Week* and *Fortune* make use of an ORGANISM metaphor, the latter also employs a KINGSHIP metaphor, as does *The Economist*. The British magazine also realizes a MACHINE metaphor for marketing. While we can thus find quite a range of different metaphors, single dominant metaphors are partly elaborated on in great depth, too. A case in point is the subtle construction of market participants as rivals and contenders or, in more questioning terms, allies and partners in the *Business Week* sample. It is because of this richness that the latter sample is reproduced in its original form, a richness that also shows in its functional grammar features. Although durative/intensive (i.e. extending over a period of time, see Table 3.3 on p. 58) trajectory with progressive aspect is prominent in all articles, the *Business Week* text combines these features with additional completive trajectory and predecessive aspect to achieve maximum dynamics and emphasis on the present, and thus support the metaphoric movement model. Going through the sample texts will show how these similarities and differences play out in the articles.

Metaphor frequency

Relative metaphor frequencies are the same in all four samples, with the WAR metaphor being the most prominent in quantitative terms. Of the 26 metaphoric expressions the *Business Week* sample contributes, those of war are most frequent, albeit under-represented when compared to the whole corpus (42.31 per cent as opposed to 69.54 per cent). Similarly, the overwhelming majority of metaphoric tokens in *The Economist* text in fact stem from the WAR metaphor, which, with 72.73 per cent, is even over-represented when compared to the whole corpus. In the *Fortune* text too, an absolute majority of 60.87 per cent of metaphoric expressions is accounted for by the WAR metaphor. Although metaphor is used sparingly in the *Financial Times* article, five of the eight metaphoric expressions attested are in fact instantiations of the WAR metaphor. Because of this dominance, it is mainly the WAR metaphor that accounts for metaphor concentration in the four articles. Another parallel is that the SPORTS metaphor ranks second in all texts, closely following the dominant WAR metaphor. The relevant figures are 34.61 per cent in *Business Week*, 27.27 per cent in *The Economist*, 21.74 per cent in *Fortune* – making it slightly under-represented in that publication when compared to the overall 25.5 per cent – and exactly a quarter in the *Financial Times*. Further, all samples show very parsimonious use, or even no instances, of the GAMES metaphor (23.08 per cent in *Business Week*, no occurrences in *The Economist*, 17.29 per cent in *Fortune*, and a single occurrence in the *Financial Times*). Interestingly, the two British publications both convey a fairly low percentage of the GAMES metaphor. By contrast, the two US magazines together account for three-quarters of all metaphoric expressions of games. It is therefore obvious that the GAMES metaphor is highly culture-specific.[13]

As the lexical fields have already shown, the GAMES metaphor is particular in yet another respect, namely in showing significant semantic and lexical overlaps with the SPORTS metaphor. Accordingly, the articles include ambiguous expressions such as the juxtaposition 'e-commerce players invade Asia' (BW, line 29), which could, by virtue of the dual nature of *players*, be classified as a threefold cluster of war, sports and/or games. The article from *The Economist*, devoid of metaphoric expressions of games, nevertheless contains the highly ambiguous 'who will win' (EC, line 40). While the phrase could in fact be an instance of any of the three cluster metaphors, the total lack of the GAMES metaphor elsewhere in the text rather renders this phrase a hybrid, combining both the SPORTS and the WAR metaphors. A very similar example is to be found in the *Fortune* text: again, expressions of sports and games convey a high degree of convergence. In fact, all four instances of the GAMES metaphor therefore have to be cross-classified as metaphoric expressions derived from sports ('a game of inches' [FO, lines 1 and 90] as well as 'has played this game' [FO, line 52]). Consequently, there is only one instance of the SPORTS metaphor that really stands on its own: 'turf' (FO, line 46). In the light of this syntactic and semantic juxtaposition, it is doubtful whether the nominal 'win' (FO, line 14) could be anything but a realization of either the SPORTS or the WAR metaphors, or of a blend of both. Finally, the *Financial Times* shows 'rip-off' (FT, line 5) as the one realization of the GAMES metaphor, an expression that is itself metaphorical, drawing on violent physical action as its source. Elsewhere, the metaphor is largely reduced to the technical expressions *stake(s)* and *red chip* (BW, lines 35, 65 and 71).[14] It follows that the conceptualization of market participants as players is negligible in the samples. Indeed, the infrequent GAMES metaphor is mainly employed to support the more dominant metaphors in the cluster.

If the GAMES metaphor is quantitatively and qualitatively weak in the samples, the alternative ROMANCE metaphor is almost non-existent. It features in neither *The Economist* nor the *Fortune* article, and does not record any occurrences of lexical field items in the *Business Week* sample either. However, the latter provides three expressions that could qualify for a PARTNERSHIP metaphor (BW, lines 42, 64 and 76). The partners here are either other market participants or prospective customers, and the expressions thus question the dominant scenarios of warlike aggression or contention without being as systematic. The only realization of a lexeme from the alternative field occurs at the end of the *Financial Times* article (FT, line 34): the notion of brand owners as consumers' friends contradicts the dominant metaphoric scenario, and is granted additional weight by closing the article. It is this specific position of the alternative metaphor that will be probed further when analysing the position and function of clusters within the samples.

Metaphoric scenario

Apart from the *Financial Times* article, all centre on two related movement scenarios, namely contenders moving aggressively in their fight over territory (WAR metaphor), or runners moving fast across a racing turf towards a finishing line (SPORTS metaphor, more specifically a RACING metaphor). This dual conceptualization is most prominent in the *Business Week* article, which also constructs the movement of weaker participants, despite being fast, as being less co-ordinated.

In that first sample, the hybrid phrase 'e-commerce players invade Asia' (BW, line 29) is the one example that in fact juxtaposes all three cluster metaphors. Moreover, it provides a scenario of aggressive movement into the market as a metaphoric battlefield or territory. Similar goal-orientated, even aggressive, movement features quite prominently in *The Economist* article, where the market is once more constructed as a 'battleground' (EC, line 6) over which 'war has been declared' (EC, lines 6–7). The expression 'NetApp moved right on to EMC's home turf' (EC, line 31) echoes both *Business Week*'s 'bruising battle for cyberturf', (BW, line 2) and *Fortune*'s 'turf war' (FO, line 46). Conceptualizing the market as a narrow, bounded space too small for two companies to be active in, puts the focus on a metaphoric fight for space (for example, 'battling for market share' [FO, line 2]). A much intensified instance of the fighting-for-scarce-spatial-resources scenario is the following quotation from the *Fortune* sample: '"It's a death struggle to incrementally gain share"' (FO, lines 31–2; see also FO, lines 41 and 46–7). Referring to the fought-over space as either 'territory', 'battlefield' or 'turf' shows how the SPORTS metaphor can be used in juxtaposition with, and as a substitute for, the WAR metaphor.

The second scenario, the metaphoric notion of fast, goal-orientated movement, is introduced in the by-line of the *Business Week* sample. There, it is interwoven with the fighting scenario, betraying a tight conceptual link between the two ('a bruising battle for cyberturf' [BW, line 2]). The scenario is elaborated on in the first paragraph (BW, lines 3–12) by expressions such as 'her operation isn't up to speed yet' (BW, line 4). Here, the company is metonymically equated with its management and metaphorized as a runner in a race. This notion is extended in BW, line 12, where the company's CEO is quoted as admitting that they have 'a big challenge catching up'. Metaphoric racing is made even more explicit in BW, lines 32–3 ('front-runners'; 'at the head of the pack') and in BW, line 39 ('front-row places'). Similar occurrences can be found in the *Fortune* text (for example, 'companies remain under pressure to pick up the pace' [FO, lines 27–8]), thus maintaining the overall motif of dynamic movement.

The same motif is reflected in 'EMC and NetApp did not compete head to head' (EC, line 24), which sets the tone for the spatial conceptualization pervasive in *The Economist* sample. Throughout the article, the market is metaphorized as a three-dimensional container with different strata: the phrases 'being squeezed in the middle are computer makers' (EC, lines 26–7) and 'NetApp has moved upmarket fast' (EC, lines 28–9) both denote vertical movement. Horizontal space and lateral movement can be found in 'a bridge between [the] systems' (EC, line 36) and 'differences between the firms shrink' (EC, lines 43–4). Not only does the author construct markets as containers, but s/he also introduces a second orientational metaphor, namely GOOD IS UP. Accordingly, there is an ameliorative attitude at work in EC, lines 28–9: 'NetApp has moved upmarket fast, as its products have become better'. Similar evaluation is at work in FO, lines 22–30. Here, the reader is provided with factual information about two companies' market positions, along with the spatial metaphoric expressions usual in that context ('declined', 'inched up', 'dropped', 'sank'), all of them instantiations of the primary MORE IS UP metaphor.

As noted above, the *Business Week* article introduces a third form of metaphoric movement, namely fast, uncoordinated movement. The phrase 'Ong has been scrambling to hire staff' (BW, lines 7–8) is echoed in BW, line 23: 'Why the flurry now?' The interrogative status of the second instance helps to structure the text both by linking back to 'scrambling', and by determining the following text, which now requires an answer. A conceptual metaphor MARKETING IS FAST, UNCOORDINATED MOVEMENT, however, is not entrenched in media discourse on marketing and sales. It not only lacks creative extension, but unconventional usage with different semantic connotations cannot be attested either. Moreover, explicit statements about conceiving of a topic in metaphoric terms are scarce, too, a rare example being '[the company] also licenses its technology to other Internet companies – selling "picks and shovels for the gold-rush", as Vertical One's boss . . . puts it' (MS EC 40). Also, the *Business Week* writer is alone in using that metaphor: it is largely absent from *The Economist* sample and does not feature in the *Fortune* or the *Financial Times* texts at all. However, the seemingly paradoxical relationship between uncoordinated and goal-orientated movement, evidenced in the first paragraph of the *Business Week* sample, could well be systematic in the corpus (see *changes . . . have left* [the company] *scrambling to catch up* [MS BW 27]).

So far, we can see that metaphoric movement in its goal-orientated form collapses with either the SPORTS or the WAR metaphor ('three front-runners have emerged' [BW, line 32], and 'Unilever's latest offensive against archrival Procter & Gamble' [FO, lines 10–11]). These scenarios are supplemented by yet a third form of movement in the *Business Week* article, a focus producing a spill-over effect throughout that sample. Thus we learn that '60 million Asians will be hopping on the Net' (BW, lines 27–8), that 'portals are not simply rolling over' (BW, lines 39–40), and that 'Hong Kong will become a springboard into China' (BW, line 69).[15] All three movement scenarios – antagonistic and aggressive, fast and goal-orientated as well as fast and uncoordinated – are combined in the following instruction offered by the *Business Week* writer: 'As the three main contenders push forward, others must move quickly to avoid becoming also-rans' (BW, lines 82–3).

Again, the *Financial Times* shows different features. While the writer also uses the well-known spatial metaphor for markets, the metaphor does not result in metaphoric races or fights over space. Rather, the text constructs companies as arranging and rearranging their position in the bounded space in a non-goal-orientated and non-violent fashion ('Tesco [is] positioning itself' [FT, line 11]). Another difference between this last sample and the other texts is constituted by the fact that the antagonism between two protagonists (retailers and brand owners), while being expressed through the WAR metaphor, is not about metaphoric space but about the abstract notion of branding and retail policies (for example, the highly conventional 'brands are fighting to justify their high prices' [FT, line 2]). Elsewhere, metaphoric expressions of war enter the text whenever the relationship between brand owners and consumers, or brand owners and critics, is described.

Consumers in fact form an important third party in all four articles

– after all, they represent the ulterior motive for marketers' endeavours. Interestingly, they are nevertheless always found as the static object of dynamic marketing activities. This particular relationship is most often described by the third most frequent type in the corpus – that is, *target*. Consumers and their metonyms are the object of the dispositive processes the lexeme governs ('companies are targeting Asia', 'target the region' [BW, lines 13–14 and 47], 'brands are increasingly targeting younger people' [FT, lines 26–7]). Indeed, it is not only in the marketing and sales corpus at hand that *target* collocates with *audience* and *people*; similar collocations can be observed in both the BNC (which also shows *market* as a collocate) and the BoE (in the latter, *target* collocates with *audience* and *group*). This finding in fact corroborates Michaelson's (1987) statement that 'the competition is not the target . . . the market is the target' (p. 11). A description other than *target* is *The Economist*'s presentation of the market as a passive entity which is 'up for grabs' (EC, line 47). While *grabbing* certainly conveys aggression, *The Economist* author still does not go as far as his/her *Business Week* counterpart. On the other hand, intensification can be witnessed in FO, lines 78–9, where the reader learns that 'Unilever blitzed 24 million homes'. Even if the process enacted upon consumers changes from metaphoric violence to romance, prospects are still positioned as the passive object of marketers' activities, the only difference being that these are no longer aggressive but rather persuasive (for example, 'to attract users to its portal' [BW, line 42]). Thus, the ROMANCE metaphor can also parallel the antagonistic force schema when used to position prospective customers at the receiving end of a process. The concept of marketing as action of any kind being directed at consumers meets with an interesting twist at the end of the *Financial Times* sample. The phrase 'making an enemy of consumers' (FT, lines 32–3) has consumers change from being the passive objects of marketers' aggression into potentially more active adversaries. The term *enemy* is contrasted sharply with *friends* in the obligation expressed – albeit in a form attenuated by the initial 'maybe' – in the final sentence (FT, lines 32–3). Here, the author takes an unusually explicit instructional perspective, signalling an attempt to change the metaphors dominant in marketing discourse.[16]

Metaphor chains

The dominant scenarios decribed above evolve as metaphoric chains within the texts. However, these chains are interrupted whenever facts and figures are provided (BW, lines 23–8, as well as the lines and paragraphs omitted from the other samples). An interesting functional parallel can be drawn between these literal stretches full of figures and the 'scores, distances, times, heights, and weights . . . recorded and compared [in sports coverage]', which help to lend 'an apparently factual validity to claims to superiority' (Bryson, 1990, p. 176). Here, as elsewhere, literalization is employed, seemingly to grant objectivity to a text and thereby make the text more trustworthy and acceptable, including its metaphoric constructions in other parts.

Notwithstanding such interruptions, the links in metaphoric chains interact in particular ways, largely elaborating on one another. Such elaboration can, for example, be witnessed for the WAR metaphor in the headline and by-line of the *Business Week* article or the specification of the metaphoric battle as 'offensive' and 'counteroffensive' (FO, lines 10 and 85). The SPORTS – here, RACING – metaphor is elaborated on in BW, line 32 ('three front-runners have emerged'). However, elaboration, while prominent, is not the only relationship between the links. In *The Economist* sample, the metaphoric chains also involve an aspect of subtle questioning: the expression '"NetApp killer"' (EC, line 35) is taken up again in EC, line 42, stating that '[he] doubts whether it will kill NetApp any time soon'. Yet questioning remains a subordinate feature; the links in the metaphoric chains largely elaborate and extend (and, more often still, simply echo) each other. Echoing is particularly used with highly frequent, technical metaphors such as *launch* (repeated five times in the *Business Week* and three times in the *Fortune* articles). An exception is, again, the *Financial Times* text: although its metaphor scarcity precludes any complex metaphor chains, the article is unique in including an instance of negation (FT, lines 32–4). In addition, this negation is provided at a particular sensitive point in the article, namely at the end, thus carrying considerable weight and making for a more argumentative, if not instructional, stance of the text producer. If used more pervasively, it could well lead to a more hybrid cognitive model underlying marketing discourse.

Intensification, attenuation and literalization

While echoing, elaboration and extension across metaphoric chains serve to intensify a particular metaphor, questioning, or even negating, obviously attenuate it. As we shall see, literalization is ambiguous in that respect, being employed to achieve both effects simultaneously.

Intensification is the one dominant characteristic of the *Fortune* text, indicating a rather homogenous underlying model. It is achieved by a variety of means, including prefixes ('archrivals' in FO, line 3; and 'hyperspeed', in FO, line 21), attributes ('"death struggle"' – FO, line

31) or augmentative trajectory ('fiercest competition' – FO, line 38). Intensification is also at work in FO, line 7, where the progressive aspect and intensive trajectory of 'a battle is raging' relate back to 'battling for market share' (FO, line 2), while the collocate *rage* intensifies the WAR metaphor. The fourfold repetition in 'P&G and Unilever have to slog it out for every fraction of every share in every category in every market' (FO, lines 33–4) is another intensifying device, culminating in 'that's a lot of slogging' (FO, line 35). Yet, the WAR metaphor is also attenuated elsewhere, for example in 'its latest strategic initiative' (FO, line 44): while *strategic* can be seen as a faint echo of war vocabulary, *initiative* is clearly non-militaristic.

Attenuation is more pronounced in *The Economist* article. On the whole, the author seems undecided whether to embrace the WAR metaphor fully, attenuate it somewhat, or ascribe it to business people by quoting them on it. While the WAR metaphor is used very explicitly at the beginning to define the topic ('Store wars' – EC, line 1), attenuation is present from line 9 onwards. The antagonism between market participants is paraphrased there as 'the two firms [are said to] champion different approaches' (EC, lines 9–10). Searls (1997) notes that, as 'sports is a sublimated and formalized kind of war, the distances between sports and war metaphors in business are . . . small' (para. 8). Seen as such, juxtaposing a metaphoric expression of sports with a realization of the WAR metaphor helps to further lessen the very explicit military expressions of the headline and EC, lines 3–8.

Matters are less clear with the expression 'bunfights' (EC, line 9). By replacing the semantic components [+SERIOUS] and possibly [+LETHAL] evident in *fight* with [-SERIOUS], the usage of *bunfight* in the above sample text represents an instance of attenuation. However, it also evokes the intensified *gunfight* as well. Such interlacing of intensification on the one hand and attenuation on the other finds its most striking example in the simile of BW, lines 89–93:

> South Korea's Daum Communications Corp. . . . has appealed to anti-Japanese sentiment by boasting . . . that it will repel Softbank's invasion just as Koreans defeated Japanese intruders more than 500 years ago.

Here, the reference to a literal war is clearly an intensification. Yet it is the Japanese–Korean war (AD 1592–98) the company alludes to, rather than the guerrilla war Koreans fought against the Japanese occupation between 1910 and 1945. By drawing on a historical war rather than one still straining relations between Japan and Korea more than half a century later, current taboos are avoided (for a parallel example involving the American Civil War, see Eubanks, 2000, pp. 141–2). The quotation's position in the text nevertheless underscores its intensified nature: The marketing strategy of 'playing up . . . local roots to appeal to nationalist customers' is already mentioned in BW, lines 40–1, yet the writer saves the example for the end of the text to give it as much emphasis as possible. In the *Business Week* sample, the WAR metaphor thus not only serves to define the topic in the initial position ('Portal combat' – BW, line 1). In its intensified reification towards the end of the text, it also meets a persuasive function by anchoring the writer's preferred metaphoric conceptualization in the minds of the readers.

We have seen before that three of the four articles metaphorically construct the abstract notion of the market as a narrow space. Interestingly, narrow metaphoric space is literalized in the *Fortune* text: the observation that 'shelf space is . . . tight in stores these days' (FO, line 63) is a means of lending seemingly 'objective', non-metaphoric truth to the notion of the market as a bounded space of limited capacity – after all, there is *literally* not enough space for all the products offered. Furthermore, literalization is linked here to quoting a credible source as another way of reinforcing supposed objectivity. Switching between literal and metaphoric competition for space continues in FO, lines 70–4. There, various options for succeeding in a competitive surrounding are discussed in a simulated dialogue. The final answer ('there's only one way to blow a box of Tide off the shelf' [FO, line 72]) elaborates on the FIGHT FOR TERRITORY metaphoric motif by intensifying it in a novel expression. If we consider that, in the text, brands metonymically represent the companies marketing them ('Tide has made itself an American brand icon' [FO, line 59]), metaphorically shooting a representation of the brand comes very close to obliterating the company itself. Literalization does not always work, though. In the prediction that '[the] tablets will be everywhere. Literally' (FO, line 78), it is the very claim to non-metaphoricity that actually enhances the metaphor (Goatly, 1997, p. 173). Consequently, a signalling device meant to lend 'objective truth' to a statement has quite the opposite effect.

A reverse movement, from literal to metaphorical, can be found in the *Financial Times* text. Here, the author metaphorizes the emotional aspect of brands. At the beginning of the article, we find personalized brands described as actively 'exploiting people's insecurities and desires' (FT, line 6), with passive customers identified as 'prone to the desires and insecurities that emotional branding seeks to exploit' (FT, lines

27–8). In terms of emotions elicited by brands, we can also find 'pleasure' (FT, line 7) an example of the strategy known as 'emotional branding' in marketing. While the above instance involves literal feelings, the final notion of brands as friends (FT, line 34) is clearly a metaphoric extension. Although not very frequent, the concept of brands as metaphoric friends is still present elsewhere in the corpus (see Table A.3) and is also corroborated by anecdotal evidence from primary corporate discourse – for example, by British Telecom's brand-as-friend campaign ('BT', n.d.).

Primary and secondary discourse

The FRIENDSHIP metaphor is not the only instance in which writers for business magazines take up concepts from business people. However, while the *Financial Times* author strongly endorses the metaphor, contrasting it with different metaphors prevailing elsewhere in marketing discourse, metaphors from primary business discourse can, of course, meet with a whole range of reactions from journalists. It is noteworthy that, in most cases, the metaphors proposed by business are at least echoed and thereby reified, if not actively extended, in business media discourse. Thus, the CEO's statement in the *Business Week* article ('we have a big challenge catching up' [BW, line 12]) is linked both anaphorically to 'cyberturf' and 'isn't up to speed yet' (BW, lines 2 and 4) and related cataphorically to its echo in BW, line 53 ('rivals want to catch Yahoo') and its elaboration later in the article (for example, 'front-runners' or 'AOL is trying hard to keep pace' in BW, lines 32 and 67). Another case in point is the quotation 'e-commerce players invade Asia' from the same article (BW, line 29). While the metaphoric expression is quoted here from a 'credible source' – a classical way of supporting one's own argumentation (van Dijk, 1993, p. 235), it is later employed in its nominalized form by the writer himself ('in response to the foreign invasion' [BW, line 88]). Such chains, involving both primary and secondary discourse, show that business people and journalists in fact share the metaphoric concept in question.

In other instances, it is business people who extend the shared metaphor. The *Fortune* text, for example, includes the following quotation from primary corporate discourse: ' "it's a death struggle to incrementally gain share" ' (FO, lines 31–2). While this conceptualization ties in seamlessly with the article's WAR metaphor, it is also phrased to maximize its persuasive power, combining declarative status with intensification. What is more, the metaphor thus intensified is claimed by the article's author only two lines later and elaborated on throughout the paragraph (FO, lines 33–40). Finally, the obligation represented by 'P&G and Unilever have to slog it out' (FO, line 33) again helps to present a particular metaphoric conceptualization as common consent.

Elsewhere, journalists are not as ready to support marketers' metaphors. An example of such reserve can be found in text from *The Economist*. In EC, line 35, the writer quotes the expression 'NetApp killer', introducing it with 'touted as a "NetApp killer"'. The choice of words here betrays a pejorative attitude on the part of the author of the article. The phrase is echoed in the next paragraph ('[he] doubts whether it will kill NetApp any time soon' [EC, line 42]), again representing indirect speech. By this device, the writer manages to echo, and thus firmly establish, the WAR metaphor in the article while at the same time ascribing it to an out-group. Similar ascribing processes are at work in the *Financial Times* sample. In contrast to *The Economist* writer, however, the author here only indirectly quotes anonymous sources, ascribing both metaphor and pejorative attitude to them. Means to do so are either agentless passive ('labelled as the devil' [FT, line 1]) or questioning perceived opinions ('[a]re brands an appalling rip-off' in FT, line 5).

Finally, the metaphors found in primary discourse can, of course, also differ from those employed by journalists. The *Fortune* sample, for example, features a company employing an ORGANISM metaphor (' "Path to Growth" '; FO, lines 44–5). While this conceptualization still conveys the goal-orientated movement prominent in the *Business Week* sample, it does not at all match the *Fortune* text's overall focus on WAR and SPORTS metaphors. In the company's (internal) marketing and public relations communication, the WAR metaphor seems to be shunned as potentially being offensive.

So far, the analysis has dealt with the frequency of cluster and alternative metaphors in the sample texts as well as with metaphoric scenarios of movement across space, and with metaphor chains. Further, it has addressed issues of intensification, attenuation and literalization, and the relationship between primary and secondary discourse in terms of metaphor usage. Let us now look more closely at clusters and chains to see how they interact to structure the articles.

Article structure

The first thing to be noticed is that the central metaphor is established right from the beginning of the articles – in fact, as early as in their headlines. Further, the headlines function as attention-getters by using word plays. Thus we find *Business Week* introducing the WAR metaphor with a variation on the collocation *mortal combat* (reference data from the BNC). The *Fortune* sample's headline ('A game of inches', [FO, line 1]), although no word play, is another metaphoric expression denoting the article's topic, thus setting the agenda for the text to come. The *Economist* headline ('Store wars' [EC, line 1]) is again an example of how metaphor can co-occur with other tropes or additional schemes (Steen, 1999, p. 94), and even be backgrounded by them (Gibbs and Steen, 2002). As in the *Business Week* example, the article's heading consists of a word play – here alluding to popular culture ('Star Wars') and bringing 'forth a scenario of sheer conflict entailing the crudest form of survival of the fittest' (White and Herrera, 2003, p. 294), which is combined with additional assonance. However, this powerful combination should not make us lose sight of the fact that the headline introduces the WAR metaphor defining the topic. As in the other samples, the *Financial Times* title, too, serves to set the metaphoric agenda. In contrast to previous metaphorizations in headlines, however, this one is ascribed rather than claimed, as indicated by the word-play on 'labelled'. In short, all four headlines introduce the metaphor framing the text. Still, these metaphors differ from one another, setting the stage for subsequent metaphoric structuring.

The dispersion plot of the *Business Week* text file shows that clustering is concentrated in the first half of the text, particularly at the very beginning. It is clear that metaphor is used to establish the conceptualization of the article's topic straight away (headline and by-line) and to elaborate on it briefly afterwards (BW, lines 4 and 9) in order to entrench the dominant cluster of WAR and SPORTS metaphors at an early stage. In this context, the by-line ('a bruising battle for cyberturf' [BW, line 2]) defines the market simultaneously as a racing ground and a territory fought over, providing a prototypical cross of the two most dominant metaphors. In fact, this dual metaphorization corroborates Boers' (1999) observation that 'abstract competition . . . is often structured in terms of RACING . . . or in terms of a FIGHT' (p. 47). On the whole, however, metaphoric expressions of war can be found throughout, and specifically at the very start of the text, whereas the SPORTS metaphor shows a sketchier pattern, being most prominent towards the middle of the sample. The WAR metaphor hence meets a defining function, while the SPORTS metaphor, is used rather argumentatively. The WAR metaphor again clusters towards the end, where it is intensified through the literalization discussed above (BW, lines 89–93). It thus helps to persuade readers to accept a preferred metaphoric model, or reinforce models they already hold. The metaphor regains its initial dominance at the end of the text and therefore functions to frame the article. As mentioned above, realizations of the GAMES metaphor are patchy. The few there are mainly occur just before or slightly after the middle of the text, with one appearing towards the end. However, the metaphor's mid-text concentration is too weak to indicate any argumentative function. Also, we could see that it is either restricted to technical expressions (for example, *stake*) or converges with the SPORTS metaphor, which it thereby supports.

When looking at *The Economist* text, it shows that most metaphoric expressions cluster towards the end of the text and in the opening paragraphs, with metaphors thinning out in the middle. Similar to the patterns observed in the *Business Week* article, the WAR metaphor is most prominent in the opening and closing paragraphs of the text (EC, headline; lines 6 and 45–7), whereas the few occurrences of the SPORTS metaphor can again be found towards the middle. There we find a company being described as 'the cheerleader for a technology' (EC, line 16), extending 'the two firms champion different approaches' (EC, lines 9–10). Further, the companies are said not to 'compete head to head', with one invading 'EMC's home turf' (EC, lines 24 and 31). The WAR metaphor's weakness in mid-text is also qualitative, as its only two occurrences ('"NetApp killer"' and 'kill NetApp' [EC, lines 35 and 42]) involve the writer's questioning stance as discussed above. However, the metaphor reappears as an unproblematic conceptualization towards the end. In thus framing the text as a whole, the WAR metaphor is once more employed for defining and persuasive purposes.

Although the same overall structure can be observed in the *Fortune* sample, the three macro slots of beginning, middle and end are filled differently. While the WAR metaphor is both quantitatively most frequent and qualitatively intensified in the text (for example, 'the fiercest competition' or 'locked in battle for more than 35 years' [FO, lines 38 and 39–40]), the SPORTS metaphor functions to frame the article ('game of inches' [FO, lines 1 and 90]). The metaphor, although infrequent, is thus employed at key points in the text. The cluster analysis further shows that metaphoric expressions are spread fairly evenly across the text, despite the second half showing more stretches without any relevant expressions. Clustering increases again towards the end of the text. While the SPORTS metaphor also occurs towards the middle ('nobody has played this game better than Tide' [FO, lines 52–3] and the hybrid expression 'turf war' [FO, line 46]), the WAR metaphor is much more prominent in that position (especially in FO, lines 31–40), indicating its argumentative function. Moreover, the author here builds up a very elaborate chain of metaphoric expressions of war, intensifying the metaphor with almost every new instantiation. This mid-text intensification of the WAR metaphor, together with the SPORTS metaphor frame, makes for a very powerful conceptual cluster.

As in so many respects, the *Financial Times* again differs from the other publications in the corpus. As for distribution of metaphoric expressions across the text, it is remarkable that these cluster mainly at the beginning. Apart from only two more metaphoric expressions of war ('targeting younger people' and 'making an enemy of consumers' [FT, lines 26–7 and 32–3]) and one example of an alternative metaphor right at the end ('how they can be their friends' [FT, lines 33–4]), no more relevant metaphoric expressions are found after the first quarter of the sample. Hence, metaphors mainly serve a defining function in this article. Given this initial metaphor dominance, it comes as no surprise that FT, lines 5–13 display all the three cluster metaphors to conceptualize brands: 'the continuing battle . . . between Levi Strauss . . . and Tesco' (FT, lines 8–9), 'Tesco positioning itself as a consumer champion' (FT, lines 11–12) and '[a]re brands an appalling rip-off' (FT, line 5). Although relevant metaphoric expressions are scarce afterwards, we do find that the sample's topic is framed metaphorically. In contrast to the other articles, however, framing is not homogeneous. Rather, while brands are presented in different metaphoric terms at the beginning, the author ultimately takes an instructional perspective, proposing an alternative metaphoric conceptualization of brand owners as 'friends' (FT, line 34). This extreme personalization intensifies the earlier reference to a brand as a 'champion' (FT, line 12). Here, the author shows that a cluster metaphor, namely SPORTS, can be extended to an alternative metaphor. Far from necessarily having to support the WAR metaphor as in the other samples, it can even go so far as to contradict it.

A similar development of the SPORTS metaphor can be witnessed in the *Business Week* article informing the reader that 'CMGI and Intel . . . have teamed up with Pacific Century Cyberworks' (BW, lines 74–5). This non-violent elaboration of the metaphor ties in with other attenuations of the antagonistic RIVAL schema in the article: expressions such as 'a rival group' or 'rivals want to catch Yahoo' (BW, lines 36 and 53) are attenuated to 'contenders' (BW, line 82), 'alliances' (BW, lines 16, 88 and 95) and, finally, 'partnerships' (BW, lines 64 and 76). By contrast, the *Fortune* author does elaborate the SPORTS metaphor by referring to football: 'like football and trench warfare, this is a contest of sweat, mud and inches' (FO, lines 13–14). This conceptualization is unusual in that it mentions both source and target space (Cameron and Low, 1999, p. 80) and furthermore spells out which semantic features are drawn upon in the metaphoric blend (Low, 1999, p. 64). Most importantly, however, it juxtaposes the SPORTS (or, more specifically, FOOTBALL) and the WAR metaphor, thus betraying the tight conceptual links between the two domains.[17]

In this respect, the *Fortune* article is diametrically opposed to the *Financial Times* text: in the latter, the WAR metaphor may be the most frequent, but end stress and thus persuasive weight is granted to an alternative metaphor. Consequently, the conceptual role of consumers changes along with that of marketers.

Alternative metaphors

On the whole, occurrences of the alternative ROMANCE metaphor are few and far between, too scarce in fact to account for any systematic clusters or chains. While this metaphor is therefore very weak indeed, it is not the only non-dominant one to surface in the articles. The *Business Week* text, for example, also features other non-violent, non-competitive metaphors beside the dominant cluster. One of these is MARKETS ARE ORGANISMS, as evidenced by the phrases 'the world's fastest-growing Internet markets' and 'homegrown portals' (BW, lines 17 and 39). MARKETS ARE ORGANISMS has been well-documented as a conceptual metaphor in marketing (Heiss, 1994), yet in the corpus, its realizations, while numerous, are restricted to highly conventional expressions such as *organic/rapid growth* or *the company/industry/market has thrived*. Some of those formulaic examples can, be found in the *Fortune* article, for example, among them 'slow-growth industries' (FO, line 12); 'to eke out growth' (FO, lines 18–9); 'growing at hyperspeed' (FO, lines 20–1); and ' "Path to Growth" ' (FO, lines 44–5). (Significantly, the author here tends to integrate the ORGANISM metaphor into a movement scenario.) So while Hunt and Menon (1995) may be right in claiming that 'the organism metaphor has arguably been the most popular metaphor in marketing theory' (p. 86), it is not as productive as the WAR or SPORTS metaphors.[18]

The *Business Week* text also introduces the metaphor COMPETITION IS HEAT, as realized in 'the competition for good content is becoming heated' (BW, lines 47–8), where the metaphor serves to intensify the prevalent movement dynamics. Apart from that local function, the domain of temperature is indeed quite productive in the corpus as a whole. Creative extensions are both produced by the writers themselves (*while it's a cold winter indeed for other retailers, Kohl's execs insist they can weather any storm* [MS BW 8]) and developed from quotations. An example of the latter can be found in MS BW 14, in which the quote '*we don't understand why* [the brand] *is so hot right now*' gives rise to no less than six elaborations on metaphoric *hot* in the 941-word article. Moreover, metaphoric construction of a topic can be quite explicit by providing both source and target (*the Ibiza season has . . . turned into a marketing hothouse* [MS FT 52]). The choice of semantic features transferred is also clear from the context of the metaphoric expressions, as in the following example:

> a small number of consumers . . . can turn a grass fire into a conflagration . . . a handful of hipsters . . . were able to 'tip' Wolverine's Hush Puppies shoes into a national revival.   (MS BW 17)

Although the corpus does not feature metaphor users negotiating or struggling over the metaphor's semantic features, the majority of criteria to identify a conceptual metaphor as being entrenched and productive are in fact met (see Low, 1999, p. 64). Beyond that, COMPETITION IS HEAT can, in view of the dominant WAR metaphor, be explained as an extension of the embodied metaphor ANGER IS HEAT (Lakoff, 1994). The general entrenched metaphor in this context is INTENSE EMOTIONS ARE HEAT (Kövecses, 2000), of which we indeed find an example in the *Business Week* text ('rivals are trying to ignite nationalist passions' [BW, lines 88–9]). It is the common source space *heat* shared by both metaphoric competition and anger that calls the independence of COMPETITION IS HEAT into question. As it is related conceptually to anger, if not aggression, it hardly functions as an alternative in marketing discourse.

Two more non-cluster metaphors can be found in *The Economist* article. On the one hand, dominant market participants are metaphorized as monarchs ('the company dethroned IBM' [EC, line 12; see also Table A.6 on p. 216]). A parallel expression is 'laundry king' (FO, line 67). On the other, *The Economist* writer also introduces the metaphoric concept COMPANIES ARE MACHINES ('EMC's legendary sales machine' [EC, line 45]). This metaphor is again very much entrenched in both primary and secondary marketing discourse. First, it is extended creatively: apart from the collocation *marketing/sales machine*, which occurs four more times in the corpus, we also find '*this company . . . as a machine for research*' (MS EC 41). This creative extension is itself elaborated on in another quotation in the same article: *'ideas shoot out of* [the company's founder] *like a Van de Graaff generator'.*[19] Elsewhere in the corpus, text producers are also explicit about conceptualizing one domain in terms of the MACHINE domain (*'Pfizer is a marketing machine'* [MS FO 6]). Finally, text producers also clarify what features are in fact transferred in the blending process:

> [The company] becomes huge. Then there's a different set of rules . . . and . . . it's not my gig. It becomes a machine. I don't want to be pushed around in a job situation'.   (MS FO 25)

So can the MACHINE metaphor be called a viable alternative to the metaphors investigated? While it is certainly very productive on its own, it should still be noted that it has been discussed in relation to the WAR metaphor: Morgan (1997, pp. 15–16), for example, traces the large-scale industrial rationalization and mechanization known as Taylorism back to Frederick the Great's organization of the Prussian army and his reduction of soldiers to machines. In addition, Clausewitz (1952) also employs this Cartesian notion of a machine-like army quite lavishly (p. 160 and elsewhere).[20] Hence, the MACHINE metaphor is certainly more productive but less independent of the dominant cluster than is the ORGANISM metaphor.

To sum up, we can see that it is either the WAR or the SPORTS metaphor that frames three of the four articles, with GAMES and alternative metaphors showing sketchy patterns at best. Things are different with the *Financial Times*, and while this text is also the one with the lowest metaphor count, its introduction of an alternative metaphor in a textually salient position should not be underrated. However, other non-cluster metaphors tie in with the dominant metaphors conceptually, thus supporting them. The prevailing cluster brings about scenarios for marketing defined by antagonistic or fast, goal-orientated movement through a narrow space. As a last step, let us see how these metaphoric scenarios are underscored by grammatical patterns.

Functional grammar patterns

The very dynamic model the *Business Week* text is based on is sustained by the prevailing use of progressive aspect together with durative/intensive trajectory – as in, for example, 'some of the biggest names in cyberspace are stepping up their Asian operations' (BW, lines 15–16). An additional feature is completive trajectory coupled with predecessive aspect, as in 'three front-runners have emerged' (BW, line 32). Together, the two devices help to direct the reader's attention to the current state of affairs while also providing information about the past and its relation to the present. The two grammatical features more often than not combine with one of the cluster metaphors, as in 'AOL is trying hard to keep pace' (BW, line 67) or 'AOL . . . has launched its service' (BW, lines 36–7). Another case in point is the following quote from *Fortune*: 'the rest of the world has been growing at hyperspeed' (FO, lines 20–1). Here, the dynamic metaphoric scenario is reinforced by both the intensifying prefix as well as durative trajectory. Intensive trajectory and progressive aspect are also there in *The Economist* text ('venture capitalists are rushing to back storage start-ups' [EC, omitted]) as is completive trajectory combined with predecessive aspect ('[it] has suddenly become a battleground' [EC, lines 5–6]). However, as the RACING metaphor and the related scenario of dynamic movement are not as evident as in the *Business Week* article, the grammatical device is proportionately less prominent in *The Economist*. Interestingly, the *Financial Times* text features progressive aspect and durative trajectory mainly in its opening paragraphs, which also record the highest density of cluster metaphors. Thus we find 'brands are fighting' (FT, line 2) as well as 'continuing battle' (FT, line 8), 'Levi fighting to stop this activity' (FT, line 14) as well as 'brand owners are being thrown on to the defensive' (FT, line 23). This co-occurrence of particular grammatical with particular metaphoric features speaks of a functional relationship between the two. Indeed, all four articles show that dynamic versus static scenarios are conveyed through grammatical devices together with metaphors rather than through word classes.

After this analysis of eight parameters in four sample texts, the following discussion summarizes the findings from this qualitative investigation in relation to the quantitative data, presents a conceptual model underlying media discourse on marketing and sales and shows the impact this model has on both cognition and discourse.

4.2.1. Four sample texts

bold type: metaphoric expression of war

bold italics: metaphoric expression of sports

bold underlined: metaphoric expression of games

italics: metaphoric expression of romance

An asterisk indicates a relevant metaphoric expression that was not included in the lexical fields.

Business Week

1   Portal **combat**
2   In Asia, a **bruising battle** for *cyberturf*
3   Mary Ong, the CEO of newly formed Lycos Asia Pte Ltd. (LCOS), is the first
4   to admit that her operation isn't up to *speed* yet. Since U.S. Internet
5   powerhouse CMGI, which owns the Lycos Web portal, announced in
6   September a joint venture with Singapore Telecommunications to set up
7   customized versions of Lycos in 10 Asian cities, Ong has been scrambling to
8   hire staff, find office space, and get the business started – pronto. Lycos
9   **launched** its Singapore site in December, when it also announced plans to
10 go online in Malaysia and the Philippines. With rivals such as Yahoo! [*sic*] Inc.
11 already well established, Ong knows that Lycos can't afford to lose any more
12 time. 'We are late,' she says. 'We have a big challenge *catching* up.'
13 It doesn't make Ong's task any easier that other U.S. Internet companies are
14 **targeting** Asia, too. America Online (AOL), AT&T (T), Microsoft (MSFT) –
15 some of the biggest names in cyberspace are stepping up their Asian
16 operations, forming new subsidiaries, joint ventures, and *alliances to take
17 advantage of the world's fastest-growing Internet markets. 'U.S. companies
18 have become unbelievably more aggressive,' says analyst Rajeev Gupta of
19 Goldman, Sachs & Co. in Hong Kong. And with the November deal between
20 Washington and Beijing on China's entry into the World Trade Organization,
21 the *pace* is sure to increase as the Chinese phase out restrictions on foreign
22 ownership of local Internet companies.
23 Why the flurry now? Sheer numbers. International Data Corp. estimates that
24 online spending in non-Japan Asia will double from $2.2 billion in 1999, to
25 $5.5 billion by yearend. That's still small by American standards – the U.S. is
26 expected to spend $133 billion on Internet commerce this year – but the
27 trend is clear. By 2002, estimates IDC, 60 million Asians will be hopping on
28 the Net, spending some $30 billion on purchases. 'The year 2000 will be the
29 year that the global e-commerce *players* (**players**) *invade Asia,' says
30 David C. Michael, a vice-president at Boston Consulting Group in Hong
31 Kong.
32 Deep pockets. Already, three *front-runners* have emerged. At the head of
33 the *pack* is Yahoo (YHOO), backed by Japan's Softbank Corp., which is
34 recreating in its Asian backyard the successful investment strategy it used in
35 the U.S., buying **stakes** in a wide range of Net startups. CMGI (CMGI), which
36 owns Lycos, is behind a rival group. The third main contender is AOL, which
37 has **launched** its service in several markets and is a key shareholder in
38 Hong Kong-based Chinadotcom Corp.
39 But their *front-row* places may be in jeopardy. Homegrown portals are not
40 simply rolling over for the Americans. Some are *playing* (**playing**) up their
41 local roots to appeal to nationalist customers, while others are introducing
42 new services before the foreigners do. To *attract users to its portal, for
43 example, South Korea's Serome Technology Inc. on Jan. 5 started offering
44 free local phone calls using the Internet, and promises free calls to the U.S.
45 later this month.
46 The newcomers have one big advantage: deep pockets. As more portals,

47 both foreign and domestic, **target** the region, the competition for good
48 content is becoming heated – and expensive. Unlike the U.S., Asia does not
49 yet have an abundance of interesting Web sites. That's driving up costs.
50 'Because there are not that many content providers, everything will be more
51 expensive,' says Savio Chow, head of Yahoo's Asian operations in Hong
52 Kong.
53 Especially if rivals want to *catch* Yahoo. Following the early popularity of
54 Yahoo! [*sic*] Japan, started in 1996, Yahoo set up a Korean portal in 1997. Yahoo
55 Korea is now the market leader, with 30% market share and 23 million page
56 views daily. Yahoo has Chinese-language sites for Taiwan, Hong Kong, and
57 Singapore, and the company ranks No. 1 in a survey of popular portals in
58 several Asian countries, according to Sydney-based researcher www.consult.
59 Another edge for Yahoo is its Chinese-American founder, Jerry Yang, who
60 can promote the company and gain media attention in China in a way that
61 many others cannot. For instance, during a September visit to Beijing, Yang
62 spent half a day schmoozing with graduate students at Beijing University,
63 talking in Mandarin about what it takes to be an Internet entrepreneur. Now,
64 Yahoo is overhauling its Chinese site and forming a new *partnership* with
65 Chinese software maker Founder, a powerful 'red **chip**,' or state company
66 traded in Hong Kong.
67 Connections. As Yahoo expands, AOL is trying hard to keep **pace*. It started
68 a Japanese version in 1997 and **launched** AOL Hong Kong in September.
69 AOL hopes that Hong Kong will become a springboard into China. While AOL
70 may not have a Mandarin-speaking founder, it does have something that may
71 be more valuable in China: good guanxi, or connections, through its **stake** in
72 Chinadotcom, a Hong Kong-based portal service and the first Chinese
73 Internet company to go public on Nasdaq, raising $90 million.
74 CMGI and Intel (INTC) are counting on guanxi of a different sort. They have
75 **teamed up* with Pacific Century CyberWorks founder Richard Li. In
76 September, CMGI formed a $350 million *partnership* with Li to develop Web
77 content for the Chinese market. Meanwhile, Intel has invested $50 million in
78 PCC, which is preparing to **launch** a regional high-speed TV and Internet
79 service this year. CMGI is also going for the glitz. At the introduction of Lycos'
80 Singapore site, the company hired a local artist known as Tanya to entertain
81 guests.
82 As the three main contenders push forward, others must move quickly to
83 avoid becoming ***also-rans**.* Microsoft Corp. wants to expand its MSN
84 network. AT&T, through its Excite@Home (ATHM) subsidiary, plans to
85 **launch** broadband service in Japan in early 2000. On Nov. 10, Internet
86 search engine LookSmart Ltd. (LOOK) announced a $200 million deal with
87 British Telecommunications PLC (BTY) to develop sites in Asia and Europe.
88 Building **alliances.* In response to the foreign **invasion*, some local rivals
89 are trying to ignite nationalist passions. South Korea's Daum
90 Communications Corp., which is second to Yahoo! [*sic*] Korea, has appealed to
91 anti-Japanese sentiment by boasting in newspaper ads that it will repel
92 Softbank's **invasion* just as Koreans defeated Japanese intruders more
93 than 500 years ago. The newcomers also risk being associated with an
94 American pop culture seen by some in Asia as too violent and permissive.

Continued

95 Still, local content providers need to become part of the regional ***alliances**
96 the Americans are forming. 'We want to lock onto one of those grids so we
97 can expand our size quickly,' says Chong Huai Seng, vice-chairman of
98 Panpac Media.com Ltd., a Singapore magazine publisher. Whether Asians
99 like it or not, the Americans are coming.

(MS BW 7)

The Economist

1 Store **wars**
2 . . .
3 With the value of storage products sold doubling every year, and expected to
4 reach $34 billion by 2003, the industry is regarded as recession-proof. As a
5 result, a field renowned for its general inability to set pulses racing has
6 suddenly become a **battleground**. Within the past few days, **war** has been
7 declared between the two most significant storage companies: mighty EMC
8 and its upstart rival, Network Appliance (known as NetApp).
9 As usual in technological **bunfights**, the two firms *champion* different
10 approaches to the same problem. EMC pioneered the idea that computers
11 and storage systems are separate products that should be bought from
12 separate suppliers. The company dethroned IBM, which used to dominate
13 both the computer and the storage markets. It is now the leading supplier of
14 storage systems, with 35% of the world market.
15 . . .
16 NetApp, on the other hand, is the ***cheerleader** for a technology called
17 network-attached storage (NAS). As its acronym suggests, NAS is the mirror-
18 image of SAN. Instead of a separate storage network, NAS involves plugging
19 storage devices into a firm's main computer network. This is not always as
20 fast or reliable as using a SAN, but it is far cheaper and simpler, thanks to the
21 use of standard Internet protocols. It also means that NetApp's storage units,
22 called 'filers', can be supported and backed up using a variety of software,
23 rather than the proprietary (and expensive) tools needed to run a SAN.
24 To start with, EMC and NetApp did not compete *head to head*. EMC's
25 products are aimed at high-end applications where reliability is crucial, such
26 as corporate databases; NetApp sells smaller systems. (Being squeezed in
27 the middle are computer makers such as IBM, Compaq and Sun
28 Microsystems, which compete in both markets.) But NetApp has moved
29 upmarket fast, as its products have become better and more reliable. Yahoo!,
30 for example, uses NetApp products to run e-mail and web-hosting services.
31 On November 29th, NetApp moved right on to EMC's home *turf* by
32 announcing that its products are now compatible with IBM's database
33 software and mainframe computers, which do much of the **heavy lifting* in
34 corporate computing. EMC responded on December 5th by unveiling an
35 aggressively priced NAS server, touted as a 'NetApp **killer**', and new

36 software that provides a bridge between SAN and NAS systems. EMC has,
37 in other words, conceded that NetApp's approach has merit, and plans to
38 steal its rival's clothes.
39 Now that the two firms are competing directly and their products look
40 increasingly similar, who will win? Steve Duplessie, an analyst with
41 Enterprise Storage Group, a consultancy, is impressed by EMC's new
42 product, but doubts whether it will **kill** NetApp any time soon, because the
43 market is growing so fast. Ultimately, as the technological differences
44 between the firms shrink, it may come down to sales and marketing – and
45 given EMC's legendary sales machine, that means NetApp has a **fight** on its
46 hands.
47 Since the market up for grabs is so huge, it is worth the **bruises** . . .
48 Forrester predicts that storage will account for 17% of large firms' computing
49 budgets by 2003, up from 4% in 1999; already, spending on storage exceeds
50 spending on web servers. *Sexy* the storage business may not be; but
51 lucrative it certainly is.

(MS EC 37)

Fortune

1 A *game* (**game**) of inches
2 **Battling** for market share in a slowing industry can be a mighty dirty
3 business. Just ask laundry-soap archrivals Unilever and Procter & Gamble.
4 Look out from the top of the Empire State Building directly toward New
5 Jersey. There, right at the edge of the Hudson River, sits the Laundry
6 Institute, a small laboratory owned by Unilever. You'd never know that inside
7 this nondescript one-story building a **battle** is raging. 'We're trying to figure
8 out what to do about underarm stains,' says Jack Linard, a laundry scientist.
9 He points to the yellowed armpits of a white undershirt.
10 This is about much more than nasty stains. It's Unilever's latest ***offensive**
11 against archrival Procter & Gamble. Welcome to the down-and-dirty **fight** for
12 market share in the slowest of slow-growth industries: Consumer products.
13 Like ***football** and trench **warfare**, this is a contest of sweat, mud, and
14 inches. Here every small win – shinier floors, whiter teeth, cleaner laundry –
15 is a big one. In the $6 billion U.S. laundry market, for example, a mere
16 percentage point gain in share means a $60 million gain in revenues. So as
17 the rest of the business world braces for a slowdown, Fortune decided to turn
18 to Procter & Gamble and Unilever for a refresher course on how to eke out
19 growth in tough conditions.
20 Over the past five years, while the rest of the world has been growing at
21 hyperspeed, $52 billion Unilever and $40 billion P&G have been living in a
22 parallel slow-growth universe. Since 1996, Unilever's sales have declined an
23 average 3.6% a year. P&G's have inched up 3.6% a year. Every one of the
24 markets they compete in is barely growing, flat, or declining. Shampoo sales,

Continued

25 for instance, grew 2.4% over the past year, according to Information
26 Resources Inc.; deodorant was up 1.2%; dishwashing liquid dropped 0.5%;
27 toothpaste sank 1.5%. At the same time both companies remain under
28 intense pressure from Wall Street to pick up the ***pace**. P&G's share price
29 has fallen 20% over the past two years to a recent $70. Unilever is off 30%,
30 selling recently at $30.
31 In this kind of environment, 'it's a ***death struggle** to incrementally gain
32 share,' says Burt Flickinger, a former P&G brand manager who now works as
33 a consumer products consultant. P&G and Unilever have to ***slog** it out for
34 every fraction of every share in every category in every market where they
35 compete. And that's a lot of ***slogging**. Both companies own hundreds of the
36 world's best-known brands – Crest, Pampers, Ivory (Procter & Gamble);
37 Dove, Vaseline, Lipton (Unilever) – competing in some 140 countries. But
38 perhaps the **fiercest** competition is taking place in the U.S. market for
39 laundry detergent, where P&G's Tide and Unilever's Wisk have been locked
40 in **battle** for more than 35 years.
41 Both companies badly need to win ground here. P&G CFO Clayton Daley
42 told analysts in January that Tide is crucial to 'getting P&G back on track.'
43 And Unilever has chosen Wisk as one of 14 brands in the U.S. – out of 1,600
44 worldwide – to lead its latest strategic initiative, officially called 'Path to
45 Growth.'
46 What makes this ***turf** war so **brutal** is simple: There isn't much territory to
47 gain. Last year, volume in the U.S. fabric-care market was flat. And at $6
48 billion a year, the market is already so big that it can't get much bigger.
49 'People aren't getting any dirtier,' points out Ann Gillin Lefever, a consumer
50 products analyst at Lehman Brothers. The only way to win share: take it from
51 the competition.
52 In recent years nobody has ***played** (**played**) this ***game** (**game**) better than
53 Tide. While the rest of the industry stagnated, Tide's sales climbed by 41%,
54 to $1.8 billion over the past five years. It now owns 40% of the market. Its
55 strategy? First, Tide spends more than $100 million a year promoting its
56 brand name by advertising on TV, billboards, subways, buses, magazines,
57 and the Internet. It sponsors a Nascar racecar and youth soccer leagues. It
58 holds nationwide publicity stunts, such as its recent Dirtiest Kid in America
59 contest. Tide has made itself an American brand icon – right up there with
60 Coke or McDonald's.
61 . . .
62 Every new Tide on the shelf is an inch of territory nabbed from some other
63 brand. 'Shelf space is so tight in stores these days that,' says Susan Chachil,
64 a category manager at Kmart, 'when something new comes in, something
65 else has got to go out.'
66 . . .
67 But that was then. Unilever – the undisputed laundry king in such overseas
68 markets as South America and Southeast Asia – has made growing Wisk a
69 top priority in the U.S., and it's loosening the purse strings to do it . . .
70 So how do you make things worse for a strong brand like Tide? Cutting
71 prices won't work; Tide'll only match them. Advertise more? Tide'll just
72 outspend you. There's only one way to ***blow** a box of Tide off the shelf:
73 Come out with something bigger, better, and newer. And that, finally, is what

74 Unilever believes it's got.
75 ...
76 **Armed** with a new $80 million budget, last November Unilever **launched** the
77 tablets in the U.S. under the name Wisk Dual Action Tablets. Over the next
78 few months Wisk tablets will be everywhere. Literally. On Jan. 7, Unilever
79 **blitzed** 24 million homes with tablet samples delivered in Sunday
80 newspapers. Later this month it will roll out a series of TV ads aimed at a
81 younger, hipper market. One spot features sultry music, the film running in
82 slow motion as a good-looking guy gets splashed by a passing car.
83 ...
84 But Wisk shouldn't start counting its profits just yet. Tide – surprise! – has
85 already **launched** a *counteroffensive: Tide Rapid Action Tablets. Tide has
86 also fired the first **shot**. Its new ads show a side-by-side comparison of Tide's
87 and Wisk's tablets plopped into beakers of water. In the spot Wisk doesn't
88 dissolve as well as Tide. It's a small point – most consumers don't wash their
89 clothes in beakers anyway – but already Wisk is threatening to challenge
90 Tide's claims in court. In a *game* (**game**) of inches, after all, every inch
91 counts.

(MS FO 4)

Financial Times

1 Labelled as the devil of the consumer society
2 Brands: Leading brands are **fighting** to justify their high prices and to dispel
3 their image as symbols of a global economic system gone wrong writes
4 Richard Tomkins.
5 Are brands an appalling **rip-off**, enriching their corporate owners by
6 exploiting people's insecurities and desires? Or are they worth every penny
7 of the price premium they command because of the pleasure they bring?
8 It is an old question that has been given new life by the continuing **battle** in
9 Europe between Levi Strauss, the US clothing company, and Tesco, the
10 supermarket chain that sells Levi's jeans at discount prices.
11 On the one hand, you have Tesco positioning itself as a consumer
12 *champion* by obtaining Levi's jeans on the grey market and selling them for
13 much less than authorised stores.
14 On the other, you have Levi **fighting** to stop this activity out of a belief that its
15 brand is devalued when its jeans appear in a supermarket alongside shelves
16 full of soap powder, tea bags and pickled gherkins.
17 So far the brand owner has come off worse – not so much in the European
18 Court of Justice, whose interim ruling on the dispute last month set new
19 standards of inscrutability, but in the court of public opinion, where Levi has
20 been found guilty of anti-consumer protectionism.
21 How the case will end is anybody's guess. But it has come at a bad time. It
22 has had the unfortunate effect of highlighting some awkward questions about

Continued

23 brands just as brand owners are being ***thrown*** on to the *****defensive** by anti-
24 globalisation protesters and their sympathisers.
25 . . .
26 A particular concern is that brands are increasingly **targeting** younger
27 people, who are more prone to the desires and insecurities that emotional
28 branding seeks to exploit. Many parents today despair at their children's
29 obsession with brands, a phenomenon unknown in their own younger days.
30 . . .
31 A global brand, it seems, is worth a lot less now than it was just a year-and-a-
32 half ago. Maybe brand owners should be spending less time making an
33 **enemy** of consumers in the courts and more time wondering how they can
34 be their *friends*.

(MS FT 91)

4.3 Discussion: socio-cognitive impact and possible alternatives

The corpus analysis verifies the claim that 'war provides the strategic language which structures almost all [marketing] discourse' (Desmond, 1997, p. 344). Starting from the original lexical fields, it can be seen that there are conceptual links within the cluster, with the domain of war permeating the other two domains either directly or indirectly. When looking at metaphoric instantiations of the lexical fields, the field of war shows the highest percentage of items realized. Moreover, the WAR metaphor is both most frequent and most entrenched in the corpus. In concrete sample texts, it tends to occur at the beginning and end, thus providing a conceptual frame for the topic in question. The SPORTS metaphor, on the other hand, rather features towards the middle of the samples, although the two metaphors can swap roles (as in the *Fortune* text). The GAMES metaphor is by far the least frequent one in the cluster and does not occur in any salient textual position. Although word class analysis revealed the corpus to be nominally biased, the models conveyed in the sample texts are dynamic rather than static. This dynamic nature is brought about by use of the progressive tense in combination with intensive/durative trajectory as well as by strategic use of metaphors of fast and goal-orientated or antagonistic movement. Further, cluster metaphors are mainly extended and elaborated in chains, tying in with the intensification so prominent in the *Fortune* sample. However, there is also subtle (*The Economist*) or even explicit

(*Financial Times*) questioning of the WAR/SPORTS cluster, making for a metaphorical hybrid in the *Financial Times* article. As for alternative metaphors, we find evidence not only of ROMANCE but also of ORGAN-ISM and MACHINE metaphors. While scarce, these metaphors have the potential to feature as viable non-violent and non-competitive alternatives to the dominant cluster.

The analysis of the four sample texts gives rise to the assumed conceptual model shown in Figure 4.1. The remainder of this section discusses its impact on discourse and cognition as well as on the socio-economic sphere those are embedded in. In this context, the focus will be on the gendered nature of the model. As for its organization, please recall that the elements are ordered from centre to periphery, with arrows indicating dependence relations.

The central metaphor, MARKETING IS . . . MOVING IN A BOUNDED SPACE, can be traced back to a primary metaphor, which, being by nature very generic, in itself does not reveal much about the particularities of media discourse on marketing. However, it entails two different specific forms of movement, namely MARKETING IS . . . FAST MOVEMENT on the one hand and MARKETING IS . . . ANTAGONISTIC MOVEMENT on the other. The former can again be sub-divided into MARKETING IS . . . FAST, UNCOORDINATED MOVEMENT (evidenced by phrases such as 'Ong has been scrambling to hire staff' [BW, lines 7–8]) and MARKETING IS . . . FAST, GOAL-ORIENTATED MOVEMENT, which translates into the RACING metaphor witnessed particularly in the *Business Week* sample. The second entailment of the central metaphoric concept, namely MARKETING IS . . . ANTAGONISTIC MOVEMENT, finds its specific expression in MARKETING IS . . . WAR OVER TERRITORY and, on the same level, MARKETING IS . . . A FOOTBALL MATCH. The FOOTBALL metaphor, which featured very prominently in the *Fortune* sample, is ambiguous, containing both competitive and playful elements. Its latter aspect is incorporated in the more general metaphor MARKETING IS . . . PLAYING A GAME.[21]

Although the GAMES metaphor is fairly general, I have nevertheless located it on the fringes of the model as it is neither frequent nor salient. The least prominent cluster metaphor in quantitative terms, it also never takes a central position in any of the four texts: nor can it be found in the qualitatively important slots at the beginning and end, and it does not elaborate on or question the dominant metaphors. Moreover, it is altogether absent from one of the four samples (*The Economist*). Elsewhere, it is mainly restricted to technical terms or collapses with the SPORTS metaphor (as in 'nobody has played this game

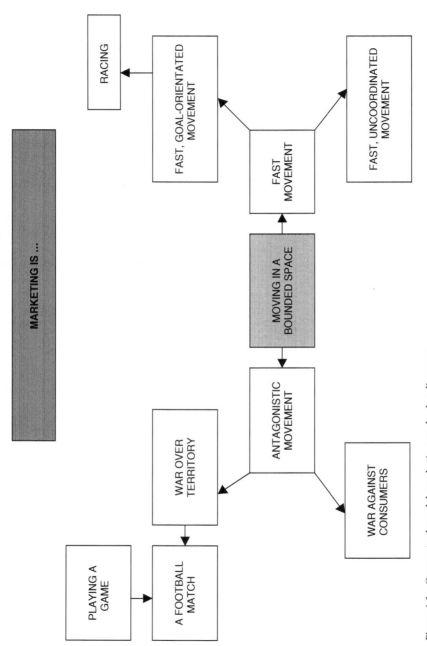

Figure 4.1 Conceptual model marketing and sales discourse

better than Tide' [FO, lines 52–3]). Therefore, Eubanks' (2000) observation about popular marketing handbooks as meshing 'horrendous war images with liberal doses of game metaphors' (p. 145) does not hold true for magazine and newspaper texts on marketing: doses of the GAME metaphor are all but liberal.[22]

Yet, the 'horrendous war images' are definitely there, lending particular importance to the model's antagonistic force schema. While the fast, goal-orientated movement scenario refers to several parties moving from one point to another one ahead of them, the force schema rather encapsulates movement by two parties against each other, the aim being to push the opposing party back behind its starting point. Although both concepts are highly competitive, the more aggressive form of competition is obviously antagonistic movement.[23] The similarities between the WAR and the SPORTS (in particular the FOOTBALL) metaphor are spelt out in the *Fortune* sample, leading to their juxtaposition at the same level. Although the SPORTS metaphor is less frequent than the WAR metaphor, it definitely serves as its conceptual support and even functions as a bracket in the *Fortune* sample. Further evidence of the tight conceptual links between the two metaphors is derived from group schema theory, according to which both armies and sporting teams can be seen as being relational or comparative groups, being 'constitutionally competitive, or concerned with [their] status relative to other groups' (Augoustinos and Walker, 1995, p. 123). The fact that these two groups are drawn upon to describe metaphorically groups in marketing helps to render the latter intrinsically relational and competitive, too.

The picture that emerges is one of a largely (albeit not entirely) homogeneous discourse centring on WAR and SPORTS metaphors, with non-competitive metaphors in a non-dominant position. The dominance of the most frequent metaphors is further underscored by their being employed to frame topics, thus fostering and reifying particular conceptual models. At the discourse level, usage of such metaphors positions writers and readers in particular roles *vis-à-vis* each other. The fact that dominant metaphors define a topic at the beginning of the texts and also recur at their end indicates their persuasive interpersonal function. In this context, recalling the readership structure of the four magazines is worthwhile, to see who the text producers in fact write for. Looking at readers' occupations and gender, it shows that readers are in fact 90 per cent male, with most of them holding senior management positions: 63 per cent in the case of *Business Week* (*Business Week*, 2002a), 52 per cent for *The Economist* (*The Economist*, 2002), and 69 per cent of *Fortune* readers (Time Inc. *Fortune*®, 1998). As for the readership of the *Financial Times*, 38 per cent hold board-level positions and an additional 28 per cent are directors or department heads (information provided by Sarah Griffiths, Advertising FT Newspaper UK). In addition to this, the way direct quotations from business people are elaborated on in the four articles show that the dominant metaphors are largely endorsed by journalists and marketers alike. The centrality of the WAR metaphor in primary marketing discourse is corroborated by Raghavan (1990), who states that 'there is sufficient reason to believe that [the military metaphor] represents the way in which most managers think about competitive maneuvers' (p. 7; see also Cleary and Packard, 1992, p. 232). In view of this, authors of journalistic texts on marketing seem to echo, if not imitate, the metaphors found in corporate discourse – that is, those used by their readers. Theoretically, use of direct quotes could, of course, be selective to fit the metaphors proposed by journalists. Yet, if one considers the imbalance of (discursive) power between corporate elites and journalists, the derivative nature of magazine and newspaper texts, and a general reader-orientation, it seems more plausible that journalists emulate the ones they report on – that is, their audience. It seems that the writers' chief aim is to entertain and flatter their readers through imitation rather than to challenge their defining power by proposing alternative conceptualizations on a large scale.

As represented by the model in Figure 4.1 and the relationships between discourse participants sketched out above, metaphors have an impact not only at the textual level but also at the level of cognition and discourse. What, then, about the socio-economic framework that both discourse and cognition, and the texts they give rise to, are embedded in? The framework in question is late capitalism, and the social practice of marketing is one of its central aspects. Participants at this level are marketers and customers, the relationship between them being characterized metaphorically as aggression on the part of the former, directed against the latter: indeed, 'market' seems to denote 'something you do *to* customers' (Searls and Weinberger, 2000, p. 76; original emphasis). Moreover, the MARKETING IS WAR AGAINST CONSUMERS metaphor in fact re-accentuates the bounded space marketers fight over. The territory to be gained or lost is obviously the market; that is, people and their cognitive make-up. This notion of fighting for consumers' minds is also embraced by Michaelson (1987, p. 108), who proposes that the military components of psychological attack and propaganda have their business parallel in advertising. Advertising is a marketing weapon that demonstrates its firepower in capturing shares of mind.

Quoting Ries and Trout (1986), Desmond (1997, p. 344) notes that 'as the mind of the consumer forms the territory on which the battle is waged, this must be penetrated and possessed'. Seen as such, minds-as-territories can be penetrated and colonized, a notion strongly reminiscent of van Dijk's (1996) concept of power through mind control in discourse (p. 84). Interestingly, the term 'territory' is doubly metaphoric in a marketing context: minds are metaphorized as territories, which are in turn conceptualized as a (female) body to be penetrated (Opitz, 1992, p. 40). The somewhat surprising fact that the technical term *market penetration* occurs only twice in the corpus may indicate a growing sensitivity towards the lexeme's aggressively sexual overtones. Then again, it may just be coincidence. In any case, it is exactly those connotations that, from a gender perspective, are central to the socio-cognitive impact of the above model.

The two most prominent cluster metaphors, WAR and SPORTS, are masculinized to a high degree. Of course, there are 'masculine' and 'feminine' sports (for example, football versus figure skating),[24] begging the question as to why the lexical field includes only the former. The reason is a simple one: non-coincidentally, the most popular types of sports in Western culture are at the same time the 'masculine' ones, a bias that can be traced historically. At the heyday of nineteenth-century colonialism, sports came to be regarded as the perfect training for future male empire leaders, be it in the spheres of politics, the military or business. Physical education was seen as 'instilling physical and mental toughness, obedience to authority, and loyalty to the team' (Kidd, 1990, p. 34). This view of sports as an important practice to maintain the prevailing social order persisted well into the second half of the twentieth century (Messner, 1992, p. 19) and obviously entailed an attempt to exclude women from all but a very few types of sport (Kidd, 1990, pp. 35–7). Although women have by now become a part of almost all kinds of sports practised, such marginalization still finds a contemporary reflection in the fact that media coverage of male athletes is a hundredfold that of professional women athletes on prime-time TV (Sabo and Jansen, 1998, p. 208).

It is this marginalization of women, and simultanous glorification of men, that links the socio-cultural domains of the military, sports and business (Pietilä, 1990, p. 4). Further, social links entail cognitive inter-relations between the three domains, and more often than not the connections are metaphoric. Consequently, it can be said that

> the foundation metaphors that animate the language games that operate within these disparate arenas of power are nearly interchangeable.   (Sabo and Jansen, 1998, p. 203)

Thus we find that media coverage of sport events, especially competitive and contact sports, is shot through, as it were, with metaphoric expressions of war (Malszecki, 1995). And there are numerous realizations of the SPORTS metaphor in military discourse and coverage of war (Schott, 1996, p. 26), most notably in the case of the 1991 Gulf War (Jansen and Sabo, 1994; Lakoff, 1992, p. 472). Indeed, 'the metaphors of sport have insinuated themselves into war (and by extension, business)' (Malszecki, 1995, p. 225). The domains of war and sports are thus in a two-way metaphoric relationship, with each of them functioning as either the source or the target input space for the other. By contrast, metaphoric transfer between war or sports on the one hand, and business on the other is unidirectional: there is no entrenched metaphor *WAR IS BUSINESS (although literally, war is big business indeed). Rather, war and sports are so tightly related as to form a blend, which then serves as the source domain for metaphoric mapping in marketing discourse. What makes the war/sports blend such a suitable source input space for marketing are the masculinized characteristics shared by both domains. Each domain has brought forth a prototype of hegemonic masculinity, the oldest of which is the soldier. The technology-driven decline in the importance of physical strength in warfare then called for a substitute prototype of hegemonic masculinity. This was found in the athlete, who represents

> the male body as strong, virile, and powerful [and has] taken on increasingly important ideological and symbolic significance in gender relations.   (Messner, 1992, pp. 168–9)

The athlete is related to the businessman by virtue of the fact that his qualities 'are synonymous with high performance on the battlefield, in the political sphere, and in science, technology, and industry' (Sabo and Jansen, 1998, p. 203). Mapping the blend of soldier/athlete on to the businessman establishes the latter as yet another paragon of hegemonic masculinity, who is even replacing the older soldier prototype from which he derives (Connell, 1998; Wörsching, 1999). Obviously, the links between the two prototypes are very tight.[25]

Metaphorically, constructing the businessman as a representative of hegemonic masculinity has an impact on gender relations that should not be underestimated. It far exceeds the practical issue of how comprehensible metaphoric expressions of war and sports are for women, who usually lack cultural experience of either (Burke, 1992, p. 255; Tannen, 1994, p. 121).[26] More importantly, WAR and SPORTS metaphors can be used to

> police the borders that secure the gender system within discrete binary categories that require hyperbolic and hierarchical renderings of difference. (Jansen and Sabo, 1994, p. 9)

Winsor (1996, p. 39) similarly widens the scope by claiming that 'parallels [between militarism, business, and sport] tend to exclude women further from accepting and being accepted by their corporate peers'. Indeed, reinforcing the cognitive and discursive links between the three spheres helps to secure the socio-economic framework of late capitalism, of which marketing is just one sub-division, as an arena of mainly male power. Despite women entering marketing in increasing numbers (Business Women's Network, 2002, p. 298), the masculinized conceptualization of marketing is still being reinforced. The most obvious reflection of such reinforcement can be found in an intensified usage of WAR and SPORTS metaphors in both corporate and media discourse. The argument could also be reversed: media discourse is ancillary in maintaining the status quo by reifying the cognitive underpinnings of marketing as a social practice. In some respects, the quantitatively and qualitatively heavy use of the WAR/SPORTS cluster witnessed in the corpus can be seen as a substitute act of masculinity, thus mirroring 'the difference between men who cheer football matches on TV and those who run out into the mud' (Connell, 1995, p. 79).

It has to be conceded that, in particular contexts,

> the military metaphor generates augmented understanding of a competitive situation . . . and thus has the ability to foster creativity in formulating competitive strategies. (Raghavan, 1990, p. 81)

What makes alternatives desirable, however, is not only the wish for equal opportunities for women. Both WAR and SPORTS metaphors over-emphasize the competitive aspects of marketing, incorporating the 'instrumentalism, aggression, and the zero-sum concepts of competition that dominate corporate capitalism' (Jansen and Sabo, 1994, p. 6). They thus fail to account for the more creative and co-operative aspects of the field (Jäkel, 1997, p. 208). By underscoring 'inappropriate interorganizational and personal competition and conflict' (Cleary and Packard, 1992, pp. 232–3) these metaphors may not even make good business sense. What, then, are the candidates for alternative metaphors?

First, there is the MARKETS ARE ORGANISMS metaphor, as evidenced by conventional expressions such as 'the world's fastest-growing Internet markets' (BW, line 17); 'the market is growing so fast' (EC, lines 42–3); or 'the rest of the world has been growing at hyperspeed' (FO, lines 20–1). Searls and Weinberger (2000) also propose MARKETS ARE CONVERSATIONS. This notion is interesting in so far as it represents the metaphorization of an originally literal concept: after all, 'the first markets were filled with talk' (ibid., p. 75). In late capitalism and its abstract, intangible markets, however, 'buying and selling is itself a kind of conversation: one spoken in goods, services, and money' (Searls Group, 1999, para. 48), with the actual sale 'merely the exclamation mark at the end of the sentence' (Searls and Weinberger, 2000, p. 75).[27] Searls and Weinberger see the Internet as the driving force behind changing metaphoric concepts of marketing, since it enables consumers to emancipate themselves from corporate market communication by interacting in cyberspace, thus re-enacting word-of-mouth advertising on a global scale as so-called 'viral marketing'. Although the question remains in how far this online communication between consumers is in fact a *metaphoric* conversation, MARKETS ARE CONVERSATIONS is nevertheless an interesting alternative. In the corpus, however, *conversation* itself appears only twice as a metaphoric expression (MS BW 17 and MS FT 69). Similarly, metaphoric *speak* only shows two tokens as well (MS FO 10 and MS FO 32). Finally, there are nine metaphoric instances of *talk*, five of which feature online 'conversations'.

Furthermore, a whole range of RELATIONSHIP metaphors present themselves as viable, non-aggressive alternatives. While by no means frequent (see Table A.3 on p. 198), expressions deriving from those metaphors include *partnerships* replacing the *fights* between companies (BW, lines 64 and 76), or *friendships* between companies and consumers (FT, line 34). It is particularly the growing importance of Relationship Marketing that makes this alternative metaphor seem promising, because theorists in the field regard the WAR metaphor as 'quite inappropriate or even disastrous for . . . relationship marketing' (Hunt and

Menon, 1995, p. 84). Finally, alternative metaphors for marketing need not be entirely new ones. After all, new metaphors largely emerge through recombination and re-accentuation of already entrenched conceptual blends, and it could well be possible to re-accentuate the cluster metaphors so as to arrive at alternatives. The SPORTS and the WAR metaphors, for example, not only emphasize the antagonism between in-group and out-group but also reinforce in-group cohesion. The SPORTS metaphor in particular can give rise to the metaphoric notion of *teams* (as in 'they have teamed up' [BW, lines 74–5]), which 'can also be used to increase organizational effectiveness' (Cleary and Packard, 1992, p. 233). On a related note, Morgan and Bales (2002) list derivatives of WAR and SPORTS metaphors under both competition and co-operation in their threefold – competition, co-operation and connection – model of metaphor families. The competition family furthermore includes the GAMES metaphor, which is seen as being related more closely to the SPORTS than to the WAR metaphor. The conceptual link here resides in the fact that the last alone involves death, whereas the former two do not. It is SPORTS and WAR metaphors, however, that find their way into the metaphor family of co-operation, as they can be extended to give rise to metaphoric *teams* (ibid., para. 12).[28] WAR, SPORTS and GAMES metaphors certainly all embody aspects of teamwork; yet users of such re-accentuated metaphors should keep in mind the highly ambiguous nature of the concepts, which also incorporate antagonism, aggression, winning at the expense of others, or even obliteration.

In conclusion, we can see that the WAR/SPORTS cluster is very much masculinized, and that by drawing on it extensively, media discourse on marketing and sales helps to construct texts characterized by gendered cognitive schemata. In doing so, journalists serve to reinforce a conceptual model and discourse defined by aggression, and ultimately help to maintain marketing as a male-defined practice. It is because of these far-reaching consequences that business publications should emancipate themselves from their readers' perceived agenda and the corporate discourse on which they report. Instead of reproducing marketers' overly competitive in-group schema, it would be worthwhile to enforce alternative metaphors.

Let us now see how business magazines and papers fare when it comes to mergers and acquisitions.

5
Business Media on Mergers and Acquisitions: Metaphors of Evolutionary Struggle

PENTHESILEA: Yes you, you and all the others. You are modern-day robber barons, whose proceedings in the world are certainly not p.c. . . . But when it's about modern management, you deal with psychology and esoterics alright. You facilitate courses in . . . 'Metaphors for Managers' . . . Only because men of your generation could not go wild in a war, you have to bumble about in the whole world.

(Johnson, 2001, pp. 31, 36)

This second empirical part is structured like the first one: after establishing basic lexical fields, a corpus of magazine and newspaper texts on mergers and acquisitions (M&A) is scanned for metaphoric occurrences of the units in previously established lexical fields. These comprise fighting, mating and feeding, and are combined to form an umbrella field of evolutionary struggle. The quantitative analysis again shows the FIGHTING metaphor as having the highest number of items selected from the relevant field and to occur most frequently in the corpus, with MATING and FEEDING ranking second and third. Having thus ascertained absolute and relative frequencies, the analysis is again broadened by a qualitative investigation into four sample texts, one from each publication in the corpus. This second part of the analysis reveals striking differences between metaphor frequencies in the overall corpus as opposed to individual sample articles. There is, furthermore, no uniform way of bracketing texts. However, the metaphoric scenario to emerge is similar in all four cases: companies are entities in a bounded space that is subject to external pressure, forcing the companies to move in relation to each other to survive. Although EMPIRE-BUILDING and DANCING could be alternatives to that scenario, the qualitative analysis shows that they in fact support the dominant cluster metaphors. This chapter, too, is rounded off by discussing the conceptual model possibly underlying media discourse on M&A and the impact it has on the wider socio-economic framework in which the texts are situated. As that model involves a temporal sequence of companies first watching and then attacking each other with obliterating, unifying or incorporating intentions, the model can, in fact, be cross-classified as a script. Again, that model or script will turn out to be highly masculinized, even more so than the marketing model as it not only promotes (metaphoric) aggression but also involves explicit gendering through the MATING metaphor.

First, however, let us look at the literal basis of this metaphoric script.

5.1 Quantitative analysis

5.1.1 Lexical fields

In M&A discourse, we find an overarching EVOLUTIONARY STRUGGLE metaphor, comprising the three factors driving natural selection, namely fighting, mating and feeding. These three closely interrelated sub-domains are represented in one table (see Table 5.1). The metaphoric expressions of evolutionary struggle found in M&A discourse incorporate the components [+HUMAN] and, more generally, [+ANIMATE]. In some cases, category membership has been determined by consulting small-scale dictionaries. For example, *courtship*, a seemingly cultural, and hence human, notion, in fact has a sub-entry relating to mating behaviour in animals in all three reference works ('Courtship', 1995a–c). On the other hand, *glutton* was categorized as [+HUMAN], as only one of the dictionaries gives a specialized meaning, synonymous with *wolverine* ('Glutton', 1995). Finally, *desire*, in spite of being a conscious, and hence human, feeling, was pinned down as [+ANIMATE] by virtue of being a near-synonym of *lust*.

As can be seen from Table 5.1, metaphor clusters in M&A discourse originate from a lexical continuum, in which the focus shifts from fighting over mating to feeding, rather than from three discrete fields. Each sub-field again contains 35 lemmas, which comprise a total of 206 lexemes, more than half of which are nouns. Verbs, accounting for a bit more than a quarter, rank second, with adjectives being placed third. Table 5.2 provides the analysed figures for the three continuous sub-fields. Again, nominal bias in each case will translate into an analysis of relative instead of absolute frequencies.

In the first sub-field, 'fighting', the five lemmas *defence (defense)*, *hostility*, *raid*, *victim* and *vulnerability* replace *blitz*, *campaign*, *cut-throat*, *launch* and *trench*, which featured for marketing and sales (see Table 4.1).

116

Table 5.1 Lexical sub-fields 'evolutionary struggle'

[+ANIMATE]			[+HUMAN]		
Noun	Verb	Adjective/adverb	Noun	Verb	Adjective/adverb
FIGHTING					
assault	to assault	–	armour, arms, army	to arm	–
attack	to attack	–		to backfire	
			battle, battle(-)/field, battleground	to battle	embattled[1]
blood	to bleed	bloody		to beleaguer	–
			bomb, bombshell	to bomb, to bombard	–
bruise	to bruise	–			
brutality	–	brutal	casualty		–
			conqueror, conquest	to conquer	–
enemy defence	to defend	defensive	defeat	to defeat	–
	–	inimical			
–	–	fierce	front	–	–
fight, fighter	to fight	–			
hostility	–	hostile	manoeuvre	to manoeuvre	–
killer, killing	to kill	–	raid, raider	to raid	–
			soldier	–	soldierly

Noun	Verb	Adjective
surrender	to surrender	—
survival, survivor	to survive	—
victim	—	—
vulnerability	—	vulnerable
MATING		
courtship	to court	—
desire	to desire	desirable
target	to target	—
troops	—	—
veteran	—	—
victory	—	victorious
war, warfare, warrior	—	warlike, warring
weapon, weaponry	—	—
affair	—	—
affection	—	affectionate
altar	—	—
arms (body part)	—	—
bed, bedfellow	—	—
consummation	to consummate	—
dalliance	to dally	—
divorce	to divorce	—
embrace	to embrace	—
fiancé, fiancée	—	faithful
flirt, flirtation	to flirt	flirtatious, flirty
honeymoon	—	—
husband	—	—
infatuation	—	infatuated
kiss	to kiss	—
love, lover	to love	lovable

Table 5.1 Continued

| | [+ANIMATE] | | | [+HUMAN] | |
Noun	Verb	Adjective/adverb	Noun	Verb	Adjective/adverb
lust	to lust	lustful	maiden	–	–
			marriage	to marry	–
mate	to mate	–	nuptials	–	nuptial
			passion	–	passionate
rape	to rape	–	relationship	–	–
			romance	–	romantic
sex	–	sexual, sexy	spouse	–	–
			suitor	–	–
			wedding	to wed	–
			wife	–	–
			wooer	to woo	–
FEEDING					
bite	to bite	–	appetite, appetizer	–	appetizing
–	to chew	–			
–	to choke	–			
–	–	delicious	course	–	–
–	to devour	–	diet	to diet	dietary

digestion, indigestion	to digest	–	dinner	to dine	–
			dish	–	–
feeder, food	to feed	–		to eat	eatable, uneatable
			feast	to feast	edible, inedible
–	to gobble (up)	–	glutton, gluttony	–	gluttonous
greed	to gorge	–			
	–	greedy			
hunger	to hunger	hungry	helping	–	–
–	–	insatiable			
–	–	juicy			
morsel	–	–	meal	–	–
–	to nibble	–			
nourishment	to nourish	–			
predator	–	predatory			palatable, unpalatable
prey	to prey (up)on	–			
–	–	ravenous			
–	to spit out	–			
starvation	to starve	–			
–	to swallow	–			

Table 5.2 Relative frequencies of word classes in mergers and acquisitions cluster,[2] numbers and percentages

Lexical field	METAPHOR	Noun		Verb		Adjective/adverb		Totals	
		Lexical field	Metaphorical expressions	Lexical field	Metaphorical expressions	Lexical field	Metaphorical expressions	Lexical field	Metaphorical expressions
fighting	FIGHTING	46	300	21	83	11	99	78	482
		58.97%	62.24%	26.92%	17.22%	14.10%	20.54%	100%	100%
mating	MATING	38	115	15	15	15	8	68	138
		55.88%	83.33%	22.06%	10.87%	22.06%	5.80%	100%	100%
feeding	FEEDING	24	34	19	26	17	6	60	66
		40.00%	51.52%	31.67%	39.39%	28.33%	9.09%	100%	100%
Totals		108	449	55	124	43	113	206	686
		52.43%	65.45%	26.70%	18.08%	20.87%	16.47%	100%	100%

Note: see the notes of explanation to Table 4.5 on page 74.

The second lexical sub-field, 'mating', is also already familiar from the chapter on marketing and sales discourse. There it came under the heading of 'romance' and served as the basis of a possible alternative metaphor. In media discourse on M&A, it now takes centre stage as the foundation of the second cluster metaphor. Again, the field has been slightly altered. Whereas the lexical field in the first case also comprised three terms originating from the more general domain of relationships (*family*, *friend* and *heart*), these three items have now been replaced by *relationship*, *maiden* (nominal form) and *rape*. The inclusion of the latter item obviously requires some explanation. At first sight, including that lemma in a lexical field of mating may indeed come as a surprise. Running a search on that item was in fact motivated by the dominance of the FIGHTING metaphor. Its prominence, combined with the equally central nature of the MATING metaphor, made it seem plausible that hostile takeovers could be conceptualized as rapes. Another incentive to include the item was Hirsch and Andrews' (1983, p. 148) observation that 'reference to rape is not uncommon' in M&A texts. As the authors unfortunately fail to provide any evidence, searching the corpus for that term was intended to validate or reject their claim. The search proved a somewhat surprising absence of *rape* as a metaphoric term, which gives rise to various possible explanations (see section 5.3).

Apart from *rape*, however, the field of mating as a whole seems to be diametrically opposed to that of fighting, an opposition that apparently does not square with the above notion of a continuum. However, one has to distinguish between the aspects of *love* on the one hand and *sex* on the other. It is the latter in particular that overlaps with the lexical sub-field 'fighting' in general, and with war in particular. In fact, quite a few war terms serve as metaphoric expressions in the sexual domain: Ammer (1999, pp. 69–70) names *combat zone* as a term for a red-light district as well as the slang expression *blonde bombshell* (ibid., p. 39; another example is *sex bomb*). Conceptualization of sexuality in terms of aggression finds its more general expression in the meaning of *weapon* as *penis* and *shoot* as *ejaculate* (Wilkinson, 1993, pp. 36 and 42).[3] On a less explicit note, the term *knight*, although too ambiguous to be included under the heading of either fighting or mating, has a specific meaning in M&A discourse: featuring in the metaphoric expressions *black knight* and *white knight*, the term is akin to the notion of the knight in shining armour, combining military and romantic virtues.[4] These examples indicate that the fields of fighting and mating are not as distinct as they seem to be at first glance; in fact, the qualitative analysis will reveal that there are tight conceptual and textual links between the two.

The third sub-field, 'feeding', not only completes the M&A cluster but also represents a break away from the metaphors of the previous section by introducing a new domain. It is qualitatively related to the field of mating in much the same way that mating is connected to fighting: the metaphors SEXUALITY IS WAR and HAVING SEX IS EATING make for a continuum on which the three sub-fields are located. As for the semantic overlaps between mating and feeding, only the items *honeymoon* and, less directly, *consummation* indicate a relationship between the two domains. However, the generic metaphor DESIRE IS HUNGER (Deignan, 1997, pp. 30–2) suggests that the conceptual links between the fields are much more pervasive, a hypothesis corroborated by qualitative analysis. Tables A.4 and A.5 (see pp. 209 and 212) show that [+ANIMATE] lemmas are much over-represented for the FEEDING metaphor, accounting for 87.5 per cent of all metaphoric expressions of feeding. On the other hand, it is the [+HUMAN] elements of the mating domain that make up the overwhelming majority (78.26 per cent) of all attested metaphoric expressions of mating. While [+HUMAN] elements help to attenuate the aggression inherent in the evolutionary struggle scenario, the specific MARRIAGE metaphor is still linked to the FIGHTING metaphor in intricate ways, showing the two to be just different means to the same end of surviving in an intrinsically competitive environment. These findings show that the prominence of [+ANIMATE] lemmas in the 'feeding' field and the dominance of [+HUMAN] lemmas in the 'mating' field are not arbitrary features but rather something that journalists draw on for particular purposes. All told, we can see that the M&A cluster is substantially different from that of marketing and sales, as the three domains are located on an 'evolutionary struggle' continuum rather than constituting distinct fields. Within this continuum, even domains that otherwise seem opposed – such as fighting and mating – can be integrated. It will be the task of the qualitative analysis to follow that lead.

Alternative metaphors are difficult to pin down in media texts on M&A. One apparent candidate is M&A ACTIVITY IS EMPIRE-BUILDING, as suggested by phrases such as *part of the GM empire is Subaru* (MA EC 42) or [the] *chief executive was ousted in a boardroom coup* (MA FT 12). Table A.6 (on p. 216) illustrates the occurrences of this metaphor. However, when looking at the data more closely, it shows that the EMPIRE metaphor is in fact linked quite tightly to the FIGHTING metaphor, as evidenced by the connection between items such as *territory* (empire domain) and *conquer* ([+HUMAN] fighting domain). Moreover, there is definitely a link between the fields of empire and romance, seen by, for example, terms such as *courtly*, or by the *knight* looming in the wings

Table 5.3 Lexical field 'dancing'

Noun	Verb	Adjective/adverb
ball, ballroom	–	–
ballet	–	–
beat	–	–
boogie	to boogie	–
–	–	cheek-to-cheek
choreographer, choreography	to choreograph	–
circle	to circle	circular
dance, dancer	to dance	–
figure	–	–
–	to follow[5]	–
foxtrot	to foxtrot	–
harmony	to harmonize	harmonious
pirouette	to pirouette	–
lead	to lead	–
polka	to polka	–
promenade	to promenade	–
rhythm	–	rhythmic
rock ('n'roll)	to rock	–
round	to round	–
rumba	to rumba	–
samba	to samba	–
spin	to spin	–
step	to step	–
–	to sway	–
swing	to swing	–
swirl	to swirl	–
–	to swivel	–
synchronicity	to synchronize	synchronous
tango	to tango	–
tempo	–	–
turn	to turn	–
twirl	to twirl	–
twist	to twist	–
verve	–	–
waltz	to waltz	–

of not only empires and mating, but also fighting. Thus the EMPIRE metaphor is related to the cluster metaphors in multiple ways rather than constituting an unrelated, alternative means of conceptualizing M&A.[6]

The alternative lexical field included finally is that of dancing, detailed in Table 5.3. This field, too, was informed by previous knowledge of the discourse at hand, including anecdotal evidence, and composed with the help of thesauri and glossaries. The idea that dancing as a non-violent, non-competitive form of movement could give rise to metaphor was already proposed by Lakoff and Johnson (1980, p. 5).[7] Furthermore, Eubanks (2000, p. 109) notes that 'dance metaphors . . . are present, though rarely, in the standard language of trade and economics', an observation warranting investigations into whether M&A language shows the same phenomenon. Anecdotal evidence includes *fruitless merger dances* (*The Economist*, 1997, p. 90) and *Pfizer would consider other dance partners should its bid fail* (MS FO 6). Interestingly, the two examples suggest that the DANCE metaphor, too, could be conceptually related to the MATING metaphor, and the qualitative analysis will ascertain that metaphoric expessions of dance are indeed used in relation to those of mating.

The lexical field 'dancing' is remarkable in that among its 65 lexemes, nouns and verbs show relatively similar distribution figures (50.77 per cent and 41.54 per cent), whereas adjectives/adverbs are extremely scarce (7.69 per cent). This particularity is related to the fact that most items denoting movement show dual nominal and verbal forms (for example, *turn, to turn* or, more specifically, *polka, to polka*). In the next section, we will, among other findings, see how the word class patterns of the lexical fields translate into metaphoric expressions.

5.1.2 Absolute and relative frequencies

The upshot of the quantitative analysis is that the lexical field of fighting records the highest number of items realized metaphorically. Moreover, the related FIGHTING metaphor is most frequent in the corpus in both absolute and relative terms, accounting for the lowest type–token ratio of all three cluster metaphors. Second and third on these parameters are the MATING and the FEEDING metaphors. In terms of word class distribution, it will be seen that the nominal bias of the lexical fields is reinforced in the case of metaphoric expressions. While such nominal over-representation can be witnessed for all three cluster metaphors, the FIGHTING metaphor also shows an over-representation of adjectives, while the FEEDING metaphor records such over-representation for verbs.

In detail, metaphoric patterns in the M&A corpus are similar to the ones in the marketing texts in so far as the lexical field 'fighting' once more proves to be the one drawn upon most often for metaphoric expressions: as many as 34 out of its 35 lemmas (97.14 per cent) are in fact realized as metaphoric expressions in the corpus. The sub-field of mating is second, with 23 out of 35 (65.71 per cent) lemmas instantiated as metaphoric occurrences. It can also be seen that, with the exception of *maiden*, all items marked as old-fashioned are indeed realized, with some of them – *suitor, court* – showing quite a substantial number of ocurrences. Accordingly, the field of feeding trails behind, with only 16 out of 35 lemmas (45.71 per cent) to be found in metaphoric usage. When it comes to absolute frequencies, the FIGHTING metaphor proves to be the one most often drawn upon in metaphoric expressions, representing more than two-thirds of all attested metaphoric types (482 of the overall 686 metaphoric expressions in the corpus, equalling 70.26 per cent). What is more, the FIGHTING metaphor accounts for the three most frequent types (*target, hostility* and *battle*) and their 211 tokens. Those three types make up about a third of all metaphoric occurrences (30.76 per cent) and less than half of all metaphoric tokens of war (43.78 per cent). The second and third places in terms of frequency are taken by the MATING metaphor (20.12 per cent) and, far behind, the FEEDING metaphor (9.62 per cent), respectively.

It should be kept in mind, however, that productivity shows in the degree of a metaphor's conventionalization rather than in its frequency. In that respect, the most frequent type, *target*, again features as a technical metaphoric expression, since all its occurrences are in fact metaphoric. The same holds true for *hostile* and *battle*. Typical phrases in which those conventionalized expressions feature are the following: *they could easily become an acquisition target* (MA FT 6); *Gas Natural was unlikely to make a hostile bid for Iberdrola* (MA FT 7); or *France's banking battle may have finished messily* (MA EC 31). In terms of collocations, it is less than surprising that *target* no longer co-occurs with *audience* or *market* as it did in the marketing corpus, but with *company*, as in *the quality of the target company's resources* (MA FT 44).[8] On the other hand, there are also more novel extensions of the FIGHTING metaphor such as the following: '*there's only three things you gotta remember: shoot, move, and communicate*' (MA FO 4). This example is interesting in more ways than one. First, the marked juxtaposition can be considered a creative metaphoric extension. Moreover, the quote is inserted at the beginning of the text, later to be taken up again by the author, who elaborates on it to close her article (*his chances improve if he continues to shoot, move, and communicate as well as he has in the past*), thus framing the topic. Interestingly, the quote stems from literal military service and is then transferred explicitly to the world of business. It is worth noting that business discourse features a number of male executives who literalize the FIGHTING metaphor by making reference to their experience in the armed forces and thus ground the metaphor in gender-specific social practice (examples include Katzenbach and Santamaria, 1999; Kilbane, n.d.; see also MS BW 15).[9] Finally, the list of activities also spells out what features are blended. Although the article lacks any struggle over semantic features, it becomes clear that the FIGHTING metaphor is deeply entrenched. If further evidence is needed, it is provided by explicit metaphorizations such as *whatever metaphor works best, the fact is that Boeing is a company at war with itself* (MA FO 21) or novel collocations such as *just recently he pulled the trigger on a merger* (MA FO 4).

Frequency of the domains is congruent within the cluster, both with regard to lexical items realized and to metaphoric expressions. In this context, the type–token ratios follow the ranking of overall frequencies, with the FIGHTING metaphor showing a ratio of 0.07 and hence the most pronounced variation. Because of its low rate of lexical units being realized metaphorically, the MATING metaphor records a higher ratio of 0.17. Finally, the FEEDING metaphor, showing the lowest number of items realized, is also the least frequent one, resulting in a type–token ratio as high as 0.24. As in the marketing corpus, there is thus a correlation between the number of lemmas realized metaphorically on the one hand and variation in terms of type–token ratio on the other. On the basis of the three cluster metaphors, overall metaphor density in the M&A corpus is 4.17 per 1,000 words, and thus lower than in the marketing corpus, where it was 5.3.

If we add the sparse 20 occurrences of the DANCING metaphor, this density rises to 4.3/1,000 words. Of the combined 706 tokens of cluster metaphors and the alternative metaphor, the latter accounts for a meagre 2.83 per cent, illustrating its less than marginal quantitative representation. Consequently, judging from the quantitative findings alone, the alternative's impact on both that discourse and the related conceptual model can be expected to be all but negligible. Its weakness is also reflected in the low selection figures of 12 out of 35 lexical items (34.28 per cent), which, together with absolute frequencies, correspond to a type–token ratio of 0.6. Interestingly, one of the two most frequent lemmas, *dance* itself, betrays rather novel extensions. We find *the Asian automotive world's latest mating dance* (MA BW 21) as well as *'SDL was the beautiful prom queen standing in the middle of the dance floor without a partner'* (MA FO 2; see section 5.2). Another quotation from primary discourse to draw on the culture-specific prom image is the following:

> Jeremy Elden of Germany's Commerzbank likens the current merger madness to 'the rush to find a partner, any partner, at a school dance after the big boys have picked the best ones'.　　　　(MA EC 29)

It is obvious that these examples very much support, if not collapse with, the MATING metaphor, raising the central issue of gendering or even gender stereotyping.

Before dealing with these findings in more detail, however, let us have a look at word class distribution. To that end, Table 5.2 shows how nouns, verbs and adjectives/adverbs are spread across the lexical sub-fields as contrasted with their spread over the metaphoric expressions (reproduced in Tables A.4 and A.5 on pp. 209 and 212).

The patterns in Table 5.2 differ from those in the marketing corpus. There, the nominal bias of the lexical field was maintained by all metaphors, with verbs always being placed second and adjectives/adverbs third. In the M&A corpus, however, things are different. Although the predominance of nouns in the lexical sub-fields is reflected by a nominal bias in the metaphoric expressions too, all three metaphors show orders of verbal and adjectival expressions different from those witnessed in the marketing and sales cluster. Thus adjectival expressions rank second in the case of the FIGHTING metaphor (20.54 per cent), outstripping the verbal forms (17.23 per cent). This particular figure sheds some more light on the conventionalized nature of metaphoric expressions, as almost two-thirds of these adjectival forms are represented by a single type, namely *hostile*. Indeed, *hostile bid* and, to a lesser extent, *hostile takeover* feature as a collocation not only in the present purpose-built corpus but also in the BoE.[10] Adjectival expressions are therefore over-represented, while verbal ones are under-represented, a significant difference from the patterns observed in marketing and sales discourse. Verbal metaphoric expressions of mating also drop when compared to verbs in the respective lexical sub-field. Adjectives, which were on par with verbs in the lexical sub-field of mating (both accounting for 22.06 per cent) plunge by almost three-quarters when used metaphorically – that is, to 5.8 per cent. As for the FEEDING metaphor, the order nouns–verbs–adjectives is finally preserved. However, the percentage changes from lexical sub-field to metaphoric expressions are more pronounced, making for substantial over- and under-representations.

The exception to the above patterns is constituted by the alternative metaphoric expressions of *dancing*, which, given the movement implied in the original lexical field, show a surprisingly noun-heavy pattern with no adjectival forms whatever (see Table A.6 on p. 216). The absence of any adjectival forms of the DANCING metaphor ties in with Eubanks' (2000) study on TRADE IS A DANCE, in which 'no discussant mentioned familiar attributive qualities of dance such as grace, rhythm, or expressiveness' (p. 115). So, do these irregularities mean that the metaphoric concept of MATING is a static one? In a partial answer, such assumptions are to be treated carefully by all means, the more so since the qualitative analysis of sample marketing texts showed that there is not necessarily a correlation between word-class distribution and the nature of an assumed underlying conceptual model.

On a different note, what is the significance of the FIGHTING metaphor's dominance in terms of selection, productivity and frequency? The discussion of media discourse on marketing argued that the WAR metaphor is highly gendered, the more so since it is there supported by the equally masculinized SPORTS metaphor. The significance of the dominant FIGHTING metaphor in M&A discourse is similar to that in marketing as it betrays a masculinist stance in itself. Hirsch and Andrews (1983, p. 148), for example, observe that the overall imagery in M&A discourse is one in which 'the acquiring executive is macho and the target company is accorded the female gender'. This will probably strike the critical reader as the metaphorization of Katschnig-Fasch's (1999) claim that masculinity is prototypically expressed in the image of the conqueror and winner, and thus requires femininity as a mode of defeat (p. 71). Yet if the WAR metaphor thus points to a stereotypical and highly charged gender dichotomy underpinning M&A discourse, how can we then account for the MATING metaphor as part of a metaphor cluster? Does the inclusion of this 'feminized' metaphor not indicate a difference from the marketing corpus?

Paradoxical as though it may seem, mating does not necessarily contradict fighting. True, both are diametrically opposed in that they cover the two poles of a prototypical gender binary, with romance being ascribed to the realm of femininity just as much as fighting is regarded as quintessentially masculine; the two, in fact, constitute each other. Apart from that, however, the MATING metaphor, especially when crossing over into the area of sexuality, in fact supports the FIGHTING metaphor in very subtle ways (just recall the overlaps between the respective lexical fields). To begin with, there could well be, as Reardon (1985, p. 53) notes, a connection between objectifying ('targeting') and idealizing women, and between violence against and the chivalrous elevation of women. As will be seen in the next section, the corpus indeed yields qualitative evidence of Hirsch and Andrews' (1983) statement that the targeted company is metaphorically female. Aggression and more gentle ways of persuasion thus come to represent two means to the same end – that is, acquiring the targeted company. With regard to this Janus-headed issue, Hirsch and Andrews (1983) mention the

metaphoric expressions *black knight* and *white knight* as indicating a scenario of 'chivalry in which the distressed damsel is either undone or
rescued' (p. 148). Seen as such, the MATING metaphor works just like
the SPORTS metaphor did, namely in support of the overriding FIGHTING
metaphor, attenuating and intensifying it at the same time.

Can this permeation of the MATING by the FIGHTING metaphor also
be witnessed with the FEEDING metaphor? Chapter 2 illustrated how
takeovers and feeding share a common generic space, in that one entity
incorporates another in both cases, thus nullifying the incorporated
entity's existence. When we look further at which items from the original lexical field are in fact realized, it shows that the focus of the
FEEDING metaphor is rather on the aspect of extinction: we mainly find
instantiations of both the feeding animal's/eater's motivation (*appetite,
greed, hunger*) and ways of feeding/eating that are marked as [+AGGRES-
SIVE] (*devour, gobble, gorge*).[11] Other forceful stages in the feeding/eating
process, such as *bite* and *spit* are also realized, while *eat* itself is not. The
conceptual links between aggression and feeding are perhaps best captured by the quote *other midsize players . . . are wolfed down by predators*
(MA BW 23). If moreover, we consider the conceptual links between
mating and feeding, which are condensed in the metaphor DESIRE IS
HUNGER, then even the quantitative findings suggest that the cluster of
FIGHTING–MATING–FEEDING is conceptually coherent. Isolated instances
of the alternative DANCING metaphor also indicate that it is akin to the
MATING metaphor, raising the issue of what concept *could* serve as an
alternative.

This leaves us with the question why journalists see fit to employ the
cluster in the way they do. One incentive could be to reify M&A as a
male social practice much like marketing, while at the same time using
the MATING metaphor seemingly to attenuate any inherent aggressiveness. In this context, the astonishing lack of *rape* as a metaphoric expression could help to conceal the fact that the MATING metaphor also
holds the potential to intensify further the already dominant FIGHTING
metaphor.

To sum up, the media text corpus on M&A is very much characterized by an overarching EVOLUTIONARY STRUGGLE metaphor, which can be
broken down into a threefold metaphor cluster of FIGHTING, MATING
and FEEDING. Of these three, the FIGHTING metaphor is selected
most often (almost all of the 35 items in the basic lexical field are realized), most frequent (accounting for 70 per cent of all instances of
cluster metaphors), most varied (showing the lowest type–token ratio,
namely 0.07) and hence very much entrenched in the corpus. Highly

conventionalized metaphoric expressions drawing on it, for example the collocation *hostile takeover*, are balanced by more creative extensions. The MATING metaphor ranks second with reference to entrenchment, variation and frequency; and the FEEDING metaphor is third, and last. The alternative metaphor defined for M&A media discourse, DANCING, is selected remarkably rarely – only about a third of the items from the lexical field are indeed realized in metaphoric form – and also extremely scarce, adding up to less than 3 per cent of all attested metaphoric tokens. As far as word class distribution is concerned, all lexical fields are characterized by a more-or-less pronounced nominal bias. We find a particularly marked over-representation of nouns in the case of the MATING metaphor, with the FIGHTING metaphor betraying a noun-heavy pattern as well. Still, it is adjectives that are the second most frequent word class with the latter. This is all the more remarkable because adjectives are under-represented everywhere else, most notably in the case of the DANCING metaphor, which does not occur in adjectival form at all. However, it appeared that the model informing media discourse on M&A, despite the more adjectival nature of the prominent FIGHTING metaphor, is no less dynamic than the one for marketing.

In the next section, the above broad quantitative findings will prove to be a starting point for in-depth qualitative analysis.

5.2 Qualitative analysis of sample texts

In this section, four sample texts will be analysed for metaphor frequency, metaphoric scenarios, metaphor chains, intensification and attenuation, primary and secondary discourse, overall article structure, alternative metaphors and functional grammar patterns. Results show that the frequency patterns established for the corpus as a whole cannot be sustained for individual texts. Still, a very similar metaphoric scenario emerges in all four articles: once more, the market is conceptualized as a bounded space in which companies find themselves. In addition to the marketing scenario, however, this space is also subject to external pressure, causing the companies inside first to circle and then to attack each other. In accordance with the three cluster metaphors, the threefold goal of such assaults is obliteration, unfication or incorporation. The dominant metaphors are again organized in chains, elaborating, echoing or extending each other. Interestingly, questioning and negating is delegated to struggles between executives and journalists over semantic features. Just as there is no uniform frequency pattern, article structure also differs from one text to the other. Thus, we may find the MATING metaphor as a text bracket (*The Economist* sample) or have the salient textual macro slots occupied by different metaphors or combinations of them (*Fortune* and *Financial Times* texts). Although there are no pervasive grammatical features to support the central scenario, it is nevertheless intensified by means of hyperbolic language and additional metaphors. While such additional metaphors prove to be pervasive, alternative metaphors are non-existent, making for a powerful, because multi-faceted, metaphoric scenario.

Metaphor frequency

The *Business Week* article includes nine cluster metaphors, seven of which are in fact instances of the FIGHTING metaphor, while two represent metaphoric expressions of feeding. In this respect, *The Economist* sample differs markedly from the *Business Week* text. The article, representing the introduction to a series of merger reviews, contains 13 instances of cluster metaphors and all three metaphors are represented. Interestingly, it is the MATING metaphor with its seven realizations that features most prominently. It should also be noted that, in line with the [+HUMAN]/[+ANIMATE] distribution patterns in the corpus as a whole, it is mainly the [+HUMAN] sub-set of the MATING metaphor that has been realized in the *The Economist* sample. As for the other two metaphors, the four instances of the FIGHTING metaphor add up to just under a third of the 13 tokens, while the FEEDING metaphor is realized only twice.

The remarkable dominance of the MATING metaphor in *The Economist* text is in fact representative of the spread of cluster metaphors across the publications in the corpus: while *The Economist* accounts for just under 30 per cent of all cluster metaphors, its percentage of the MATING metaphor is 43.48 per cent (see Table A.4 on p. 209). However, since the *Financial Times* is under-represented when it comes to the MATING metaphor (just under 15 per cent compared to a quarter on the whole), its remarkable use by *The Economist* is clearly not culture-specific. Nor is it a hallmark of magazines compared to newspapers: in both *Business Week* and *Fortune*, percentages for the MATING metaphor are roughly the same as overall percentages (27.54 per cent compared to an overall 29.85 per cent, and 14.49 per cent as compared to 15.8 per cent, respectively). Because of *The Economist*'s anonymity policy it is impossible to say whether the gendered nature of the MATING metaphor explains its prominence in that publication. However, checking the other three publications for a link between metaphoric expressions of mating and the authors' gender reveals that there is no correlation between the two parameters.[12] Therefore, *The Economist's* pronounced usage of the MATING metaphor is most probably an idiosyncrasy.

To proceed, the *Fortune* text contains only five metaphoric expressions derived from the defined M&A cluster. Of these, three relate to the FEEDING metaphor and one each to the FIGHTING and the MATING metaphors. Apart from *The Economist* text, the *Fortune* sample thus represents another instance in which the frequency order of metaphors is not congruent with that witnessed in the overall corpus. Clustering across the text, too, is idiosyncratic: the first half of the article is devoid of relevant metaphoric expressions, with the five instances being spread evenly across the latter half.

Finally, the *Financial Times* sample is again rather untypical of the publication in that it far exceeds its average article length (1,264 words compared to 628). The article contains nine cluster-related metaphoric expressions, two-thirds of which are derived from the FIGHTING metaphor. A further two are accounted for by the FEEDING metaphor, while the MATING metaphor is realized only once. Thus we can see that, in contrast to the marketing samples, the M&A texts are very heterogeneous in terms of metaphor frequency and do not at all mirror metaphor distribution in the overall corpus. Notwithstanding such diversity, however, the articles still manage to construct very similar metaphoric scenarios.

Metaphoric scenario

The scenario emerging in the *Business Week* article is one in which companies are motivated by external pressure to move in relation to each other in a bounded space representing the market. Movement mainly takes the form of first circling and watching, then attacking. Such an attack has the twofold purpose of obliteration (FIGHTING metaphor) or incorporation (FEEDING metaphor). In any case, the ultimate goal is following the 'law of the jungle' (a motif to be spelled out in the *Fortune* sample, see below). The underlying model is hence rather dynamic, and as it also shows a temporal dimension, it can be cross-classified as a script.

In particular, the *Business Week* writers construct the social practice of M&A as a container to be entered. They do so by addressing 'Germany's ... entry into the game' (BW, lines 19–20), an expression echoing the GAMES metaphor of marketing and sales texts. Other examples of the MARKETS ARE CONTAINERS metaphor are 'entree to Europe's biggest markets' (BW, line 46) and its near-echo 'entree to the major markets' (BW, lines 73–4) as well as 'deregulation could send European utilities into other markets' (BW, line 51). In this last example, the companies no longer act as independent agents.

A general tendency to link marketing with M&A can be detected in the *Financial Times* text. The quotation in FT, lines 69–70 (' "they now have a second bite at the apple" '), for example, reflects the MARKETS ARE FOOD metaphor rather than M&A ACTIVITY IS FEEDING.[13] Similar connections also feature in the three other samples – for example, the marketing aspects conveyed in 'SBC . . . could be eyeing deals to give it entree to the major markets' (BW, lines 72–4), 'the threat was a change in the size or nature of a particular market' (EC, lines 23–4) and 'it's unlikely that the . . . behemoth will have enough market share to monopolize' (FO, lines 19–20). Given the fact that changes in the competitive environment, such as globalization and deregulation, are among the major causes of M&A activity (Herden and Butollo, 2002, p. 43), such intertextual connections are not particularly surprising. In the *Financial Times* sample, however, the tendency is very pronounced, with metaphoric expressions being one of the main indicators. Indeed, the *Financial Times* text repeats a number of metaphoric expressions already discussed in section 4.2. The phrase 'companies have been scrambling to establish scale' (FT, lines 40–1) can be read as a variation on lines 7–8 of the *Business Week* marketing sample on p. 98 ('Ong has been scrambling to hire staff'). Similarly, the RACING metaphor so prominent in that article is also present in the *Financial Times* text ('every industry . . . is in a race for global domination', FT, lines 41–2). Defining features from other marketing texts are there, too. In FT, lines 30–4, the author discusses the issue of tight space on supermarket shelves, a topic which served as a literalization device in the *Fortune* text on marketing (see p. 101).

To return to the M&A text from *Business Week*, the scenario involving the market as a bounded space or container is spelt out in the metaphorization of deal-making companies as 'bold movers' (BW, line 42) and their activities as 'moves' (BW, line 76). One of the goals of such movement, extinction through incorporation, finds its expression in 'TotalFina's $49 billion gulp of French rival Elf Aquitaine' (BW, lines 37–8). It is interesting to note that this chunk of text combines the FIGHTING metaphor with that of FEEDING: the 'rival' who in the marketing texts was seen in a battle or race against the agent, now becomes someone to be incorporated, and hence obliterated. The sentence is thus a good example of how metaphoric expressions of feeding can support the aggressive FIGHTING metaphor. Movement of a different kind is present in 'Bell South Corp. . . . outmaneuvered France Telecom to grab a 60% stake in . . . E-plus' (BW, lines 69–70), showing the complexity of at least three moving parties.

As noted above, the conceptual model that emerges is M&A ACTIVITY IS MOVEMENT IN REACTION TO EXTERNAL PRESSURE. Pressure is exerted upon the closed system of a number of companies, either by 'shareholders and boards' (BW, line 6) or by politicians (BW, line 58), leading to more-or-less aggressive rearrangements within that system, either through obliteration by fighting or forceful incorporations by feeding. So movement is in fact somewhat more complex than the antagonistic pushing and parallel racing so characteristic of media discourse on marketing. Rather, we are now confronted by several entities in a bounded space which change position in relation to each other, targeting (BW, line 22) and assaulting (BW, lines 1, 37 and 64), incorporating (BW, lines 32 and 37) or 'outmanoeuver[ing]' (BW, line 69) each other. It also seems that agents in that space are monitoring each other closely. This aspect is conceptualized metaphorically by watching other companies ('U.S. telecoms are also keeping a close eye on what goes on across the Atlantic', 'SBC . . . could be eyeing deals' [BW, lines 68–9 and 72–3]). Such metaphoric watching is in fact a derivative of the generic metaphor CONSIDERING IS LOOKING (Kövecses, 2002, p. 231) or THINKING IS PERCEIVING (Lakoff and Johnson, 1999, pp. 238–40).

Similarly, the scenario to emerge in *The Economist* sample is also characterized very much by dynamic relational movement. Because of the additional MATING metaphor in that article, the goals are now threefold, either obliteration (FIGHTING metaphor), unification (MATING metaphor) or incorporation (FEEDING metaphor). As for unification, it is the sexual aspect of the MATING metaphor that *The Economist* article emphasizes. The phrase 'companies . . . have jumped into bed with each other' (EC, line 9) is an example of the entities being involved in relational movement along those lines. The metaphoric movement is here coupled with the specific M&A ACTIVITY IS HAVING SEX metaphor: The two entities do not attack or incorporate but join each other in a sexual encounter. It is not coincidental that the same paragraph describes Europe as 'the hottest merger zone of all' (EC, lines 11–12). In fact, the attribute refers back implicitly to the sexual metaphor by virtue of the embodied metaphor LUST IS HEAT (Deignan, 1999, p. 191; Lakoff, 1987, p. 410).

The notion of metaphoric heat is also present in the *Business Week* article. Its first paragraph (BW, lines 2–8) introduces the notion of pressure as quoted from primary discourse and subsequently taken up by the author (BW, lines 5 and 8). The metaphor is then extended by the concept of heat: 'another hot twelve months on the European merger scene' (BW, line 9), and, in nominal terms, 'Jospin is putting the heat on France Telecom CEO' (BW, lines 58–9). The quasi-juxtaposition of the two metaphoric concepts to link paragraphs (BW, lines 8–9) betrays the well-known embodied concept of an increase in pressure leading to an increase in temperature, as reflected in much-studied metaphors such as ANGER IS HOT FLUID IN A CONTAINER (Gibbs *et al.*, 1997; Lakoff and Kövecses, 1983). Thus, the market-as-bounded-space is not only subject to pressure but that pressure also causes heat, forcing companies in that space to move around and against each other.

The various goals of those movements are flexible and interchangeable. For example, while 'the threat may have come from another predator' (EC, line 29) includes an obvious enough conceptual link between *threat* and *predator*, the subsequent phrase ('Bayerische Vereinsbank sought a merger with a Bavarian rival' [EC, lines 29–30]) is not as straightforward semantically: after all, it is not immediately clear why a company should want to move actively towards an adversary. However, this phrase in fact constitutes the linguistic realization of the rather paradoxical phenomenon of the 'white knight': an originally negatively evaluated company comes to be seen as positive when negative evaluation shifts towards another company. Accordingly, metaphoric movement changes in intent from obliteration to unification. The third option would be incorporation, as in the conventional 'management was scared of being gobbled up' (EC, line 31), one of the article's two realizations of the FEEDING metaphor. Setting up merging as an alternative to either obliteration or being extinguished through incorporation clearly conveys how closely related those goals are.

The fourth paragraph of *The Economist* sample (EC, lines 32–6) links the FIGHTING and the MATING metaphor on the syntactic level by establishing a metaphoric spatial relationship between the two: a company is depicted as moving away from one negatively evaluated FIGHTING space ('When a company merges to escape a threat' [EC, line 32]) and toward a more positively viewed MATING space ('it often imports its problems into the marriage' [EC, lines 32–3]). It seems that a standstill is not a viable option in the bounded space in which the market participants find themselves. Rather, a company always has to be moving in relation to one or several others, albeit with different intentions. The emergent model thus looks rather dynamic. The latter sentence also constructs a link between metaphoric fighting and mating, proving that the M&A cluster is indeed conceptually coherent.

The relative prominence of the FEEDING metaphor in the *Fortune* article emphasizes incorporation as the main goal of metaphoric movement.

Adding the FIGHTING metaphor leads to an evolving metaphoric scenario in which both the FIGHTING and the FEEDING metaphors draw on the notion of ruthless natural selection by directing aggression towards another company. As for extinction through incorporation, the metaphorical hunger of acquirers brings their counterparts under equally metaphorical siege ('beleaguered Rite Aid' [FO, line 45]). Although it is present in all four articles, we shall see below that the FEEDING metaphor is by no means universally accepted. In particular, it is corporate representatives who sometimes choose to abandon it in favour of seemingly less aggressive conceptualizations. One of the indicators of media and corporate representatives struggling over metaphoric representation is the fact that the overtly aggressive FIGHTING and FEEDING metaphors are seemingly attenuated by using the MATING metaphor.

In the *Fortune* text, the author realizes that metaphor through the term *sexy* ('Who knew fiber optics could be so sexy?' [FO, line 52]). This particular attribute links back to 'attractive' in FO, line 17, which is in turn anaphorically related to '"the beautiful prom queen"' of FO, line 13 (see p. 157). The closing line of the article employs a particular sub-meaning that *sexy* has acquired – that is, one synonymous with the metaphoric meaning of '*cool*', *fashionable* or *trendy* (and possibly *short-lived*). According to the Oxford English Dictionary, evidence of this usage in business publishing dates back to 1970. While the semantic expansion does not contain an explicit component [+EROTIC], this association is, according to some views, 'optional but conspicuously available'.[14] Considering that the *Fortune* article connects the term *sexy* to 'beautiful prom queen' (FO, line 13) and 'whether the deal makes JDSU more attractive' (FO, lines 16–17), there could well be a hidden constituent [+EROTIC]. However, the first quote denotes SDL company, the second JDSU and the last line of the article finally refers to the whole industry. So if *sexy* indeed includes connotations along the lines of (sexual) desire, those would be associated only loosely with the above metaphoric construction of companies.

Let us for a moment return to the 'prom queen' quote mentioned above: in FO, lines 12–14, a corporate representative is cited as describing an acquired company as '"the beautiful prom queen standing in the middle of the dance floor without a partner"'. As elaborated on below, the primary source here differs from the writer of the article, who had referred to the same company as a 'rival' (FO, line 5). By turning a rival into a partner, the quoted source reconstructs the corporation in question, changing movement goals from obliteration to unification.

However, the ulterior motive is still market domination, and to that end other market participants must be 'neutralized', by whatever means. Consequently, the mating concept subtly supports the dominant FIGHT-ING metaphor, all the more so as the company taken over is constructed as a static female, with the acquirer featuring as the active and victorious male suitor.

While this feature of the underlying model is only implicit in the *Fortune* article, other examples from the corpus spell out the relationship between the FIGHTING and MATING metaphors quite blatantly. Consider MA BW 16: the title is the phraseological *If you can't beat 'em*, the complementary phrase to be inferred is *join 'em*. However, the complement is provided in an adapted form: *It may marry its Hong Kong rival.* At first sight, the words *marry* and *rival* seem to have the mutually exclusive semantic components [+TOGETHER] on the one hand and [+OPPOSED] on the other. Their syntactic connection, however, does make sense against the background of *If you can't beat 'em, join 'em*, constructing metaphorical violence and metaphorical marriage as two means to the same end. A parallel syntactic and semantic interlacing of the two cluster metaphors can be found in MA EC 17:

> At a recent conference, Ron Sommer of Deutsche Telekom, Germany's former telephone monopoly, joked that suitors in the telecoms industry now need fat chequebooks and a bunch of flowers. And if gallantry is rebuffed? Throw away the flowers and call in the tanks.

By integrating two seemingly opposed metaphors, the model becomes all the more powerful, even co-opting potentially alternative metaphors such as the DANCING metaphor.

This strength leaves little room for counter-discursive conceptualizations of M&A, in the media or elsewhere. While readers are offered a seemingly broad range of various conceptualizations from a number of different sources, they are in fact presented with one, albeit complex metaphoric EVOLUTIONARY STRUGGLE model only. In the case of *Fortune*, such pseudo-objectivity is coupled with the rather informal style of 'conversationalization' or 'synthetic personalization' (Fairclough, 1995a, p. 139). The resulting pseudo-intimacy between writer and reader is evidenced by, for example, direct address ('If you scratched your head' [FO, line 4]), hinting at supposedly shared knowledge (the title pun) or expressions such as 'gotten . . . into trouble' (FO, line 7) and 'sexy' (FO, line 52). A strong integrated conceptual model and conversationalization would each be persuasive enough on their own; together they can become downright compelling. Metaphoric models presented in such a framework acquire extra weight as unproblematic common sense, exerting a strong influence on discourse and readers' cognition alike.

Finally, the uncontested scenario to emerge in the *Financial Times* text is again one in which companies operate in a bounded space governed by the laws of nature to develop in a particular direction. In this environment, the key to evolutionary success lies in size: companies that are not big enough become victims by being once more either extinguished through obliteration or incorporation (as expressed by metaphoric expressions of fighting and feeding) or forced into a union with an adversary (as conveyed by the MATING metaphor).

We find all three cluster metaphors in the *Financial Times* article's opening paragraph, with the FIGHTING metaphor being realized most frequently. As noted above, the central model equates feeding ('devoured' [FT, line 1]) and fighting ('brutal', 'casualty list' and 'victims' [FT, lines 2, 5 and 6]), as two forms of aggressive behaviour. Further still, weak companies appear as being helpless and affected by anonymous forces stronger than them, which coerce them into a union with adversaries ('victims . . . have been driven into the arms of rivals' [FT, lines 6–8]). If we look at the second instance of *drive* later in the article ('most dotcom retailers will be driven out of business' [FT, line 59]), it becomes clear that those weaker companies are faced with a choice of either yielding to an adversary or being obliterated altogether. In any case, they are constructed as passive entities. (In *The Economist* sample, by contrast, companies still actively 'sought a merger with a . . . rival' [EC, line 30]). Used as such, the MATING metaphor comes across as an attenuated form of violence and coercion.

As noted in section 5.1, the umbrella metaphor combining fighting, mating and feeding is that of evolutionary struggle. The respective scenario is hinted at in the opening stretches of the *Fortune* article ('JDS Uniphase is poised to become king of the fiber-optics jungle' [FO, line 2]) and spelt out explicitly in the long middle part of the *Financial Times* text. This particular metaphoric chain starts with 'So as some companies die, others should spring up in their place' (FT, lines 16–17), with the belief of necessity indicating a cause–effect relationship seen as a law of nature. The same view of business can be found in an elaboration on the 'winner-takes-all society' (FT, line 20): 'two or three companies at the top take a vastly disproportionate share of the market, making it difficult for others to thrive' (FT, lines 20–2). The EVOLUTIONARY STRUGGLE metaphor ties in here with the metaphor MARKETS ARE

FOOD, so that being active in one and the same bounded space becomes in itself a competition for vital but scarce resources. The fourth paragraph of the article further opens with an explicit development ('as the business-to-consumer market develops' [FT, line 19]), the end point of which is represented by the above-mentioned 'winner-takes-all society' ('it is becoming [a] winner-takes-all society' [FT, lines 19–20]). Again, it is a primary source that spells out the EVOLUTIONARY STRUGGLE metaphor underlying this self-propelled development (' "It's a natural evolution in the industry" ' [FT, lines 27–8]). The EVOLUTIONARY STRUGGLE metaphor is highly persuasive in that it constructs a social practice – that is, economic activity – as a seemingly objective and inevitable development. Belief of certainty and declarative status underscore that point. That particular construction is reified by the journalist taking up the metaphor ('there is a natural tendency towards monopoly' [FT, lines 48–9]).

As the *Financial Times* writer presents fighting as a natural entailment of evolutionary struggle, it is constructed as equally certain and inevitable. Therefore, the underlying model is dynamic in that it shows flexible goals but is nevertheless not very adjustable. In any case, however, this dynamic scenario is so pronounced that the only impossible type of movement seems to be no movement at all. So while the model may construct fighting and mating – specified in *The Economist* text by the [+HUMAN] varieties war and marriage – as a hybrid metaphorization of M&A, the conceptual cluster is nevertheless coherent. It is by means of this coherence that the underlying model gains in persuasive power and is likely to have quite a sustainable impact on cognition and discourse. By presenting the readers with such an intricate link between seemingly mutually exclusive metaphors, and by not questioning them through alternatives, the *Financial Times* author goes some way towards establishing the model firmly in both discourse and the readers' cognition.

Let us now look at the role that metaphor chains play in the establishment of the central metaphoric scenario.

Metaphor chains

The most prominent metaphoric chain in the *Business Week* text involves the FIGHTING metaphor. Its elements echo each other – for example, in the repetition of *hostile* (BW, lines 64, 67 and 89) in combination with other elements such as 'target' (BW, line 22) or 'battle plans' (BW, line 90).[15] A creative elaboration is the expression 'rapid-fire dealmaking' (BW, line 18). On a more general note, aggressive movement is organized in chains, too, starting with the headline itself ('big

grab' [BW, line 1]). In accordance with the dominant metaphoric scenario, this movement no longer aims at the market – as it did in the
marketing texts – but at another company that is acquired. Further evidence of this scenario can be found in the repetition of the term in
'Olivetti's grab of Telecom Italia' (BW, line 37) and 'to grab a 60% stake
in . . . E-plus' (BW, line 70). We can thus see that each instance of the
metaphoric chain of grabbing elaborates on the previous ones.

While it is the MATING metaphor that is most prominent in *The Economist* article, its third paragraph (EC, lines 21–31), signals a switch from
the MATING to the hitherto absent FIGHTING metaphor. This is constructed in the form of a chain throughout the paragraph, with 'threat'
serving as the main link (EC, lines 22, 23, 26 and 29). The paragraph
begins by introducing the notion of the 'defensive merger' – that is, one
brought about as a reaction to a 'threat', and closes by introducing the
FEEDING metaphor into the chain ('scared of being gobbled up' [EC, line
31]). This exemplifying metaphoric chain constructing M&A as fighting
is continued in the fourth paragraph (EC, line 32), which links it directly
to the MATING metaphor ('When a company merges to escape a threat,
it often imports its problems into the marriage' [EC, lines 32–3]). This
connection shows the common goal of fighting and feeding to be
posing a threat, while mating is depicted as escaping such threats. Thus
the metaphoric chain established in EC, lines 21–33, once more betrays
the conceptual links between the three cluster metaphors.

Although the *Fortune* text does not show any persistent use of particular metaphors, the direct quotations still make for local metaphor
chains at the article's beginning (FO, lines 5–14) and in mid-text (FO,
lines 26–31). The metaphoric chain evolving in FO, lines 5–14, falls into
the questoning category, including as it does different conceptualizations of a particular company ('rival' versus 'prom queen'). It is not
totally clear which conceptualization is meant to define the topic in this
initial position, yet the term 'sexy' in the very last line (FO, line 52)
goes some way towards suggesting that it is the MATING rather than the
FIGHTING metaphor. The dual characterization as rival or prom queen
may on the surface seem contradictory. However, it has already been
pointed out that the primary source, in promoting the latter, may do
so mainly for the sake of attenuation. In this case, the goal of market
domination stays the same, and the introductory chain still functions
to highlight two different aspects of one and the same underlying
model. Mere questioning becomes fully-fledged negating in the mid-
text chain (FO, lines 26–31), which again features corporate representatives and journalists struggling over metaphoric meaning, this time

involving the FEEDING metaphor. It should be noted that this particular chain is taken up by a primary source later in the article ('acquisition-hungry' [FO, line 36]). So if the FEEDING metaphor is to serve any argumentative function, it does so by showing the conflict it can foster between primary and secondary discourse.

An elaborating FIGHTING metaphor chain is present throughout the *Financial Times* text. However, it is interrupted after FT, line 13, and only resumed in FT, line 53 ('survive'), after a long interlude of 820 words (of a total of 1,264 in that article). We are thus confronted with a case of M&A being framed metaphorically as an evolutionary fight in defining and persuasive ways. The substantial middle part of the article is devoted to establishing the overarching EVOLUTIONARY STRUGGLE metaphor. This important feature of the structure of the *Financial Times* text will be elaborated on p. 150; for the time being, it should be noted that the article also develops a chain involving a SIZE metaphor, which often takes on distinctly hyperbolic overtones and thus comes to function as an intensification device not only in the *Financial Times* but also in media discourse on M&A in general.

Intensification and attenuation

The notion of size is a hallmark of media discourse on M&A. In the *Business Week* example, we have a metaphoric chain starting straight from the title. The initial 'big' – to be repeated in BW, lines 18 and 29, as well as in 36 (in the comparative) and 77 – finds its first echo in the expression 'giant bond issues' (BW, line 15), to be followed by the hyperbolic 'wagonloads of money' (BW, line 27). An embodied relationship between size and weight is reflected in the reference to big companies as 'cash-rich heavies' (BW, line 54), whereas the expression 'monster deals' (BW, line 56) adds the aspect of something superhuman. These findings tie in with Pieper and Hughes' (1997) observation that

> [the] language of hyperbole was also used repeatedly by the media [in reporting on the Time-Warner/Turner merger]. This language employed terminology which described the executives and their companies in larger-than-life terms. (para. 77)

Further examples of metaphor combined with hyperbole can be found later in the article, corroborating Searle's (1979/1983, p. 97) observation that 'many metaphors are exaggerations'. Some of these later instances are expressions of the primary metaphor MORE IS UP – for example, the attribution 'valuations are astronomical' (BW, line 57). Another vertical spatial metaphor is present in 'bottomless appetite' (BW, line 14). Since it is here combined with the FEEDING metaphor, it could well be triggered by the physical experience of food going down inside the body. Apart from that, 'bottomless' is also an intensification adding to the hyperbolic augmentation witnessed elsewhere. A further intensification device, built into the corpus as a whole, is the types of items realized from the field of feeding. As noted above, it is mainly aggressive types of feeding/eating which have found their way into the corpus. Thus, we find 'blue chips . . . will either be taken over or will gobble up somebody else' (BW, lines 31–2), which equates the two input spaces FEEDING and TAKEOVERS. Another intensification, this time drawing on the FIGHTING metaphor, can be found in the attribution 'rapid-fire dealmaking' (BW, line 18).

Intensification in *The Economist* also takes place in the form of hyperbolic language in connection with SIZE metaphors, albeit to a lesser degree than in the *Business Week* sample. Attributions such as 'Titanic league' (EC, line 17) or 'immense losses' (EC, line 19) are echoed later in the article, both in their comparative and superlative forms ('greater scale' [EC, line 27], and 'biggest financial-services firm' [EC, line 52]).

The title of the *Fortune* article introduces a very similar form of hyperbole, again to be found in the subsequent superlative expressions 'largest tech merger in history' (FO, lines 4–5) and 'the SDL purchase is the biggest yet' (FO, line 12) as well as in other phrases incorporating augmentative attitude ('massive acquisition' [FO, line 8], 'demand . . . is enormous and getting bigger' [FO, line 43] and 'the combined JDSLU–SDL behemoth' [FO, line 19]). In terms of nominal hyperbole, *behemoth* occurs eight times in the M&A corpus, followed by five occurrences of *titan* (see also the expression 'Titanic league' [EC, line 17]). However, both are dwarfed by the 36 tokens the corpus records for the nominal form of *giant* alone.

Finally, the *Financial Times* article also includes the kind of hyperbolic language so characteristic of M&A discourse. The respective chain starts in FT, line 11 ('one internet leviathan') and continues until just before the re-entry of cluster metaphors in FT, line 53. Hyperbole is achieved mainly through attribution 'the very largest dotcom companies' (FT, lines 52–3), as well as by primary sources – '"The big are getting bigger"' [FT, line 24]).

Apart from the SIZE metaphor, media texts on M&A also quite frequently incorporate an ANIMAL metaphor to intensify hyperbolically the metaphoric scenario they sketch. A case in point is the headline of the *Fortune* text, which, just like the title of *The Economist* marketing text, hints at popular culture (for another pun on the same topic, see MS EC 15). A variation of the Hollywood film title 'Gorilla in the Mist', it elaborates on the ANIMAL metaphors popular in business and, in particular, M&A discourse (see also the two occurrences of *gorilla* in the marketing and sales corpus – MS FO 6 and MS FO 36). Apart from the well-known *bulls* and *bears* of the stock exchange,[16] the specific terminology also knows *cats and dogs* to denote speculative shares (Investopedia, 1999–2002, n. par.) and *stags*, which refers to 'an investor or speculator who subscribes to a new issue with the intention of selling them soon after allotment to realise a quick profit' ('Stag', n.d.). In an M&A context, we find high-growth companies (that is, in excess of 20 per cent in sales revenues per annum) called *gazelles* (Investopedia, 1999–2002, n. par.), *pigeons* denoting likely targets (Hirsch, 1986, p. 833), hostile bidders and targeted companies referred to as *foxes* and *lions* (Hirsch, 1986, p. 804) as well as the term *shark repellent* to describe an activity intended to stave off would-be acquirers (Investopedia, 1999–2002, n. par.). Also popular is *elephants* as a name for very large companies: in quite a daring cross between the ANIMAL and MATING metaphors, an executive of a small-scale company having alliances with two larger corporations is quoted as saying 'We're like a mouse sleeping with two elephants' (MA EC 26). To return to the *Fortune* text, the term *gorilla* is elaborated on in FO, lines 2–3 ('jungle', 'swing along'), resulting in a whole primordial scenario instead of just an isolated metaphoric expression. Although it is not attested in the present corpus (but see MS FO 6), White and Herrera (2003) also discuss metaphoric references to companies as dinosaurs, which reflect the jungle scenario in M&A media discourse. The title of the *Fortune* article thus not only brings in the ANIMAL metaphor on the one hand and forges a bond between writer and reader by alluding to supposedly shared knowledge about popular culture on the other, but also evokes the image of the proverbial jungle in which the evolutionary forces of natural selection rule.

As far as attenuation is concerned, it has already been noted that corporate representatives, when quoted, tend to play down the aggression inherent in the FIGHTING and FEEDING metaphors, instead rejecting (FO, lines 30–1) or trying to attenuate them by drawing on the MATING metaphor. The next sub-section will investigate the intricate relations between media and corporate representatives when it comes to M&A.

Primary and secondary discourse

The Economist article does not rely on quotes at all, and it is therefore unclear whether the author proposes his or her own model to be incorporated by the reader, or whether metaphorizations originating from primary discourse are supported. The latter is clearly the case in the *Financial Times* sample, where the author elaborates on and extends rather than questions the metaphors proposed by corporate representatives. This cognitive and discursive support most notably involves the EVOLUTIONARY STRUGGLE metaphor, where the view of primary sources of 'a natural evolution in the industry' (FT, lines 27–8) is taken up in the notion of 'survival' (of the fittest) (FT, line 62). It stands to reason that readers are expected to do the same, the more so as the model is granted much defining, argumentative and persuasive force, and is, moreover, never contested, not even for the sake of the argument.

Convergence between corporate and media representatives ends here, however. As elaborated on pp. 151–2, the text from *Business Week* shows a marked difference between corporate and media discourse in terms of grammar: journalists prefer to express mere possibility, ascribing belief of certainty to the corporate representatives they quote. This difference is telling. Obviously, the authors seek to hedge their claims, leaving declarative status to primary sources. Such endeavours convey a certain sense of responsibility towards readers in the sense of not wanting to mislead them by presenting informed speculation as fact.

Yet the most blatant cases of disagreement can be found in the *Fortune* text. Its pervasive use of direct quotations, which make up about a fifth of the whole text, is perhaps its most striking feature. In switching between journalistic comment, quotes of primary sources and factual information, the text very much resembles the TV news programme discussed in Chapter 2. In two cases (FO, lines 28–31, and FO, lines 50–1) the citations are embedded in the question-and-answer format of a simulated dialogue. The highly dynamic nature of this device is underscored by the direct quotations fostering metaphorization in often unconventional, or even controversial, ways. For example, it is interesting to note that the 'prom queen' quotation discussed earlier (FO, lines 12–14) in fact contradicts a previous identification of the same company: in FO, line 5, SDL was referred to as the acquirer's 'rival'. Yet a representative of corporate M&A discourse, who furthermore advised the acquirer on the restructuring, offers a strikingly different metaphorization. His conceptualization serves two functions: first, drawing on the MATING metaphor attenuates any aggressiveness involved in the acquisition. In their case study of the media coverage of takeovers, Herrera and White (2002) notice that the WAR metaphor was at some point abandoned in favour of the MARRIAGE metaphor, as the latter was perceived to be less face-threatening. In the words of the authors, 'it downplays the loser dimension' (ibid., p. 238). Similarly, Bastien (1989/2000, p. 369) observes that the WAR metaphor is characteristic of what he dubs the 'exploitive conformative acquisition', while the MARRIAGE metaphor tends cognitively to govern the 'synergistic merger'. Second, while the acquiree may be mollified by the attenuation inherent in the MATING metaphor, in particular its [+HUMAN] subset, it is also weakened by being allocated the more static female gender, making the metaphor rather double-edged. Seen in this light, the MATING metaphor here helps to weaken, if not to 'emasculate', a rival (and at the same time strengthen the acquirer's position) while putting up a smokescreen of attenuation.

The FEEDING metaphor, first introduced in a reported interview exchange (FO, lines 28–31), is another contested issue in the *Fortune* article. Again, primary sources differ from journalists in how they conceptualize the topic. The metaphoric term 'indigestion' (FO, line 29) is used as an unproblematic expression by the writer. Indeed, the lemma *digestion* is the second most frequent realization of the FEEDING metaphor in the whole corpus (see Tables A.4 and A.5 on pp. 209 and 212). However, the item, though taken up, is negated by the executive quoted: ' "We don't digest them; we integrate them" ' (FO, line 30; see also FO, line 39, for additional usage of *integration* in corporate discourse). The two sentences are juxtaposed, differing only with regard to polarity. One of the speaker's obvious intentions is to attenuate the FEEDING metaphor, which he apparently perceives as signalling too much aggression against the acquired companies. The syntactic structure is repeated, this time in the form of an identification (' "It's not acquisition frenzy; it's a well-thought-out strategy" ' [FO, lines 30–1]). By virtue of the parallelism between the two pairs of sentences, the FEEDING metaphor is here linked to, if not equated with, the M&A ACTIVITY IS INSANITY metaphor.

In fact, that metaphor is quite well established throughout the corpus, for example in the phrase 'the deal mania raging next door' (BW, line 30). Although the more clinical terms *sane* and *(in)sanity* cannot themselves be found in the corpus, there are a combined 18 instances of *craziness, crazy; frenzied, frenzy; mad(ness)* and *mania, maniac(al)*. However, these tokens show a high degree of conventionalization, occurring mainly in combination with *merger* or *acquisition* (as in *merger mania* [MA BW 4; MA BW 10; MA FO 15], *merger frenzy* [MA BW 20; MA FO 3], *acquisition frenzy* [MA FO 2] or *merger madness* [MA EC 29]). It should be noted, however, that this tendency to form nominal compounds does not translate into statistically confirmable collocations in the corpus. By contrast, the BoE does record *merger* as collocating with *mania*, yet its frequency (9 out of 817 occurrences of the node word) is very low. Regardless of statistics, the dramatization and intensification achieved by these combinations are mirrored by the author's use of hyperbole, as discussed above.

The common denominator shared by *indigestion* and *acquisition frenzy* is the notion of illness. To counter this illness aspect, the speaker quoted by the *Fortune* writer introduces the notion of strategy, a concept taken from the [+HUMAN] and hence attenuating sub-category of the FIGHTING metaphor. The FEEDING metaphor, on the other hand, indeed shows a proximity to the ILLNESS metaphor, as corroborated by creative extensions as the one below:

> Post bubble bulletin: Earnings anemia
> Can bring on corporate bulimia.
> Can't keep down everything that you bite off?
> Spin off! Sell off! Kill off! Write off!
> Reflex responses to burning question:
> How to cure asset indigestion.
> (Sprung, 2002, p. 10)

This aspect of the FEEDING metaphor sheds some light on why the speaker quoted in FO, lines 30–1, may be rejecting it: not only is it perceived as being too aggressive against the acquiree, but it could also reflect unfavourably on the acquirer's state. It should therefore come as no surprise that an additional primary source, while still drawing on the FEEDING metaphor, avoids its [+ILL] aspects, choosing instead the neutral expression ' "when you're acquisition-hungry" ' (FO, lines 35–6).

The above discrepancies are largely constituted by the fact that – at least in this example of media discourse on M&A – the author obviously regards the more overtly aggressive FIGHTING and FEEDING metaphors as being unproblematic, and has no qualms about using them lavishly. By contrast, corporate representatives, who have to take the interests of various stakeholders into account, including the acquiree's, are obviously much more reluctant openly to embrace the aggressive movement scenario. If we recall *Fortune*'s and other publications' readership demographics, primary sources emerge as playing a dual role: as corporate representatives they use the media as a mouthpiece, seeking to attenuate overly aggressive metaphors. However, as the readers they largely are at the same time, they might very well share the cognitive model proposed by the journalists.

In the remainder of this section, the insights gained so far will be combined in a discussion of the articles' overall structure. Moreover, they will be tested to see whether any alternative metaphors countering the central scenario can be discerned and what role functional grammar patterns have with regard to this scenario.

Article structure

In the *Business Week* sample, the FEEDING metaphor is locally restricted to the first half of the text, while the FIGHTING metaphor is distributed evenly throughout. This article thus shows no remarkable metaphor clustering in any part. As could be seen from the marketing texts, an article title often introduces the main metaphor defining the topic. In the case of the *Business Week* sample, however, the first metaphoric expression of feeding occurs only in BW, line 14 ('bottomless appetite'), while the first realization of the FIGHTING metaphor is postponed until BW, line 18 ('rapid-fire dealmaking'). From there onwards, however, the FIGHTING metaphor continues to be realized throughout the text and this pervasive use speaks for its defining function. Although neither the headline nor the opening paragraph includes a metaphoric expression of fighting, the main body of the article ends with the metaphor being instantiated by the static nominal – and also rather conventional – 'hostile takeover' (BW, line 89) and the more dynamic progressive aspect in 'companies are drawing up their battle plans' (BW, line 90). By means of such end stress, the FIGHTING metaphor is of some persuasive power in the text. As it does not occur before BW, line 8, however, it is doubtful whether it really frames the text.

Nor do any of the metaphors supporting it, be it the FEEDING or, linking the two, HUNTING metaphor. As for the latter, it can be found to occur not earlier than in BW, lines 45–6 ('they are hunting for acquisitions') and later in BW, lines 60–1 ('Deutsche Telekom are . . . on the prowl') as well as, in nominalized form, in BW, line 75 ('the telecom hunt could spill over into related industries'). If we look at the four types – *hunt*, *predator*, *prey* and *prowl* – in the M&A corpus as a whole, it shows that the HUNTING metaphor conforms to, if not all, then clearly the majority of criteria for an entrenched conceptual metaphor (see Low, 1999, p. 64).[17] Creative extensions can be found mainly in its combination with other metaphors, including *predators that play dirty* (MA EC 17), 'the telecom hunt could spill over' in BW, line 75, and, representing an interesting cross between aggression and mating, *Abbey National . . . is hunting for a merger partner* (MA FT 29). While the four types do not show an example of journalists elaborating on a primary source, there is a noteworthy case of metaphorization of a quotation: *'She wants to do . . . a lot more.' Yes, her plan is to hunt bigger prey* (MA FO 17). Metaphoric conceptualization is also made explicit – for example, in *'if we are aggressive, we are accused of being predatory'* (MA BW 16). This last example doubles as an instance of how the semantic features transferred are discussed, another one being the following: 'In fact what [a whispering campaign] does is the exact opposite of what a predator might hope for because it drives people together not apart' (MA FT 30). Interestingly, there is no instance of semantic deviation from the entrenched metaphoric meaning, suggesting that the HUNTING metaphor is seen as being unproblematic and is therefore not contested in discourse. The HUNTING metaphor clearly links FIGHTING and FEEDING metaphors, and its position in the dominant evolutionary struggle scenario can be traced in phrases such as in 'having survived consolidation . . . they are hunting for acquisitions' (BW, lines 45–6), where the agents switch from near-victim to aggressor.

The HUNTING metaphor is also instantiated in *The Economist* sample, where 'predator' is connected to the FEEDING metaphor (EC, lines 29–31). However, it is clearly overshadowed by the MATING metaphor determining the structure of that article. In particular, clustering patterns in this article are very clearly characterized by co-occurrences in the first half of the text, a suspension of relevant metaphors in the second half, and renewed metaphor density towards the end of the article. In this context, it becomes evident that the MATING metaphor frames the article by being used strategically in the opening stretches of the text and in its closing lines, thus both defining the subject matter as well as persuading the reader to take this specific conceptualization on board. It is superseded by the FIGHTING metaphor in the third paragraph, which also contains the article's two realizations of the FEEDING metaphor ('another predator' [EC, line 29] and 'was scared of being gobbled up' [EC, line 31]). This particular metaphor here supports the FIGHTING metaphor by virtue of being syntactically constructed as an alternative form of movement. Cluster metaphors are then suspended, to reappear in intensified form in the closing lines of the text.

In more detail, the dominant MATING metaphor is introduced in a rather unorthodox construction in EC, lines 5–6 ('corporate mergers have even higher failure rates than the liaisons of Hollywood stars'). By linking the literal and the non-literal referent syntactically in the same comparative clause, the metaphor is made explicit (Steen, 1999, p. 84). The dominant metaphoric conceptualization of mergers is thus firmly entrenched right at the beginning of the article, serving a defining function. Elsewhere, unorthodox extension is semantic rather than syntactic ('in the starry moments of courtship' [EC, line 33]). Just before mid-text, the MATING metaphor reappears in relation to the FIGHTING metaphor (EC, lines 32–3). It is quite remarkable that cluster metaphors are then all but abandoned and are only taken up again towards the end of the article.

Some of the clustering at the end of *The Economist* article is accounted for by the FIGHTING metaphor. Reintroduced in EC, lines 72–4, it takes a rather intensified form ('a company that is being bought can all too often feel like a defeated army in an occupied land, and will wage guerilla warfare against a deal'). The sentence not only combines a simile with a metaphoric expression but also uses metonymy when equating a company with its employees, thus granting extraordinary 'rhetorical weight' (Steen, 1999, p. 94) to the metaphor. Intensification of the FIGHTING metaphor is supported by belief of certainty ('will wage guerrilla warfare' [EC, line 74]). The article closes by once more instantiating the MATING metaphor ('before they book their weddings' [EC, lines 77–8]). Although the two cluster metaphors of fighting and mating are not linked syntactically here, they nevertheless occur in close enough proximity to indicate a hybrid yet coherent model incorporating the two metaphors.

Combining metaphor with adjacent tropes such as metonymy and, more importantly, simile, is in fact a recurrent feature of *The Economist* article. This penchant for similes can be read as one more way of intensifying the metaphoric model: by stating explicitly both input spaces, similes firmly entrench the metaphoric model on which the text is based.[18] In this context, it is noteworthy that the text even opens with a simile ('They are, like second marriages, a triumph of hope over experience' [EC, line 4]). This particular simile not only 'makes explicit aspects of comparison necessary for metaphor' (Goatly, 1997, p. 236) by giving both input spaces, but also by spelling out the semantic features transferred. Similarly, the final paragraph of this sample starts by providing another simile ('personal chemistry matters every bit as much in mergers as it does in marriage' [EC, lines 64–5]).[19] However, this one neither employs *like* (EC, line 4) nor a comparison, such as 'even higher failure rathes than the liaisons' (EC, lines 5–6). The author retains the comparison aspect though, only this time using an *as-much-as* construction to scale the likeness of the two domains (Goatly, 1997, pp. 237–8). As was the case earlier in the article (see especially the different types of threats provided in EC, lines 22–9), the above statement is then supported by examples.

In a nutshell, *The Economist* writer employs the MATING metaphor to bracket the text, linking it tightly to the other metaphors in the cluster. All three metaphors are also present in the *Fortune* text. After its rather complex opening combining the jungle scenario with hybrid notions of rivalry and dancing, realizations of cluster and 'alternative' metaphors suddenly drop to zero and are not resumed until halfway through the article (FO, lines 26–31). There, we find the FEEDING metaphor in an argumentative function, being negotiated by corporate and media representatives. The closing lines of the article reinstantiate the FIGHTING ('beleaguered' [FO, line 45]) and the MATING metaphor ('sexy' [FO, line 52]), with the latter linking back to the second paragraph ('"the beautiful prom queen . . . without a partner"' [FO, lines 13–14]). However, despite the conceptual links between the various metaphors, no single conceptualization in fact serves to define the topic in its entirety.

Finally, the dispersion plot of the *Financial Times* article shows a somewhat extreme pattern, with co-occurrences of the FIGHTING, MATING and FEEDING metaphors at the beginning, and a second, albeit more stretched, FIGHTING/FEEDING cluster at the end. The opening lines show very prominent co-occurrences of all three cluster metaphors, with the FIGHTING metaphor taking centre stage and being supported conceptually by the other two. After FT, line 13, metaphors of size, and of evolutionary struggle itself, prevail. Cluster metaphors are all but absent until towards the end of the article, where the EVOLUTIONARY STRUGGLE is specified as a FIGHTING metaphor again. The lemma *survival* is instrumental in this, occurring in both its verbal and nominal form: 'only . . . the very largest dotcom companies have the scale or strength to survive' (FT, lines 52–3) and '[he] foresees the survival of only three or four dotcom companies' (FT, line 62).[20] An undiluted realization of the FIGHTING metaphor closes the article ('a fight to the death' [FT, line 81]), endowing this particular view of the topic with end stress and thus much persuasive power. The closing sentence and the title, which combines the FEEDING metaphor with alliteration ('Dotcoms devoured' [FT, line 1]) very much suggest that the topic is framed in terms of the combined FEEDING and FIGHTING metaphors.

The structure of the various articles mirrors metaphor frequencies and chains in that there is no shared pattern. Still, it could be seen that the metaphoric scenarios evolving in the four samples are largely convergent. The situation is similar when looking at the use of alternative metaphors.

Alternative metaphors

It is striking that none of the *Business Week, The Economist* or *Financial Times* texts show any alternative metaphoric expressions. However, they all include a range of different metaphors (HEAT, HUNTING, INSANITY) that intensify the emergent metaphoric scenario of entities moving in relation to each other in a bounded space upon which pressure is exerted, first circling and watching, then attacking each other with the aim of obliteration, unification or incorporation. Hence, all articles reflect a complex but conceptuallly coherent model.

However, things seem to be different with the *Fortune* sample, which also includes two realizations of the alternative DANCING metaphor. Both can be found in the first half (FO, lines 13–14). But the respective expressions there feature as part of the quote ' "SDL was the beautiful prom queen standing in the middle of the dance floor without a partner" ' (FO, lines 13–14). It is therefore clear that the metaphorization is not so much derived from MERGER NEGOTIATIONS ARE DANCES or even from M&A ACTIVITY IS EMPIRE-BUILDING, but rather conceptualizes the companies involved in gender-stereotypical ways. Although the DANCING metaphor is undoubtedly present, it is telling that the acquired company is feminized and as such identified as static, with the acquirer being depicted implicitly as the dynamic male moving towards the potential dancing partner. Traditional ballroom dancing as a social practice does indeed constitute a materialization of patriarchal gender relations, with the leading role and the act of asking someone to dance reserved almost exclusively for the male partner. Particular aspects of the metaphor can hence tie in seamlessly with stereotypical concepts inherent in the MATING metaphor, making the issue of truly alternative (that is, counter-discursive) metaphors in M&A discourse a problematical one.

Functional grammar patterns

In the *Business Week* text, the time sequence of the underlying conceptual model is also reflected in alternating progressive aspect and future form. An example is 'German companies are considering big transactions' (BW, line 29) coupled with '[companies] will either be taken over or will gobble up somebody else' (BW, line 32). Careful watching before acting is further underscored by the remarkably high number of sentences containing mere possibility (for example, 'Deregulation could send European utilities into other markets' [BW, line 51], 'Novartis and

Roche may attempt to shore up their positions' [BW, lines 84–5], or 'A market crash . . . might make players queasy' [BW, lines 86–7]). Another means of conveying mere possibility is the rather frequent attribute *likely* (BW, lines 56, 76, 78 and 80). The author further contributes to (implicit) tentative trajectory by repeatedly having recourse to credible sources. These more often than not employ the future form or progressive aspect to replace possibility with certainty, betraying the different standpoints of corporate representatives compared to journalists (for example, 'Bankers predict that deals . . . will approach the $2 trillion mark' [BW, lines 10–11], or 'bankers think Fiat is preparing to sell' [BW, line 81]).

The Economist writer, by contrast, achieves entrenchment of the central metaphoric scenario through pervasive declarative status coupled with the present tense (for example, 'When a company merges to escape a threat, it often imports its problems into the marriage' [EC, lines 32–3]). As the article represents the introduction to a series of reviews, the grammar pattern here bestows a sort of incontestable truth value to the statements made.

The struggle over metaphorization emerging in the *Fortune* sample can also be seen in a tendency to use certainty. Examples are ' "We had always thought that SDL was the beautiful prom queen" ' (FO, lines 12–13) – which also employs the predecessive aspect to add a flavour of eternal truth to the statement – and ' "We don't digest them; we integrate them" ' (FO, line 30), which derives additional defining power from a clear negative–positive polarity. This complexity at the level of text translates into a hybrid yet coherent metaphoric scenario.

Grammar patterns differ vastly throughout the *Financial Times* article. The companies listed in the first paragraph, for example, are embedded in phrases of quite different grammatical function. The agentless passive in the headline reflects iconically the dotcoms' position as victims of market change. Yet we find medial transitivity in 'Eve.com . . . closed down' (FT, lines 2–3) and even active transitivity in 'Priceline Webhouse Club . . . joined the casualty list' (FT, lines 4–5). In the last example, the expression 'casualty list' refers back to 'brutal', thus rendering the war terminology explicit. While 'Urbanfetch has closed its . . . service' (FT, line 6) continues with active transitivity, the company in question is referred to simultaneously as one of several 'victims' (FT, line 6). The writer goes on to say that 'other recent victims . . . have been driven into the arms of rivals' (FT, lines 6–8), making 'victim' link active and passive transitivity as well as the FIGHTING and the MATING metaphors. Victimization is thus not necessarily reflected in transitivity. The metaphoric forces of evolution, on the other hand, are reflected most prominently in the progressive tense ('the internet shake-out is getting brutal' [FT, line 2]; see also FT, line 51), as well as in certainty combined with the future form ('it seems certain the rout will continue' [FT, line 10]; see also FT, lines 59 and 64).

Thus we can see that, while all writers draw on functional grammar patterns to cement the metaphoric scenario they propose, these patterns are by no means uniform, reflecting the much greater diversity of the M&A compared to the marketing texts.

The above results will be summarized in section 5.3, which also proposes a conceptual model underlying M&A media discourse and discusses that model's impact on discourse, cognition and the wider socio-economic sphere.

5.2.1 Four sample texts

bold type: metaphoric expression of fighting

bold *italics*: metaphoric expression of mating

bold <u>underlined</u>: metaphoric expression of feeding

italics: metaphoric expression of dancing

An asterisk indicates a relevant metaphoric expression that was not included in the lexical fields.

Business Week

1 The big grab
2 It's a statistic no one in the corporate world would have thought possible just
3 a few years ago. In 1999, the value of mergers in Europe hit $1.5 trillion,
4 almost double the $988 billion total for 1998 and approaching the record $1.9
5 trillion in the U.S. 'European chief executives are feeling pressure from
6 shareholders and boards to focus on mergers and acquisitions in an effort to
7 improve returns,' says Daniel M. Dickinson, head of European M&A at Merrill
8 Lynch & Co. in London. And when there's pressure, there are deals.
9 The elements are there for another hot twelve months on the European
10 merger scene. Bankers predict that deals involving European companies will
11 approach the $2 trillion mark this year. Taboos against takeovers continue to
12 tumble, and the euro makes big deals much easier. Having a common
13 currency allows companies across the euro zone to use their shares for
14 purchases. And fund managers' bottomless **<u>appetite</u>** for euro-denominated
15 paper means that giant bond issues can be sold to finance acquisitions. 'The
16 scarce commodity is good ideas, not money,' says John S. Wotowicz, head
17 of leveraged finance at Morgan Stanley Dean Witter in London. But the ideas

Continued

18   are there, too. The big themes for 2000: ***rapid-fire** dealmaking in telecom,
19   the rise of the cross-border deal, and Germany's full-fledged entry into the
20   game.
21   Mindshift. Germany, Europe's biggest economy, has long lagged the rest of
22   Europe in restructuring. But last year, German companies were the **targets**
23   of bids worth $265 billion – second only to Britain with $384 billion. Driving
24   the deals is a shift in the mindset of German CEOs. Not long ago most
25   German bosses didn't think that cutting deals was part of their job
26   description. They worried about potential culture clashes and about the risk
27   of criticism for spending wagonloads of money. Now, says Ernst Fassbender,
28   co-head of investment banking for Merrill Lynch in Frankfurt, the chiefs of just
29   about all sizable German companies are considering big transactions.
30   German businesses may be influenced by the deal mania raging next door in
31   France. One banker predicts one-third of the top 40 blue chips in France's
32   CAC 40 index will either be taken over or will **gobble up** somebody else in
33   2000. Still, Germany's CEOs remain skeptical. One reason: The high-profile
34   merger of Daimler Benz [*sic*] and Chrysler in 1998 has disappointed Daimler
35   shareholders.
36   Cross-border deals will play a bigger role this year. Many of last year's deals,
37   including Olivetti's grab of Telecom Italia and TotalFina's $49 billion ***gulp** of
38   French rival Elf Aquitaine, were one-country affairs. But a hefty 60% of last
39   year's European action crossed national borders, according to J. P. Morgan
40   analyst Paul Gibbs. Bankers figure such deals will increase when obvious
41   domestic merger possibilities are exhausted.
42   Financial services could well be ripe for such a shift. The bold movers could
43   be ING Group and ABN Amro of the Netherlands, Banco Santander Central
44   Hispanico and Banco Bilbao Vizcaya of Spain, and the big Swiss banks.
45   Having **survived** consolidation in their home markets, they are hunting for
46   acquisitions that will give them entree to Europe's biggest markets. ING has
47   just bought a German bank, BHF-Bank in Frankfurt, and is trying to gain
48   control of Credit Commercial de France, in which it holds a 19.2% stake.
49   Banco Santander is putting up $2 billion to back a bid by Royal Bank of
50   Scotland for National Westminster Bank.
51   Deregulation could send European utilities into other markets. Germany's
52   VEBA and VIAG merged last year. Along with RWE, they are now rolling up
53   the German electric power sector, which still has some 900 companies.
54   Bankers think it won't be long before these cash-rich heavies try to extend
55   their reach to other European markets.
56   Once again the telecom sector is the most likely source of monster deals. It is
57   consolidating fast, and valuations are astronomical. A senior Paris
58   investment banker says that Prime Minister Lionel Jospin is putting the heat
59   on France Telecom CEO Michel Bon to do a deal that makes the company a
60   world player. Former monopolies such as Deutsche Telekom are worried
61   about being eclipsed by alternative players and are on the prowl. Even British
62   Telecom, which had professed to be comfortable with buying minority stakes
63   in other European players, seems to have been jarred into a more aggressive
64   approach by British mobile king Vodafone AirTouch, which made a **hostile**
65   $134.5 billion takeover bid for Germany's Mannesmann. On Jan. 11, BT put
66   up a winning $2.5 billion bid for Ireland's Esat Telecom Group, trumping a

67   **hostile** foray by Norway's Telenor.
68   U.S. telecoms are also keeping a close eye on what goes on across the
69   Atlantic. Bell South Corp., which last year **outmaneuvered** France Telecom
70   to grab a 60% stake in Germany's No. 3 mobile operator, E-plus, could well
71   be an aggressive buyer with its partner, KPN Telecom of the Netherlands.
72   Bankers say that SBC Telecommunications, which is now invested in
73   Belgium, Denmark, and Hungary, could be eyeing deals to give it entree to
74   the major markets.
75   The telecom hunt could spill over into related industries. The AOL–Time
76   Warner merger is likely to spur thinking about such moves. Microsoft is
77   already a big investor in European cable systems and has strong links with
78   Sweden's mobile systems leader, Ericsson. More such deals are likely as
79   companies shop to fill holes in their technology spectrum.
80   Motor mergers? More traditional consolidation deals are likely as well.
81   Bankers think Fiat is preparing to sell its auto division. Peugeot could come
82   on the block, and the Quandt family, which controls BMW, may be tempted
83   to sell a stake to an outsider. The logical buyers: DaimlerChrysler, Ford, and
84   GM. And bankers say Swiss drugmakers Novartis and Roche may attempt to
85   shore up their positions in the U.S.
86   What could stop the deal parade? A market crash certainly would devalue
87   the deal currency and might make players queasy about valuations. Higher
88   interest rates, too, would make financing deals harder. An ugly local reaction
89   to a **hostile** takeover could also give pause. But there are no red flags at the
90   moment, and companies are drawing up their **battle** plans. Let the deals roll.

(MA BW 15)

The Economist

1   How mergers go wrong[21]
2   It is important to learn the lessons from the failures and successes of past
3   mergers.
4   They are, like second ***marriages***, a triumph of hope over experience. A
5   stream of studies has shown that corporate mergers have even higher failure
6   rates than the ****liaisons*** of Hollywood stars. One report by KPMG, a
7   consultancy, concluded that over half of them had destroyed shareholder
8   value, and a further third had made no difference. Yet over the past two
9   years, companies around the globe have jumped into ***bed*** with each other on
10   an unprecedented scale. In 1999, the worldwide value of mergers and
11   acquisitions rose by over a third to more than $3.4 trillion. In Europe, the
12   hottest merger zone of all, the figure more than doubled, to $1.2 trillion.
13   Can today's would-be corporate ****partners*** avoid repeating yesterday's bad
14   experiences? To help answer that question, The Economist will over the next
15   six weeks publish a series of case studies of mergers, most of which

Continued

16   happened at least two years ago so that lessons can safely be drawn. None
17   is in the Titanic league of merger disasters on the scale, say, of AT&T's 1991
18   purchase of NCR, the second-largest acquisition in the computer industry,
19   which was reversed after years of immense losses. But none has gone
20   entirely smoothly either; and all offer useful insights.
21   Most of the mergers we have looked at were **defensive**, meaning that they
22   were initiated in part because the companies involved were under threat.
23   Sometimes, the threat was a change in the size or nature of a particular
24   market: McDonnell Douglas merged with Boeing, for example, because its
25   biggest customer, the Pentagon, was cutting spending by half. Occasionally
26   the threat lay in that buzzword of today, globalisation, and its concomitant
27   demand for greater scale: Chrysler merged with Daimler-Benz because, even
28   as number three in the world's largest car market, it was too small to prosper
29   alone. Or the threat may have come from another **predator**: Bayerische
30   Vereinsbank sought a merger with a Bavarian rival, Hypobank, because its
31   management was scared of being **gobbled up** by Deutsche Bank.
32   When a company merges to escape a threat, it often imports its problems
33   into the *marriage*. Its new *mate*, in the starry moments of *courtship*, may
34   find it easier to see the opportunities than the challenges. Hypobank is an
35   egregious example: it took more than two years for Vereinsbank to discover
36   the full horror of its partner's balance sheet.
37   As important as the need for clear vision and due diligence before a merger
38   is a clear strategy after it. As every employee knows full well, mergers tend to
39   mean job losses. No sooner is the announcement out than the most
40   marketable and valuable members of staff send out their resumés. Unless
41   they learn quickly that the deal will give them opportunities rather than pay-
42   offs, they will be gone, often taking a big chunk of shareholder value
43   with them.
44   The mergers that worked relatively well were those where managers both
45   had a sensible strategy and set about implementing it straight away. The
46   acquisition of Turner Broadcasting by Time Warner comes in this category:
47   Gerald Levin, Time Warner's boss, had developed in the late 1980s a vision
48   of the modern media conglomerate, offering one piece of content to many
49   different audiences. At DaimlerChrysler, too, merger integration was pursued
50   with Teutonic thoroughness – although not skilfully enough to avoid the loss
51   of several key people. And after Citibank merged with Travelers to form
52   Citigroup, the world's biggest financial-services firm, it quickly reaped big cross-
53   profits from cost-cutting – though rather less from its original aim of
54   selling different financial services to customers.
55   When the gods are against it
56   As in every walk of business, luck and the economic background play a big
57   part. Merging in an upswing is easier to do, as rising share prices allow
58   bidders to finance deals with their own paper, and it is also easier to reap
59   rewards when economies are growing. But companies, like people, can make
60   their own luck: Boeing's Phantom Works, an in-house think-tank that has
61   speeded the integration process, developed new products and refocused the
62   company on its diverse customers, was a serendipitous creation in the
63   turmoil that followed its deal with McDonnell Douglas.
64   Above all, personal chemistry matters every bit as much in mergers as it

65 does in *marriage*. It matters most at the top. No company can have two
66 bosses for long. So one boss must accept a less important role with good
67 grace. After many months of damaging dithering, Citibank's John Reed
68 eventually made way for Sandy Weill of Travelers. It helps if a boss has a
69 financial interest in making the merger work, as the success of the union of
70 Time Warner and Turner shows: few people would have bet at the outset that
71 the mercurial Ted Turner would have been able to work with the stolid Mr
72 Levin. Without leadership from its top manager, a company that is being
73 bought can all too often feel like a **defeated army** in an occupied land, and
74 will wage guerrilla **warfare** against a deal. The fact that mergers so often fail
75 is not, of itself, a reason for companies to avoid them altogether. But it does
76 mean that merging is never going to be a simple solution to a company's
77 problems. And it also suggests that it would be a good idea, before they book
78 their **weddings**, if managers boned up on the experiences of those who have
79 gone before. They might begin with our series of briefs.

(MA EC 27)

Fortune

1 Gorilla in the midst
2 JDS Uniphase is poised to become king of the fiber-optics jungle. Is it too late
3 to swing along?
4 If you scratched your head upon hearing about the largest tech merger in
5 history, you weren't alone. JDS Uniphase's $41 billion buyout of rival SDL left
6 a lot of people wondering whether the fiber-optic company's buying spree
7 might have finally gotten it into trouble. After all, the SDL deal comes
8 immediately on the heels of another massive acquisition – JDSU's $15 billion
9 buyout of E-Tek (which closed just days before the SDL deal was
10 announced). Most companies don't spend $56 billion in decades. JDSU did it
11 in a few months.
12 Still, the SDL purchase is the biggest yet, and the most surprising. 'We had
13 always thought that SDL was the beautiful *prom queen* standing in the
14 middle of the *dance* floor without a *partner*,' says analyst Jim Jungjohann of
15 CIBC World Markets, which advised JDSU on the deal.
16 The question for investors now becomes whether the deal makes JDSU
17 more attractive – or less.
18 . . .
19 Analysts also think it's unlikely that the combined JDSU–SDL behemoth will
20 have enough market share to monopolize any one product category.
21 According to Paine Webber analyst David Wong, the largest product overlap
22 will occur with a gizmo called the 980-nano-meter pump laser. But there's a
23 worldwide shortage of them right now, and besides, Corning, Lucent, and
24 Nortel – the other major producers of fiber-optics components – are also
25 busy cranking them out to meet overwhelming market demand.

Continued

26   Like Cisco a few years ago, JDSU is finding that the best way to become a
27   one-stop shop for its customers is through acquisitions and *partnerships*, as
28   opposed to heavy amounts of R&D. But with so many different corporate
29   cultures spread across so much space, should investors fear **indigestion**?
30   'We don't **digest** them; we integrate them,' says CFO Muller. 'It's not
31   acquisition frenzy; it's a well-thought-out strategy.'
32   And so far, it has worked. Jozef Straus, former head of JDS Fitel, stepped in
33   as CEO when Kevin Kalkhoven retired in May, and management hasn't
34   missed   a   beat.   'JDS   Uniphase   takes   the   classic   underpromise-and-
35   overdeliver approach. It's an excellent method to adopt, especially when
36   you're   acquisition-**hungry**,'   says   Robertson   Stephens   analyst   Arun
37   Veerappan. Willhoit agrees. 'The company has deep management and has
38   proven thus far that it can get the job done,' he says. 'The sheer growth in
39   demand for optical components may hide any integration issues that come
40   about.'
41   And therein lies not only JDSU's biggest challenge but also its biggest
42   opportunity. As with the semiconductor market three decades ago, global
43   demand for optical components is enormous and getting bigger. Even the
44   indexes are catching on. The S&P 500 announced on July 20 that it was
45   dropping **beleaguered** Rite Aid and adding JDSU. Investors sent the stock
46   up 20% in one day, to $128. And the management of all three companies,
47   JDS Uniphase, E-Tek, and SDL, has indicated that earnings, which had not
48   yet been announced at press time, would exceed consensus estimates. With
49   forward P/E ratios upwards of 140, analysts think the market cap will only go
50   higher. 'Upwards of $500 billion in a few years? Is that a possibility?
51   Absolutely,' says Veerappan.
52   Who knew fiber optics could be so *sexy*?

(MA FO 2)

Financial Times

1   Dotcoms **devoured**
2   The internet shake-out is getting **brutal**. On Friday Eve.com, the US online
3   beauty products retailer, closed down. A few days earlier, Boxman, the
4   European compact disc retailer, and Priceline Webhouse Club, the US name-
5   your-price site for grocery and gasoline sales, joined the **casualty** list.
6   Urbanfetch has closed its online delivery service, and other recent **victims**,
7   such as HomeGrocer.com and Petstore.com, have been driven into the *arms*
8   of rivals.
9   As dotcom companies burn up their cash and fundraising opportunities
10   evaporate, it seems certain the *rout will continue. But less clear is where it
11   will stop. Could it end with just one internet leviathan dominating the
12   business-to-consumer   market?   A   Yahoo.Ebay.Amazon.com   that   serves   all
13   the consumer's needs?
14   The internet is often regarded as the most open and entrepreneurial market

15 in history. In theory, there are few barriers to entry: almost anyone can start a
16 business, without the need for large amounts of capital or a big factory. So as
17 some companies die, others should spring up in their place, offering new
18 features, better service or lower prices.
19 Yet as the business-to-consumer market develops, there are signs that it is
20 becoming an online version of the winner-takes-all society: one in which two
21 or three companies at the top take a vastly disproportionate share of the
22 market, making it difficult for others to thrive.
23 . . .
24 'The big are getting bigger,' says Tom Hyland, chair of PwC's new media
25 group in New York, which conducts the IAB survey. Sites that attract the
26 most viewers get the most advertising revenues, he says, which in turn
27 means they can offer more services and attract even larger audiences. 'It's a
28 natural evolution in the industry that will continue to play out.'
29 . . .
30 You see the result on supermarket shelves. There are far too many
31 consumer products for the space available, so retailers give priority to the
32 biggest brands. This further increases the sales of these brands, giving their
33 manufacturers even greater economies of scale – and so on, in a virtuous
34 circle.
35 Often, it is not the best product that becomes the best seller. But scale, once
36 established, is difficult to overthrow. JVC's VHS video recording system was
37 regarded as inferior to Sony's Beta, but Beta is now defunct. And in blind
38 taste tests, most people prefer Pepsi-Cola to Coca-Cola, but Coke outsells
39 Pepsi.
40 Recognising this, old-economy companies have been scrambling to establish
41 scale before it is too late. Almost every industry, from advertising to
42 telecommunications, is in a race for global domination. According to
43 Thomson Financial Securities Data, the value of mergers and acquisitions
44 announced last year rose 24 per cent to a record $3,029 bn.
45 . . .
46 If people want to go to an auction website, for example, they want the one
47 that attracts the most users: that way, buyers get the widest choice of
48 products, and sellers get the most bidders. So there is a natural tendency
49 towards monopoly, and an almost insurmountable barrier to new entrants.
50 . . .
51 To get down to practicalities, it is becoming increasingly uncontroversial to
52 argue that, in the business-to-consumer sector, only a handful of the very
53 largest dotcom companies have the scale or strength to **survive** in their
54 present form. Despite squandering billions of dollars on marketing, almost no
55 dotcom companies have succeeded in building an enduring brand: and,
56 lacking either that or a profitable business model, they face the likelihood of
57 imminent oblivion.
58 Forrester Research, the internet research company, has already forecast that
59 most dotcom retailers will be driven out of business by next year. And Robert
60 Lessin, chairman and chief executive of Wit SoundView, a US boutique
61 investment bank that specialises in the internet and technology sectors,

Continued

62   foresees the **survival** of only three or four dotcom companies in the
63   business-to-consumer world.
64   According to Mr Lessin, the internet will overwhelmingly end up as just an
65   alternative channel of distribution for 'real' corporations, because they have
66   the brands, the infrastructure, the expertise, the customers, the financial
67   resources and all the other things dotcoms lack.
68   'The fact that most of these corporations did not move fast enough to position
69   themselves for the internet is irrelevant, because they now have a second
70   **bite** at the apple,' Mr Lessin says. 'It's make versus buy – either they can buy
71   a truly troubled dotcom operation at a very depressed price, or they can build
72   it themselves. But most corporations have lost nothing by not becoming a
73   force on the internet three years ago.'
74   When the shake-out is over, will there ever be another internet start-up in the
75   business-to-consumer sector?
76   'When I invest,' Mr Lessin says, 'the first question I ask of a prospective
77   company is "Who is your physical analogy? Who are you like in the real
78   world?" And if they give me an answer to that, I won't invest.'
79   In other words, there may be no money for start-ups unless they are like
80   nothing else on earth. And they will probably need to be unlike anything else
81   on the internet, too. Who, after all, is going to finance a **fight** to the death
82   with Yahoo!, Ebay or Amazon.com? Or a Yahoobayzon, if that should
83   emerge?

(MA FT 57)

5.3 Discussion: socio-cognitive impact and possible alternatives

The four samples analysed in the last section have proved to be rather heterogeneous. Contrary to the media texts on marketing and sales, there is no single metaphor that is most frequent and/or prominent in all texts. Nor are the articles structured in uniform ways. However, while some (*Business Week, Financial Times*) favour the FIGHTING metaphor and others cast the MATING (*The Economist*) or the FEEDING metaphor (*Fortune*) in a more central role, the four texts are similar in that they all construct a complex but coherent metaphoric model of M&A, leaving little or no room for alternatives questioning that model. Instead, we find it to be intensified by very pronounced hyperbolic language and additional metaphors. The scenario is also highly gendered, both implicitly, by drawing on concepts perceived as masculine, but also explicitly, by virtue of the MATING metaphor and its stereotypical gender role allocation. No single functional grammar pattern can be discerned, and the attested formal word class distribution once more proves to be misleading as the scenario is in fact very dynamic.

This scenario finds its graphic representation in Figure 5.1, where the central schema is again the most general and also most abstract, with dependence relations being indicated by black arrows and temporal sequence by shaded ones.

The central metaphor of the model is almost the same as in the model underlying media discourse on marketing and sales (Figure 4.1 on p. 106). M&A activity, too, is essentially about entities moving in a bounded space. Given the primary embodied nature of that metaphor, it should come as no surprise that it is located at the centre of both models.[22] However, the bounded space in the M&A model is additionally subject to external pressure. The forces exerting such pressure can take various forms, ranging from concrete persons and institutions such as shareholders and boards or politicians (BW, lines 6 and 58) to abstract notions such as market change (EC, lines 23–9) or, on a superordinate level, metaphorical evolutionary struggle (FT, lines 28 and 48). In further contrast to the marketing model, the various types of movement form part of a prototypical sequence of events or script, including two stages. To make matters more complex, movement in both stages is directed at two different entities. From the standpoint of the company in question, the total of other companies in the bounded space falls into two categories, namely potential victims and potential rivals. (The company in question can itself also move between those two poles, as evidenced by *the group turned from predator to prey* [MA FT 33].) Movement in the first stage consists of circling both targets and rivals, with the intention of outmanoeuvring the latter while attacking the former in the second stage. A related intention is to gain in size, sometimes conceptualized as enlarging one's metaphorical empire (FO, line 2 and Table A.6; see also Jäkel, 1997, p. 207).[23] The FEEDING metaphor is just a variation on the FIGHTING metaphor: here, the category supplementing that of rivals is food, which has to be searched for before being eaten (and digested). Often, this search can take the form of a hunt, with the food turning into a preyed-upon animal. Evidence comes from BW, lines 45–6 and 75, as well as from the following quotation from outside the corpus:

[Time Warner chairman] Levin began feeling the hot breath of Jack Welch, chairman of General Electric . . . Time Warner would be a juicy morsel for GE . . . Levin is vulnerable because Time Warner is in disarray.   (Sloan, 1995, p. 35)

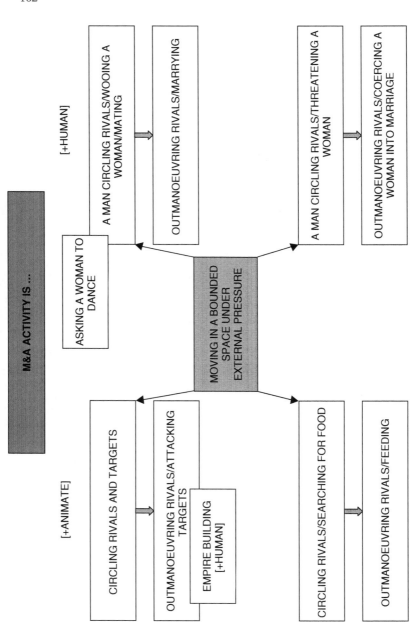

Figure 5.1 Conceptual model mergers and acquisitions discourse

The second strand in the model is represented by the MATING metaphor, more specifically, its [+HUMAN] variety, which is mainly drawn upon in the discussed texts. This again consists of a preliminary and a subsequent stage of action, with activity once more being directed at two different entities simultaneously. Unsurprisingly, the metaphor is explicitly gendered, with the male taking the active part in the interaction. Further, the MATING metaphor can be sub-divided into voluntary and compulsory types. In the former, the preliminary stage consists of circling rivals on the one hand, and wooing a woman on the other. A variety of the latter is asking a woman to dance (FO, lines 12–14). Originally classified as a possible alternative, the DANCING metaphor – which is infrequent in the corpus to begin with – thus proves to be prone to being integrated into the dominant scenario. While wooing may not seem like a form of movement at first glance, the following quote from an article dealing with the Time-Warner/Turner merger clarifies that wooing is indeed linked to positioning and re-positioning oneself in relation to others: 'For 10 months the three men circled like prizefighters, lovers or vultures' (Krantz, 1996, p. 62). The threefold simile clearly equates metaphoric violence, wooing and preying upon.[24] The second stage in the voluntary mating script is marrying, which also means outmanoeuvring rivals. Sometimes, metaphoric marriage also results in a REPRODUCTION metaphor (Pieper and Hughes, 1997, para. 74). It should be mentioned that the intention of MATING need not be marriage in all cases but can consist of any form of union, including a sexual encounter (EC, line 9). In any case, the analyses showed that the MATING metaphor and its variations are a substantial part of the cluster, and hence the conceptual model. Quinn's (1991) assessment of 'marriage [as being] too abstract an experience to . . . provide metaphors for other experiences on a regular basis' (p. 81) therefore has to be refuted. As for the compulsory variety of the MATING metaphor, its first step is posing a threat (EC, lines 29–31) to the metaphoric woman in question – that is, the company to be acquired – with the aim of forcing her into a union (FT, lines 6–8). Vicitimization thus proves to be pervasive in the model. For the sake of completeness, it should be mentioned that the victim is not completely helpless: there are indeed so-called 'takeover defence mechanisms', which mainly take the form of FIGHTING and MEDICINE metaphors. Examples include *scorched earth policy* (a defence strategy that includes selling off valuable assets to render oneself unattractive to a raider), *cyanide, dead-hand* or *poison pill,* all of which denote an 'anti-takeover finance strategy in which the potential target arranges for a long-term debt to fall due immediately and in full if it is acquired' (Hirsch, 1986, p. 831). If all else fails, there is always the *suicide pill*:

> a defensive strategy taken by a company to avoid a hostile takeover, but where the target company engages in an activity that might actually ruin their company rather than prevent a takeover.
>
> (Investopedia, 1999–2002, n. par.)

It is noteworthy that metaphoric aggression requiring such defences is not limited to the FIGHTING metaphor but spills over into the domain of mating as well. This phenomenon is captured by the metaphor M&A ACTIVITY IS COERCING A WOMAN INTO MARRIAGE. The metaphor LOVE IS WAR was already identified by Lakoff and Johnson (1980, p. 49), and given the masculinized nature of the FIGHTING domain, metaphoric war is likely to be one waged by men against women. Although gendering is rarely explicit in the corpus,[25] the broader socio-economic context of the MATING metaphor rather suggests this interpretation. A related point is that of the cognitive link between the [+HUMAN] aspects of mating and feeding – that is, marriage and eating. Apart from being conceptualized as war, love (and, by extension), lust are also metaphorized as hunger, with the object of love being seen as food (Deignan, 1997, pp. 30–2; Kövecses, 1986, pp. 67–70; Lakoff, 1987, p. 409). This double conceptualization of love/lust as both war and hunger is supplemented by the fact that the sample texts present the FEEDING metaphor as an aggressive activity supporting the FIGHTING metaphor. The cognitive links between the various metaphors in the model are tight, making for a complex yet coherent foundation of M&A media discourse. The scenario is held in place by the EVOLUTIONARY STRUGGLE metaphor and as such

> prioritises the importance of having the ability to survive in an inhospitable habitat, an environment that requires struggle and otherwise threatens the organism with extinction.
>
> (White and Herrera, 2003, p. 292)

As noted by Hirsch (1986, p. 803), this basis serves cognitive as well as socio-psychological and institutional functions for executives. Cognitive functions include rendering M&A experience more comprehensible and accessible, casting the involved parties in particular roles, pre-defining expectations as to their behaviour, providing a benchmark to evaluate that behaviour and, finally, containing an M&A experience (ibid., pp. 824–5).

The analyses have shown that, quantitatively speaking, the FIGHTING metaphor is most frequent, most often selected, most varied and most entrenched in the corpus, being followed by the MATING and then the FEEDING metaphors. Although the qualitative analysis of sample texts revealed that these figures are not necessarily reflected in all four sample texts, the FIGHTING metaphor was nevertheless constructed as the dominant part of the EVOLUTIONARY STRUGGLE metaphor. At times, it even integrates the other cluster metaphors in more-or-less subtle ways. The DANCING metaphor proves to be negligible in both quantitative and qualitative terms; moreover, its occurrence in the *Fortune* sample shows it as being co-opted into the dominant cluster. The cognitive underpinnings of the textually attested phenomena can be considered to be complex yet coherent and, because of the notion of external forces acting on the central bounded space, dynamic yet inflexible. (Again, word class distribution does not reflect accurately the dynamic or static nature of the related model.) How, then, do discourse participants employ the model to negotiate their relationships and positions?

Boyd (1995, p. 2) observes that the

> incorporation of war rhetoric as a frame for understanding the events of a hostile takeover is not limited to media accounts ... even the participating companies themselves rhetorically construct their situations in terms of war.

While this observation is corroborated by respective data in Broussine and Vince (1996), it should be kept in mind that Boyd's case study is restricted to hostile takeovers, disregarding mergers and other forms of corporate restructuring. Put differently, corporate representatives certainly do not endorse the FIGHTING metaphor in all situations and *vis-à-vis* all stakeholders. As for the situatedness of metaphor usage, Boyd shows that the 'victim' company tends to use the WAR rather than the MARRIAGE metaphor to conceptualize events. Further, it seems plausible that the FIGHTING metaphor should be more pronounced with hostile takeovers but yield to the MATING metaphor in the case of a merger. Concerning metaphor variation across classes of interlocutors, the struggle over metaphor in the *Fortune* sample showed that executives shy away from the aggressive FIGHTING and FEEDING metaphors when using the media as a mouthpiece to get their message across to stakeholders. Yet we could also see that the MATING metaphor is only a superficial attenuation: at a deeper level, it serves to support the FIGHTING metaphor by constructing metaphoric wooing as a parallel to prowling, and by drawing on asymmetric gender stereotypes victimizing the female part. In so far as it allegedly attenuates but in fact intensifies the FIGHTING metaphor, the MATING metaphor in M&A discourse closely resembles the SPORTS metaphor in media discourse on marketing and sales.

So corporate representatives seem eager, at least superficially, to tone down the face-threatening FIGHTING metaphor against their stakeholders. What role, then, do metaphors play for journalists in the relationship to their stakeholders – that is, readers? What is the interpersonal significance of journalists 'focusing on a single emblematic instance within the survival struggle in nature [to] tap a whole conceptual frame with its inherent ideology' (White and Herrera, 2003, p. 298)? We should recall that the majority of their readers are themselves executives. Therefore, it seems useful to distinguish between their roles as business representatives on the one hand and readers on the other. In the former role, they use the media to communicate particular concepts to their stakeholders, while acting as the latter, they may well employ the media to bolster up any similar metaphors they hold. This hypothesis is underscored by a parallel in marketing discourse: while the Relationship Marketing paradigm has had an impact on outgoing communication such as advertisements, in that ROMANCE metaphors play an important part there, the respective media discourse is still very much governed by the WAR metaphor (Koller, forthcoming). If the hypothesis that, in focusing on a particular metaphor, journalists emulate their readers is correct, then the metaphor usage of those readers differs according to whether they communicate internally or externally. It stands to reason that the same double standard could prevail in the discourses on M&A. The number of metaphoric expressions of fighting quoted in the texts is obviously skewed, because executives use the media to communicate with stakeholders. Therefore, such results need to be supplemented by a thorough analysis of the publications' quotation policies, and by substantial primary data. For the time being, the hypothesis that, as readers, primary discourse representatives may share the metaphors proposed by journalists while they challenge them as executives communicating externally, still waits to be tested. A concomitant hypothesis is that journalists fulfil a double role *vis-à-vis* their readers: on the one hand, they underscore their readers' conceptual model of M&A activity, whereas on the other, they also provide a vantage point to be challenged for the sake of stakeholder communication.

So far, M&A discourse has been discussed in its mutually constitutive relationship to a particular conceptual map, and as being reflected in specific textual features. Let us now look at the broadest level of analysis, namely socio-economics. To this end, we should recall that all texts in the M&A corpus were produced and published between 1996 and 2000. This time frame is particularly important in the case of M&A discourse, as the second half of the 1990s saw an unprecedented increase in corporate restructuring activity. Historically speaking, 'tender offers prior to 1970 were too scarce to warrant compiling' (Hirsch, 1986, p. 807, n. 7) and only reached a relatively modest first peak of 28 cases in 1981. Around that time (that is, by 1980), the related value of $44.3 billion was still regarded as extremely high (ibid., pp. 811–12). However, that is small fry when compared to the figures at the time the texts were written: Henry (2002, p. 72) points out that 'nearly $4 trillion worth of mergers were done from 1998 through 2000 – more than in the preceding 30 years', with the global volume in M&A activities reaching an all-time high of $3,498 billion in 2000, up from $974 billion in 1995 (Herden and Butollo, 2002, p. 40). In particular, it was cross-border mergers and hostile takeovers that contributed to this dramatic increase, with the number of the former rising by 541.38 per cent between 1990 and 1999 (Lotter, 2000, p. 89) and the latter growing by a mind-boggling 618.18 per cent from 1998 to 1999 alone (Herden and Butollo, 2002, p. 41).

It is specifically the increase in the number of hostile takeovers that is important in our context. The question of whether the dominant FIGHTING metaphor reinforced aggressive business practices or vice versa is very much a chicken-and-egg problem, but it is safe to say that the socio-economic framework sketched above did not exactly discourage conceptual models of aggression either. As for that model's socio-cognitive impact, its function in reifying gender dichotomies must not be discarded, especially because gendering is made explicit in the MATING metaphor. Not only does the central FIGHTING metaphor help to establish a male-defined cognitive, discursive and, by extension, socio-economic environment. In addition, although the MATING metaphor tends to be employed as a face-saving device and attenuation of the aggressive FIGHTING and FEEDING metaphors, it in fact ties in with them all too well. After all, the MATING script is constructed parallel to the other scripts in the model, crossed with aggression most blatantly in the case of M&A ACTIVITY IS COERCING A WOMAN INTO MARRIAGE. Metaphoric aggression in so-called romantic contexts becomes particularly salient when we focus on the sexual aspect of the MATING metaphor. As a fully-fledged discussion of the relationship between war and (male) sexuality would be far beyond the scope of this discussion,[26] the following passage from Clausewitz (1952) has to serve as a representative piece of anecdotal evidence:

> War in the real world . . . is not an extreme that *releases its tension* in a single *explosion*, but it is the work of forces which . . . at one time *swell* sufficiently to overcome the resistance of laziness and friction but are too weak at another to have any effect; thus, it is a *throbbing* of violence, as it were, more or less violent, thus *releasing the tension* and *exhausting the powers* more or less fast; in other words: *achieving the goal* more or less fast.[27]   (pp. 107–8; emphasis added)

Feminist theory on war has claimed that the patriarchal socialization of women is meant to cast them in the role of 'victims and surrogate enemies' (Reardon, 1985, p. 42). From the qualitative analysis, it can be seen that the company losing in a so-called 'takeover battle' is indeed conceptualized as female. Of further central importance is Reardon's view of the structural link between war and sexism reaching a peak in rape, which she calls 'the ultimate metaphor for the war system' (ibid., p. 40). In his work on metaphoric expressions for anger, Lakoff (1987, pp. 409–15) discusses rape as the obvious social consequence of the conceptual relationship between anger and lust, evidenced by metaphors such as ANGER IS HEAT and LUST IS HEAT. While those two metaphors have their common basis in the physical experience of increased body temperature, combining them into ANGER IS LUST, the subsequent combination LUST IS WAR is likely to be culturally motivated and best interpreted against the background of hierarchical notions of gender. Those can be sustained either by hegemonic co-optation or by force, with sexual means of violence exemplifying the latter strategy. Speaking cognitively, sexual violence finds its reflection in conceptual metaphors linking lust and aggression. The hypothetical conclusion would be that the structural connection between sexism and war is reflected in M&A ACTIVITY IS COERCING A WOMAN INTO MARRIAGE. Seen as such, the metaphor veils only thinly a metaphoric concept of rape for hostile takeovers (friendly ones being more likely to be conceptualized as marriages).

Yet, it is a striking fact that the lemma *rape* does not occur even once in the corpus. Additionally, of the 2,075 tokens in the BoE reference corpus, only 26 are examples of metaphoric usage. Outside the confines of the corpus, however, there is at least anecdotal evidence of a RAPE metaphor. The following three quotations illustrate that, given significant enough contexts and co-texts, 'many times, a single occurrence of something is more important . . . than multiple occurrences of something' (Seidel, 1991, p. 113). First, Hirsch and Andrews (1983, p. 145) quote a business lawyer using the picture of rape to describe the act of suing someone. As for secondary media discourse, a report on the takeover battle between two utility companies in Indiana and Ohio (Klein, 1993, p. A01) quotes an analyst as saying that 'Hoosiers are tired of seeing our companies raped and pillaged and taken out of state'. Finally, in their feature on the Time-Warner/Turner merger, Greenwald and Moody (1995, p. 34) quote the complaint voiced by Turner's CEO, who describes Time-Warner's behaviour towards him as 'the equivalent of female genital mutilation'.

Shocking though the above examples may be, the fact remains that a conceptual metaphor TAKEOVERS ARE RAPES is hardly ever realized. How can this be accounted for? According to the systemic view of text (and, by extension, discourse) as a string of choices, 'what is absent from a text is often just as significant from the perspective of sociocultural analysis' (Fairclough, 1995a, p. 5). The RAPE metaphor would then be conspicuous by its absence, a blind spot worth focusing on. However, it seems problematic to take absences, important as they are, as evidence in themselves. Keeping this proviso in mind, we are left with two possible reasons for the apparent metaphor gap. Since rape is a cultural taboo, the sanitizing M&A ACTIVITY IS MATING metaphor used instead should come as no surprise. In her fascinating study of the discourse of defence intellectuals, Cohn (1987) provides examples of how imagery of domestic bliss is invoked by calling production plans for nuclear weapons *shopping lists* and neutron bombs *cookie cutters*, concluding that 'the metaphors minimize; they are a way to make phenomena that are beyond what the mind can encompass smaller and safer' (ibid., p. 139). Similarly, Cameron and Low (1999, pp. 86 and 82) state that metaphoric expressions have the 'function of masking reference to unwanted or embarrassing topics', making it possible for 'participants to distance themselves from what they are talking about'. The second related function of the MATING in lieu of the RAPE metaphor is an ideological one: if mating imagery is used instead of rape imagery, it serves as a palatable 'icing' to camouflage (metaphorical) sexual violence against women and thus sustain patriarchal order. In this respect, it is related to the image of chivalry as the attenuation of metaphorical violence against women (see expressions such as *white knight* and the like). Alternatively, the hypothetical equation fighting + mating = rape (or in [+HUMAN] terms, war + marriage = rape) may simply not be conceptualized in the minds of the overwhelming majority of text producers, and the three anecdotal instances quoted above would then have to be considered idiosyncratic. The empirical data presented above rather corroborate this latter conclusion.

However, the fact remains that the company conceptualized as defeated is metaphorized simultaneously as female, indicating the possibility of sustaining power asymmetries through metaphor usage. What is more, metaphoric women are rendered powerless through the FEEDING metaphor as well, albeit more subtly so. Starting from the already mentioned generic metaphor DESIRE IS HUNGER and its entailment THE OBJECT OF DESIRE IS FOOD, Hines (1999) has shown that a person thus conceptualized tends to be female in the majority of cases. The WOMAN IS FOOD (specifically DESSERT) metaphor, she concludes, 'reduces women to the status of objects, with the attendant implications of powerlessness, inanimacy and procurability' (ibid., p. 146). The WOMAN IS FOOD metaphor – and, by extension, HAVING SEX IS EATING – has been recorded in a variety of languages, making a strong case for its universal, because embodied, nature.[28] Still, its enforced usage captures gender relations from a male perspective, constructing women as passive objects to be devoured. If we link Hines' study to the conceptual model of M&A, the defeated company is not only feminized through the MATING metaphor, but also doubly feminized and weakened by the conceptual links between the MATING and FEEDING metaphors. An example from the corpus to spell out this double weakening of metaphorical females is MA BW 23: there, a possible takeover target, which *could be forced into a shotgun marriage with a foreign suitor*, is described as possibly *dressed for a deal* and metaphorized as *easy meat in a takeover battle*.

Cognitively and discursively constructing acquired companies as female and weak while at the same time reinforcing the masculinized FIGHTING metaphor is instrumental in maintaining the related socio-economic context as a site where men are aggressive and victorious while women are granted few options apart from the loser role. So, while the metaphoric scenario admittedly meets important cognitive needs (Hirsch, 1986, p. 803), the question of whether metaphors such as MERGER NEGOTIATIONS ARE DANCING (ibid., p. 831) can be implemented successfully invariably looms large. Corpus evidence is scarce, and when the metaphor is realized it tends to be co-opted into the prevailing cluster as *mating dance* (MA BW 21) or *fruitless merger dances* (*The Economist* 1997, p. 90). Another drawback is Eubanks' (2000) observation that although

> [informants] identified *motion* as a common feature shared by business and dance . . . the group explicitly agreed that trade as a dance

would make the most sense if it referred to the dance of a couple, rather than a solo or ensemble dance performance.

(p. 115: original emphasis)

This focus on couples emphasizes the metaphor's gender at the expense of its motion aspect, thus disqualifying it as a counter-discursive alternative.[29] Furthermore, '[dance metaphors] seem excessively complex and sophisticated for basic conceptual metaphors and thus, unlikely to capture the ordinary metaphorical imagination' (Fleischmann, 2001, p. 489). It should therefore not be surprising that the few metaphoric expressions of dancing present in media discourse on M&A tend to be highly unconventional, if not idiosyncratic (for example, 'a bizarre fandango of wrongheaded acquisitions and strategic U-turns' [Bianco *et al.*, 2002, p. 49]). So, while the preliminary circling stages in the model's scripts all approximate the physical movement of dancing, the metaphor seems less than established so far, to say the least.

Still, it seems desirable to try to propose metaphors less instrumental in prolonging gender asymmetry in the texts, discourse, cognition and socio-economic framework relating to M&A. It may be a suitable time for such an endeavour, now that the heady days of the late 1990s are over.[30] Possible candidates for alternatives would be the already present ORGANISM metaphor, which could replace the 1990s term *bubble economy*, as well as a PARTNERSHIP metaphor drawing on concepts of equality rather than aggression. In addition, the ORGANISM could be combined with a hyponymic REPRODUCTION metaphor. Indeed, Pieper and Hughes (1997) have shown that the organizations resulting from corporate restructuring, or the products they introduce, are sometimes metaphorized as babies in media texts. Some examples from the present corpus are *the offspring of former state-owned telecoms giants* (MA EC 22), [the bank] *was born in 1998 of the marriage between* [two] *Munich-based banks* (MA FT 49), *the birth of AOL Time Warner* (MA BW 19), and – combining the REPRODUCTION with the FEEDING metaphor – *Germany is more fertile territory for predators* (MA EC 17).

In conclusion, it has to be granted that the very terms *mergers* and *takeovers*, being themselves metaphoric, might restrict the range of possible novel metaphors. Still, 'the flamboyant language of business takeovers' (Hirsch, 1986, p. 830) is certainly not as immune to change as the present findings might suggest.

6
Conclusion:
Gender-neutral Metaphors

THE OPTIMIST: But are you able to establish a graspable relation between language and war? THE GRUMBLER: This one, for instance: that the language most petrified as phrase and inventory shows the tendency and the willingness to regard, in a voice of conviction, impeccable in itself everything seen as reproachable in others ... THE OPTIMIST: Yes, language is a terrible burden ... THE GRUMBLER: It gets more vacant when metaphor is responsible at the material level ... When the success in our current positions was sure as a gun and the bombardment of a place a bombshell. THE OPTIMIST: Yes, all these sayings originate from the martial sphere and now we are just living in it.   (Kraus, 1926/1964, vol. 1, pp. 152 and 196)

In the introduction to this book, it was proposed that business media discourse is characterized by coherent conceptual models centring on a WAR metaphor. Such models were regarded as a masculinizing force on both that discourse as well as on related social practices. The hypothesis was tested using a theoretical framework integrating critical and cognitive approaches to language and discourse. The analysis of two central areas covered by the business media – marketing and M&A – shows that these discourses are in fact permeated by central conceptual models. These models are, first and foremost, characterized by various forms of dynamic movement in relation to, and aggression against, other entities in a bounded space. Although they may vary in their degree of hybridity, they are nevertheless coherent. In both discourses, the WAR/FIGHTING metaphor proves to be the most frequent, most varied and most entrenched. In addition, it also turned out that it is supported by the other metaphors in the cluster, even if these seem contradictory at first (as in the case of the MATING metaphor in the M&A

cluster). Obviously, such cognitive support must necessarily be rather subtle, rendering the favoured conceptual model all the more persuasive. In this context, it also showed that alternative metaphors are at best marginal and at worst negligible. What is more, they also tend to be co-opted into the dominant cluster, leaving little leeway for counter-discursive conceptualizations.

So the two discourses in question are determined by coherent, albeit more or less heterogeneous, metaphor clusters. The WAR/FIGHTING metaphor is most prominent in those clusters, translating into conceptual models characterized by aggressive competition.[1] Despite the fact that the conceptual models discussed in sections 4.3 and 5.3 require additional empirical proof along the lines of cognitive psychological experiments, a critical approach should still discuss their impact on texts, discourse, cognition and, ultimately, a broader socio-economic framework: as war – and its more general [+ANIMATE] counterpart, fighting – is highly masculinized, its quantitative and qualitative dominance as a metaphor in any discourse makes that discourse a site of male-defined mental models. Perpinan's (1990, p. 2) observation that 'almost everything in daily life [has its] own brand of militarized masculinity with a . . . language to go with it' holds true in the case of business media discourse, too. This enforced use of aggressive and competitive conceptual models can be regarded as part of a backlash against

> women moving inexorably into worksites previously occupied by men, [so that] paid work within the 'new' capitalist system of production retains values closely associated with dominant discourses of masculinity . . . locating women and notions of femininity as the 'Other'.
> (Whitehead, 2003, p. 126)

Indeed, the models suggest strongly that masculine 'attributes [such as aggressive, independent, unemotional, competitive, logical, adventurous, self-confident, ambitious] remain highly regarded in business organizations, global corporations, the armed forces, most public sector sites and professional sport' (ibid., p. 127).[2]

Excluding women by reifying business as a male arena is just one of the reasons why a change in metaphor seems highly desirable. After all, 'what sustains men in management is not just numerical advantage, but . . . the competitive, aggressive culture that speaks of masculine . . . values' (ibid., p. 131). As noted in the introduction, socio-economic realities not only determine metaphor but also 'selective use of metaphor may help create [a] reality which is unequal and . . . the metaphorical reality constructed is male dominated' (Wilson, 1992, p. 884). Apart from the disadvantages a male-defined social sphere brings to women, it is also far from being entirely beneficial for men either. This is especially true in the case of social domains conceptualized as sites of aggression. Although successful in-group members, be it soldiers or managers, can expect substantial material – and, more important still, ideational – rewards such as prestige, titles and influence, there are also serious drawbacks to in-group membership. A certain loss of individual autonomy for the sake of group cohesiveness (Augoustinos and Walker, 1995, p. 119) is perhaps the least of those disadvantages. More seriously, living in an environment conceptualized metaphorically as being highly aggressive, if not a war zone, may bring about ethical problems in making it easier to accept behaviour – such as unchecked ruthlessness and brutality – otherwise considered to be problematic (Heilbrunn, 1989, p. 18). Apart from such ethical concerns, a metaphoric state of war may well incite the psychological traits most commonly witnessed in soldiers (Keen, 1991, pp. 60–1), which can be harmful to in-group members themselves. Military and corporate identities may indeed overlap, as evidenced by executives literalizing the WAR metaphor by alluding to their past as soldiers (see, for example, the observation that 'war metaphors come easily to the decorated Vietnam veteran', MS BW 15). While some soldier qualities, such as strength, courage, willpower, decision and action, are quite positive in themselves, they tend to be accompanied by less benevolent states, among them a paranoid worldview, black-and-white thinking, repression of fear, compassion and guilt, as well as obsession with rank and hierarchy, de-individualization and outward redirection of aggression (Keen, 1991, pp. 42–3; Rumpf, 1992, p. 28). In extremis, prolonged exposure to metaphoric war and its 'cumulative effects of the horrors of fighting, sleep deprivation, and extreme psychological stress' (Goldstein, 2001, p. 258) may lead to literal combat fatigue or, in the long run, post-traumatic stress disorder, with symptoms ranging from emotional numbness, nightmares and substance abuse to a weakened immune system (Goldstein, 2001, pp. 259 and 261–2).[3]

All these possible negative results pertain to members of primary corporate communities, who, however, also represent most business magazine readers. In view of this fact, it seems plausible that journalists in fact imitate, and thus flatter, their readers by repeating their perceived cognitive models back to them. (The fact that the overwhelming majority of these readers are also men further corroborates the masculinized nature of the central metaphoric model.) Consequently, the influence that readers have on journalists should not be underestimated. But neither should the impact that media discourse can have on corporate discourse. In both cases, such clout comes with a certain amount of responsibility. To quote Pieper and Hughes (1997, paras. 39–40),

> journalists have an obligation to equally represent all sides and inter-pretations of a subject and resist influences that run counter to our 'freedom of the press' dictum. To the extent that certain frames have recurrent predominance within a media outlet and across media outlets, one must question the true objectivity and completeness of the reporting.

So secondary media discourse could well be the starting point for chal-lenging conceptualizations that are dominant but harmful in a number of ways. As far as ideology is concerned, it would certainly be

> extremely difficult for the business press, given the culture and values arising from its nature as a competitive enterprise and given the target audience ... not to weigh in decidedly on the side of free market ideology. (White and Herrera, 2003, p. 282)

However, a market economy and its inherent competition need not be conceptualized in terms of excessive aggression and antagonism. The RACING metaphor observed in the marketing corpus is a perfect example of how a metaphor can capture the idea of competition in a non-violent way and make for entertaining reading at the same time.

What is the scope for possible change in a cognitive perspective? The rising tide of neuroscience – or, more specifically, neurocomputational modelling – seems to narrow it considerably. Using structured connec-tionist models, Narayanan (1997) showed that the processing of embod-ied MOVEMENT metaphors can employ the neural system responsible for motor control. Hence, embodiment not only means that primary metaphors arise from moving in a three-dimensional space, but also that, put simply, the human brain can in fact be 'wired' for primary metaphors at the synaptic level (Lakoff and Johnson, 1999, p. 571). Moreover, connectionist systems modelling the human brain are theo-rized to learn through repeated inputs (Elman *et al.*, 1996, pp. 4–6). If we recall that complex metaphors are just recombinations and re-accentuations of such doubly embodied primary metaphors, the con-clusion that long-term exposure to particular metaphoric concepts entrenches them at a very basic physical level looms large indeed. Yet, if we accept that particular metaphors can be learned that way, the logical entailment is that they can also be unlearned by changing synaptic connection weights. Whether one subscribes to a neural theory of metaphor or not, the fact remains that it does not rule out the possibility of change.

What, then, is finally the outlook on counter-discursive conceptual models? What are the chances, means and features of 'heretical' discourses replacing 'reactionary' ones (Bourdieu, 1991, pp. 128–31)? Can the current masculinized metaphors of business media discourse be replaced by gender-neutral models? Eubanks (2000) summarizes the discontent with the WAR metaphor he encountered among informants:

> While Business Is War has for quite some time been acceptable . . . , it may be becoming less so . . . one of the biggest surprises of the focus group was the persistent complaint – across groups and genders – about war metaphors in business, which seemed to many discussants wrong-headed and passé. (p. 146)

Similar discontent surfaces in a variety of sources (Chilton, 1987; Desmond, 1997; Heilbrunn, 1989; Hunt and Menon, 1995; Malszecki, 1995; Robson, 1996; Searls, 1997; Smith, 1997). If dissatisfaction with models centring on the WAR metaphor is indeed so widespread, what strategies are there to alter them? Chilton and Ilyin (1993, pp. 12–13) present a number of ways to implement metaphoric change. First, the text producer is able both to reject the dominant metaphor in a given discourse and to prefer a different metaphor or to foster literal expression. Given the ubiquity of metaphor, the latter strategy seems difficult, if not impossible, to realize. Similarly, we could see that focusing on single metaphors alone does not suffice either, as they are part of an entrenched metaphoric model. On the other hand, novel systems may well result from a recombination of existing metaphors, yielding, for example, an alternative combination of ORGANISM and REPRODUCTION metaphors.[4]

Chilton and Ilyin go on to say that text producers, if they stick to the dominant metaphor, can still redefine its frame – defined as a 'relatively stable set of facts about a domain that are not sequentially related' (ibid., p. 12) – or its script (that is, its 'prototypical or stereotypical . . . event sequences' [ibid., pp. 12–13]). Applied to the two models presented in this book, that could, for example, mean that the frame is, in the case of M&A, no longer subject to quasi-natural forces, granting a wider range of self-determined activity to the entities in the bounded space. In the case of marketing, goal-orientated movement need not lead to the opponent's marginalization, or even destruction.

According to Chilton and Ilyin, a third way to bring about cognitive change is to keep both the dominant metaphor as well as its frame and/or script, but to focus on some aspect of that frame or script. This process, referred to as particularization, ties in with the generation of complex metaphors through re-accentuation of hitherto neglected semantic features. Thus the MATING metaphor in M&A could as well denote a consensual union involving both partners' initiative to the same degree. Similarly, the aspect of playfulness inherent in the GAMES metaphor in marketing and sales discourse could be emphasized at the expense of its more competitive features. Such a strategy demonstrates how dominant metaphors can be employed counter-discursively. The GAMES metaphor could, moreover, be combined with hyponymy, for example, by focusing on a particular non-competitive game. Alternative semantic features could also be borrowed from other cultures. One example is the writings of Ancient China's military theorist Sun Tzu from c. 500BC (Sun Tzu, 1910). Sun Tzu's views on war have informed a number of contemporary writers of popular management literature (Duchesneau, 1997; McNeilly, 1996; Saylor, 1992). Sun Tzu's basic claim is that 'all warfare is based on deception', on the 'divine art of subtlety and secrecy' (Sun Tzu, 1910, ch. 1, para. 16 and ch. 6, para. 9). Sun Tzu further states that 'to fight and conquer in all your battles is not supreme excellence; supreme excellence consists in breaking the enemy's resistance without fighting' and maintains that 'the skillful leader subdues the enemy's troops without any fighting' (ibid., ch. 3, paras 2 and 6). Engaging in physical combat is obviously only one option among various others, and one which should only be chosen in the case of certain victory. While Sun-Tzu recognizes the need for soldiers to be 'kept under control by means of iron discipline', he still advises the general to 'regard your soldiers as your children' (ibid., ch. 9, para. 42 and ch. 10, para. 24). More striking still than the PARENT metaphor is the image of a general who is 'like a shepherd driving a flock of sheep' (ibid., ch. 11, para. 17).[5] Accordingly, traits to be wished for in a general are wisdom, sincerity, benevolence, courage and strictness (ibid., ch. 1, para. 8).

No matter which strategy of changing metaphor in discourse one chooses, the effect of implementing counter-discursive metaphors such as MARKETS ARE CONVERSATION or MERGING COMPANIES ARE DEVELOPING ORGANISMS will most probably be defamiliarization, defined as

> making the routine or ordinary seem strange or different by pre-
> senting it in a novel light, by placing it in an unexpected context or
> by articulating it in an unusual manner . . . metaphoric defamiliar-
> ization thus provides epistemic access to alternative aspects of reality.
>
> (Walters-York, 1996, p. 59)

As expressed in the above extract, the power of such defamiliarizing metaphors should not be underestimated. Far from lessening a maga-zine's appeal, their 'surprise value' should help to keep news and analy-sis entertaining. Even after the defamiliarization effect has worn off, lively coverage in general is not rooted exclusively in constructing aggressive antagonism. More important still, defamiliarizing metaphors also hold the potential to constitute reality, raising the time-honoured issue of the impact of language change on ethos and attitude change. Granted, implementing gender-neutral metaphors seems almost impos-sible in a society such as 'Western' culture, which is in large part still obsessed with gender differences. Generally speaking, any defamiliariz-ing metaphor certainly requires a considerable amount of 'persuasion and indoctrination' (ibid., 1996, p. 59). Still, journalists should rise to the challenge of at least proposing non-violent metaphors. After all, the media play a pivotal role in shaping expectations about people's behav-iour. At a time when globalized markets have led to increased competi-tion, the merger bubble has been punctured and scores of all-too-literal wars still cover the globe, the media should therefore acknowledge their responsibility for reducing the literal negative impact of metaphoric lan-guage and thought.

Appendix: Corpus Data

Corpus A (Marketing and sales)

(a) Business Week

MS BW 1   Barrett, A., 'To reach the unreachable teen', *Business Week*, 18 September 2000. Available at: http://www.businessweek.com/ @@@dFzQYcQqrJxkwcA/archives/2000/b3699231.arc.htm. Accessed 22 August 2002.

MS BW 2   Brady, D., 'Zagat zigs over to the Net', *Business Week*, 20 November 2000. Available at: http://www.businessweek.com/2000/00_47/ b3708170.htm. Accessed 20 August 2002.

MS BW 3   Byrnes, N., 'Brands in a bind', *Business Week*, 28 August 2000. Available at: http://www.businessweek.com/@@IJ00VIcQJLJxkwcA/ archives/2000/b3696173.arc.htm. Accessed 21 August 2002.

MS BW 4   Capell, K., 'Novartis' marketing doctor', *Business Week*, 5 March 2001. Available at: http://www.businessweek.com/ @@*KErcocQKrJxkwcA/archives/2001/b3722111.arc.htm. Accessed 21 August 2002.

MS BW 5   Coy, P., 'Nynex, we hardly knew ye', *Business Week*, 15 November 1999. Available at: http://www.businessweek.com/ @@eqyR94cQKLJxkwcA/archives/1999/b3655098.arc. htm#B3655100. Accessed 21 August 2002.

MS BW 6   Edmondson, G., 'L'Oreal: the beauty of global branding', *Business Week*, 28 June 1999, pp. 24–8.

MS BW 7   Einhorn, B., 'Portal combat', *Business Week*, 17 January 2000, pp. 34–5.

MS BW 8   Forest, S. A., 'Don't tell Kohl's there's a slowdown', *Business Week*, 12 February 2001. Available at: http://www.businessweek.com/ @@ZK*QvocQJrJxkwcA/archives/2001/b3719096.arc.htm. Accessed 21 August 2002.

MS BW 9   Forster, J., 'Gotta get that Gatorade', *Business Week*, 27 November 2000. Available at: http://www.businessweek.com/ @@We*GNocQI7JxkwcA/archives/2000/b3709130.arc.htm. Accessed 21 August 2002.

MS BW 10   Gogoi, P., 'Rage against online brokers', *Business Week*, 20 November 2000. Available at: http://www.businessweek.com/ @@*KErcocQKrJxkwcA/archives/2000/b3708059.arc.htm. Accessed 21 August 2002.

MS BW 11   Green, H., 'Net advertising: still the 98-pound weakling', *Business Week*, 11 September 2000. Available at: http://www.businessweek. com/@@R9O7EocQrLJxkwcA/archives/2000/b3698102.arc.htm. Accessed 22 August 2002.

MS BW 12   Green, H. and Elgin, B., 'Do e-ads have a future?', *Business Week*, 22 January 2001. Available at: http://www.businessweek.com/

@@hIUy8ocQILJxkwcA/archives/2001/b3716041.arc.htm#bottom. Accessed 21 August 2002.

MS BW 13   Green, J., 'Hold on – what make of alternator is that?', *Business Week*, 13 November 2000. Available at: http://www.businessweek.com/datedtoc/2000/0046.htm. Accessed 19 August 2002.

MS BW 14   Hannon, B., 'Riding high on little wheels', *Business Week*, 4 September 2000. Available at: http://www.businessweek.com/@@@dFzQYcQqrJxkwcA/archives/2000/b3697113.arc.htm. Accessed 22 August 2002.

MS BW 15   Himelstein, L., 'This virtual broker has real competition', *Business Week*, 18 September 1996. Available at: http://www.businessweek.com/1996/30/b3485115.htm. Accessed 27 May 2000.

MS BW 16   Judge, P. C. and Green, H., 'Net branding: the name's the thing', *Business Week*, 15 November 1999. Available at: http://www.businessweek.com/@@eqyR94cQKLJxkwcA/archives/1999/b3655098.arc.htm. Accessed 21 August 2002.

MS BW 17   Khermouch, G., 'Buzz marketing', *Business Week*, 30 July 2001. Available at: http://www.businessweek.com/@@Y7sC44cQsLJxkwcA/magazine/content/01_31/b3743001.htm. Accessed 22 August 2002.

MS BW 18   Khermouch, G., 'Grown-up drinks for tender taste buds', *Business Week*, 5 March 2001. Available at: http://www.businessweek.com/@@TuimYGcQi7FxkwcA/premium/01_10/b3722132.htm. Accessed 20 August 2002.

MS BW 19   Kunii, I. M., 'A cell-phone warrior licks his wounds', *Business Week*, 15 May 2000, p. 34.

MS BW 20   Lee, L., 'Nike tries getting in touch with its feminine side', *Business Week*, 30 October 2000. Available at: http://www.businessweek.com/@@JIyt5ocQKbJxkwcA/archives/2000/b3705116.arc.htm. Accessed 21 August 2002.

MS BW 21   Leonhardt, D., 'Is baseball's marketing czar headed for the showers?', *Business Week*, 11 August 1997. Available at: http://www.businessweek.com/@@fwVbLocQH7JxkwcA/archives/1997/b3539063.arc.htm. Accessed 21 August 2002.

MS BW 22   Leonhardt, D., 'Two-tier marketing', *Business Week*, 17 March 1997. Available at: http://www.businessweek.com/@@uaauC4cQq7JxkwcA/archives/1997/b3518001.arc.htm. Accessed 22 August 2002.

MS BW 23   'Lighten up on hard-selling to kids', *Business Week*, 30 June 1997. Available at: http://www.businessweek.com/@@ZK*QvocQJrJxkwcA/archives/1997/b3533145.arc.htm. Accessed 21 August 2002.

MS BW 24   Neuborne, E., 'Branding on the Net', *Business Week*, 9 November 1998. Available at: http://www.businessweek.com/@@E6yt74cQhLFxkwcA/1998/45/b3603145.htm. Accessed 20 August 2002.

MS BW 25   Neuborne, E., 'Pepsi's aim is true', *Business Week*, 22 January 2001. Available at: http://www.businessweek.com/@@Wajvx4cQqLJxkwcA/archives/2001/b3716041.arc.htm #B3716045. Accessed 22 August 2002.

MS BW 26   Neuborne, E., 'Viral marketing alert!', *Business Week*, 19 March 2001. Available at: http://www.businessweek.com/ @@uaauC4cQq7JxkwcA/magazine/content/01_12/b3724628.htm. Accessed 22 August 2002.

MS BW 27   Smith, G., 'Fidelity.com gets serious', *Business Week*, 19 July 1999. Available at: http://www.businessweek.com/ @@v@lmY4cQIrJxkwcA/archives/1999/b3638174.arc.htm. Accessed 21 August 2002.

MS BW 28   Smith, G., 'A famous brand on a rocky road', *Business Week*, 11 December 2000. Available at: http://www.businessweek.com/ @@sztKVIcQJ7JxkwcA/archives/2000/b3711152.arc.htm. Accessed 21 August 2002.

MS BW 29   Smith, G. *et al.*, 'Marketing in Latin America', *Business Week*, 9 February 1998. Available at: http://www.businessweek.com/ @@sztKVIcQJ7JxkwcA/archives/1998/b3564010.arc.htm. Accessed 21 August 2002.

MS BW 30   Sparks, D., 'The Net: who's getting more bang for the marketing buck', *Business Week*, 31 May 1999. Available at: http://www. businessweek.com/datedtoc/1999/9922.htm. Accessed 21 August 2002.

MS BW 31   Sparks, D., 'Who will survive the Internet wars?', *Business Week*, 27 April 1999. Available at: http://www.businessweek.com/ @@R9O7EocQrLJxkwcA/archives/1999/b3661019.arc.htm. Accessed 22 August 2002.

MS BW 32   Updike, E., 'Selling the sizzle of . . . water?', *Business Week*, 27 April 1998. Available at: http://www.businessweek.com/ @@R9O7EocQrLJxkwcA/archives/1998/b3575057.arc.htm. Accessed 22 August 2002.

MS BW 33   Weintraub, A., 'When email ads aren't spam', *Business Week*, 16 October 2000. Available at: http://www.businessweek.com/ @@JIyt5ocQKbJxkwcA/archives/2000/b3703106.arc.htm. Accessed 21 August 2002.

MS BW 34   Weisul, K., 'The Net before Christmas', *Business Week*, 4 December 2000. Available at: http://www.businessweek.com/ @@KlX3uocQrbJxkwcA/archives/2000/b3710029.arc.htm. Accessed 22 August 2002.

(b) The Economist

MS EC 1   'All that glitters', *The Economist*, 17 March 2001, p. 69.
MS EC 2   'The big pitcher', *The Economist*, 20 January 2001, pp. 65–6.
MS EC 3   'The brand's the thing', *The Economist*, 18 December 1999, pp. 105–7.
MS EC 4   'Caught in the Net', *The Economist*, 26 September 1998, p. 81.
MS EC 5   'Cheap and cheerless', *The Economist*, 2 September 2000, pp. 65–6.
MS EC 6   'Come back, Ed Murrow', *The Economist*, 7 October 2000, p. 74.
MS EC 7   'Commercial brake', *The Economist*, 9 September 2000, p. 87.
MS EC 8   'Crystal clear?', *The Economist*, 15 July 2000, pp. 65–6.
MS EC 9   'A cultural revolution', *The Economist*, 10 March 2001, pp. 68–9.

MS EC 10	'Cutting the cord', *The Economist* (Telecommunications Survey), 9 October 1999, pp. 6–10.
MS EC 11	'Debunking Coke', *The Economist*, 12 February 2000, p. 74.
MS EC 12	'Direct hit', *The Economist*, 9 January 1999, pp. 57–9.
MS EC 13	'Don't look down', *The Economist*, 6 January 2001, p. 60.
MS EC 14	'The efficient adman', *The Economist*, 4 March 1999, p. 67.
MS EC 15	'Guerrillas in our midst', *The Economist*, 14 October 2000, pp. 92–5.
MS EC 16	'Hard sell', *The Economist*, 12 September 1998, p. 12.
MS EC 17	'Herr Luxury', *The Economist*, 4 November 2000, p. 100.
MS EC 18	'Hi ho, hi ho, down the data mine we go', *The Economist*, 23 August 1997, pp. 49–50.
MS EC 19	'Hot, hot, hot', *The Economist*, 20 May 2000, p. 123.
MS EC 20	'How to guess the ending', *The Economist*, 30 October 1999, p. 111.
MS EC 21	'Huddling together', *The Economist*, 10 March 2001, pp. 8–9.
MS EC 22	'In the name of experience', *The Economist*, 25 November 2000, pp. 97–8.
MS EC 23	'In search of icons', *The Economist*, 24 June 2000, pp. 120–1.
MS EC 24	'Is it a carve-up?', *The Economist*, 17 June 2000, pp. 95–6.
MS EC 25	'A land fit for consumers', *The Economist*, 27 November 1999, pp. 15–17.
MS EC 26	'Market makers', *The Economist*, 14 March 1998, pp. 73–4.
MS EC 27	'Market timers', *The Economist*, 12 September 1998, p. 90.
MS EC 28	'Marketing madness', *The Economist*, 21 July 2001, p. 58.
MS EC 29	'Media-buyers break free', *The Economist*, 27 September 1997, p. 74.
MS EC 30	'Motoring', *The Economist*, 3 March 2001, pp. 60–1.
MS EC 31	'Net wealth', *The Economist*, 17 June 2000, p. 84.
MS EC 32	'New formula Coke', *The Economist*, 3 February 2001, pp. 76–7.
MS EC 33	'One-and-a-half Nelson', *The Economist*, 25 July 1998, p. 74.
MS EC 34	'Soap powder with added logic', *The Economist*, 6 December 1997, pp. 70, 75.
MS EC 35	'Spin cycle', *The Economist*, 14 August 1999, p. 52.
MS EC 36	'Star turn', *The Economist*, 11 March 2000, pp. 79–80, 85.
MS EC 37	'Store wars', *The Economist*, 9 December 2000, p. 87.
MS EC 38	'Uneasy lies the head', *The Economist*, 24 February 2001, p. 77.
MS EC 39	'Virtual advertising', *The Economist*, 15 September 2000, p. 74.
MS EC 40	'Virtual rivals', *The Economist*, 18 May 2000, pp. 24–9.
MS EC 41	'Vox populi', *The Economist*, 15 January 2000, p. 77.
MS EC 42	'Who will sell the sellers?', *The Economist*, 30 May 1998, p. 73.

(c) Fortune

MS FO 1	Alsop, S., 'Give commercials a break', *Fortune*, 22 January 2001. Available at: http://www.business2.com/articles/mag/print/0,1643, 9109,FF.html. Accessed 21 August 2002.
MS FO 2	Borden, M., 'Why Tommy Hilfiger tanked', *Fortune*, 29 May 2000, p. 24.
MS FO 3	Branscum, D., 'The dot-com that time forgot', *Fortune*, 8 March 2001. Available at: http://www.fortune.com/indexw.jhtml?channel=artcol. jhtml&doc_id=00003158. Accessed 23 August 2002.
MS FO 4	Brooker, K., 'A game of inches', *Fortune*, 5 February 2001, pp. 44–6.

MS FO 5   Clifford, L., 'Sells like teen spirit (not)', *Fortune*, 10 July 2000. Available at: http://www.fortune.com/indexw.jhtml?channel=artcol. jhtml&doc_id=00000893. Accessed 23 August 2002.

MS FO 6   Clifford, L., 'Tyrannosaurus Rx', *Fortune*, 30 October 2000, pp. 84–93.

MS FO 7   Colvin, G., 'The future of advertising – is it okay?', *Fortune*, 2 February 2001. Available at: http://www.fortune.com/indexw. jhtml?channel=artcol.jhtml&doc_id=200551. Accessed 23 August 2002.

MS FO 8   Daniels, C., 'If it's marketing, can it also be education?', *Fortune*, 2 October 2000, p. 125.

MS FO 9   David, G., 'Who can save "dead brand driving"?' *Fortune*, 22 January 2001. Available at: http://www.fortune.com/indexw. jhtml?channel=artcol.jhtml&doc_id=00003158. Accessed 23 August 2002.

MS FO 10   Fisher, A., 'Making the brand: it's different on the Net', *Fortune*, 4 September 2000, p. 113.

MS FO 11   Fox, J., 'Look, but don't click', *Fortune*, 27 June 2001. Available at: http://www.fortune.com/indexw.jhtml?channel=artcol. jhtml&doc_id=203225. Accessed 23 August 2002.

MS FO 12   Gunther, M., 'Take your 0, and a coupon', *Fortune*, 3 April 2000. Available at: http://www.fortune.com/indexw.jhtml?channel=artcol. jhtml&doc_id=00001510. Accessed 23 August 2002.

MS FO 13   Gurley, W., 'How the Web will warp advertising', *Fortune*, 9 November 1998, pp. 66–7.

MS FO 14   Gurley, W., 'Web ads: why impressions don't matter', *Fortune*, 24 July 2000, p. 207.

MS FO 15   Hochman, P., 'TV, radio, and print are sold out. How about . . . trees?', *Fortune*, 10 January 2000. Available at: http://www.fortune.com/ indexw.jhtml?channel=artcol.jhtml&doc_id=00001605. Accessed 23 August 2002.

MS FO 16   Kahn, J., 'Do AOL's ads add up?', *Fortune*, 23 July 2001. Available at: http://www.fortune.com/indexw.jhtml?channel=artcol. jhtml&doc_id=203316. Accessed 23 August 2002.

MS FO 17   'Keep the 0010001 happy', *Fortune*, 1 June 2000. Available at: http://www.fortune.com/indexw.jhtml?channel=artcol. jhtml&doc_id=00001118. Accessed 23 August 2002.

MS FO 18   Kelly, E., 'This is one virus you want to spread', *Fortune*, 27 November 2000. Available at: http://www.fortune.com/indexw. jhtml?channel=artcol.jhtml&doc_id=00001510. Accessed 23 August 2002.

MS FO 19   Leonard, D., 'Madison Ave. fights back', *Fortune*, 18 February 2001, pp. 66–9.

MS FO 20   Lewis, P., 'AOL vs. Microsoft: now it's war', *Fortune*, 9 July 2001. Available at: http://www.fortune.com/fortune/technology/articles/ 0,15114,368282,00.html. Accessed 12 August 2003.

MS FO 21   Lewis, P., 'Not so spiffy', *Fortune*, 5 March 2001. Available at: http://www.fortune.com/indexw.jhtml?channel=artcol. jhtml&doc_id=200726. Accessed 23 August 2002.

MS FO 22   Lindsay, G., 'I want a unique logo – just like theirs', *Fortune*, 24 July 2000, p. 204.

MS FO 23   'Marketing über alles', *Fortune*, 9 April 1999. Available at: http://www.fortune.com/indexw.jhtml?channel=artcol.jhtml&doc_id=22878. Accessed 23 August 2002.

MS FO 24   McLean, B., 'Revenge of the car salesmen: the Internet is a lemon', *Fortune*, 27 November 2000. Available at: http://www.fortune.com/indexw.jhtml?channel=artcol.jhtml&doc_id=200726. Accessed 23 August 2002.

MS FO 25   Overfelt, M. and Wells IV, R. E., 'Marketing from the ground up', *Fortune*, 18 December 2000. Available at: http://www.fortune.com/indexw.jhtml?channel=artcol.jhtml&doc_id=00000012. Accessed 23 August 2002.

MS FO 26   'Protecting your privacy', *Fortune* special issue, 1 December 2000.

MS FO 27   Schrage, M., 'Don't scorn your salespeople – you will soon be one', *Fortune*, 14 May 2001. Available at: http://www.fortune.com/indexw.jhtml?channel=artcol.jhtml&doc_id=202258. Accessed 23 August 2002.

MS FO 28   Schukat, A., 'Branding is back', *Fortune*, 10 July 2001. Available   at: http://www.fortune.com/indexw.jhtml?channel=artcol.jhtml&doc_id=203377. Accessed 23 August 2002.

MS FO 29   Sellers, P., 'Seventh Avenue smackdown', *Fortune*, 4 September 2000. Available at: http://www.fortune.com/indexw.jhtml?channel=artcol.jhtml&doc_id=00000704. Accessed 23 August 2002.

MS FO 30   Serwer, A., 'Ad nauseam: rating e-broker TV spots', *Fortune*, 6 March 2000. Available at: http://www.fortune.com/indexw.jhtml?channel=artcol.jhtml&doc_id=00001837. Accessed 23 August 2002.

MS FO 31   Shaffer, R. A., 'Listen up! Pay attention!', *Fortune*, 25 October 1999, pp. 139, 142.

MS FO 32   Stein, N., 'Out for profits', *Fortune*, 14 August 2000, pp. 77–8.

MS FO 33   Tomlinson, R., Chowdury, N. and Fox, J., 'Dialing for dollars', *Fortune*, 9 October 2000, pp. 82–9.

MS FO 34   'A truly innovative dot-com ad', *Fortune*, 29 November 1999. Available   at: http://www.fortune.com/indexw.jhtml?channel=artcol.jhtml&doc_id=35174. Accessed 23 August 2002.

MS FO 35   Warner, M., 'E-commerce, without branding', *Fortune*, 3 March 2000. Available   at: http://www.fortune.com/indexw.jhtml?channel=artcol.jhtml&doc_id=40265. Accessed 23 August 2002.

MS FO 36   Warner, M., 'Hard ball in the Valley', *Fortune*, 22 September 2000. Available   at: http://www.newslinx.com/Archive/092300.html. Accessed 21 August 2002.

(d) Financial Times

MS FT 1   'Advertising', *Financial Times*, 17 July 2001. Available at: http://search.ft.com/search/article.html?id=010717000874. Accessed 23 August 2002.

MS FT 2   'Advertising scheme attacked', *Financial Times*, 22 July 1997. Available at: http://search.ft.com/search/article.html?id=970722000428. Accessed 22 August 2002.

MS FT 3   Arnold, W., 'The thud factor gives way to analysis', *Financial Times*, 11 May 1999. Available at: http://search.ft.com/search/article.html?id=990511014282. Accessed 23 August 2002.

MS FT 4   Bowley, G., 'Opel takes unusual marketing route', *Financial Times*, 31 August 1997. Available at: http://search.ft.com/search/article.html?id=970831001148. Accessed 23 August 2002.

MS FT 5   Brown, J. M., 'Marketing push helps IWP to clean up in UK', *Financial Times*, 21 November 2001. Available at: http://search.ft.com/search/article.html?id=011121000496. Accessed 23 August 2002.

MS FT 6   'Buy-out managers "ignore marketing"', *Financial Times*, 7 July 1997. Available at: http://search.ft.com/search/article.html?id=970707000408. Accessed 22 August 2002.

MS FT 7   Carter, M., 'BT goes ethnic', *Financial Times*, 27 July 1997. Available at: http://search.ft.com/search/article.html?id=970727000551. Accessed 22 August 2002.

MS FT 8   Carter, M., 'The death of traditional taboos', *Financial Times*, 18 May 1997. Available at: http://search.ft.com/search/article.html?id=970518000106. Accessed 23 August 2002.

MS FT 9   Carter, M., 'Slikies and slinkies deserve attention', *Financial Times*, 22 June 1997. Available at: http://search.ft.com/search/article.html?id=970622000362. Accessed 23 August 2002.

MS FT 10   Carter, M., 'Time to be forward-looking', *Financial Times*, 6 July 1997. Available at: http://search.ft.com/search/article.html?id=970706000363. Accessed 23 August 2002.

MS FT 11   Carter, M., 'Dancing to very different tunes', *Financial Times*, 1 May 2001. Available at: http://search.ft.com/search/article.html?id=010501001832. Accessed 22 August 2002.

MS FT 12   'CNet in $100m advertising plan', *Financial Times*, 2 July 1999. Available at: http://search.ft.com/search/article.html?id=990702012810. Accessed 22 August 2002.

MS FT 13   Cooke, K., 'Giant billboards in the skies', *Financial Times*, 15 March 1998. Available at: http://search.ft.com/search/article.html?id=980315006595. Accessed 23 August 2002.

MS FT 14   Daily, G., 'AGA to emphasize "national branding" in 2001', *Financial Times*, 4 December 2000. Available at: http://search.ft.com/search/article.html?id=001204005868. Accessed 22 August 2002.

MS FT 15   Daily, G., 'Marketing activity shines during volatile quarter', *Financial Times*, 18 May 2001. Available at: http://search.ft.com/search/article.html?id=010518007014. Accessed 23 August 2002.

MS FT 16   'Digital TV drives responses', *Financial Times*, 8 September 1998. Available at: http://search.ft.com/search/article.html?id=980908008931. Accessed 22 August 2002.

MS FT 17   'Direct selling', *Financial Times*, 27 July 1998. Available at: http://search.ft.com/search/article.html?id=980721008811. Accessed 22 August 2002.

MS FT 18   Dowdy, C., 'Branding', *Financial Times*, 14 November 2000. Available at: http://search.ft.com/search/article.html?id=001114001435. Accessed 22 August 2002.

MS FT 19   Dowdy, C., 'The branding boys have landed', *Financial Times*, 21 January 2001. Available at: http://search.ft.com/search/article.html?id=010213001267. Accessed 23 August 2002.

MS FT 20   Dowdy, C., 'Branding wars', *Financial Times*, 30 October 2001. Available at: http://search.ft.com/search/article.html?id=011030001312. Accessed 23 August 2002.

MS FT 21   Eaglesham, J., 'Law firms sell themselves short', *Financial Times*, 10 September 2001. Available at: http://search.ft.com/search/article.html?id=010910002006. Accessed 23 August 2002.

MS FT 22   'Fiery brand', *Financial Times*, 23 April 1998. Available at: http://search.ft.com/search/article.html?id=980423007300. Accessed 23 August 2002.

MS FT 23   Firn, D., 'Aortech's heart monitor gains marketing muscle', *Financial Times*, 23 May 2001. Available at: http://search.ft.com/search/article.html?id=010523009512. Accessed 23 August 2002.

MS FT 24   Fletcher, W., 'In search of integration', *Financial Times*, 22 February 1998. Available at: http://search.ft.com/search/article.html?id=980222003022. Accessed 23 August 2002.

MS FT 25   Frost, V. and Sanghera, S., 'Literary clout as a marketing tool', *Financial Times*, 22 February 2001. Available at: http://search.ft.com/search/article.html?id=010605000596. Accessed 23 August 2002.

MS FT 26   'Fund managers discover branding', *Financial Times*, 27 April 2000. Available at: http://search.ft.com/search/article.html?id=000427000102. Accessed 23 August 2002.

MS FT 27   Graham, G., 'Brand names "fail to build value"', *Financial Times*, 15 January 1997. Available at: http://search.ft.com/search/article.html?id=970115000102. Accessed 22 August 2002.

MS FT 28   Grande, C., 'Web advertising overtakes cinema spend', *Financial Times*, 12 April 2001. Available at: http://search.ft.com/search/article.html?id=010412001289. Accessed 23 August 2002.

MS FT 29   Griffith, V., 'Black consumers enter the arena', *Financial Times*, 1 June 1997. Available at: http://search.ft.com/search/article.html?id=970601000171. Accessed 22 August 2002.

MS FT 30   Grimes, C., 'Networks do battle for precious airtime dollars', *Financial Times*, 23 May 2001. Available at: http://search.ft.com/search/article.html?id=010523001101. Accessed 31 July 2002.

MS FT 31   Gubbay, J., 'A deal to bottle success', *Financial Times*, 25 May 1997. Available at: http://search.ft.com/search/article.html?id=970525000113. Accessed 22 August 2002.

MS FT 32   Guerrera, F., 'GSK in marketing blitz to promote drug', *Financial Times*, 18 April 2001. Available at: http://search.ft.com/search/article.html?id=010418001070. Accessed 23 August 2002.

MS FT 33   Guthrie, J., 'Where even a flatulent mule helps promote the product', *Financial Times*, 14 August 2001. Available at: http://search.ft.com/search/article.html?id=010814001282. Accessed 23 August 2002.

MS FT 34   Guthrie, J. and Nicholson, M., 'Britain leads name changers', *Financial Times*, 16 January 2001. Available at: http://search.ft.com/search/article.html?id=010116001502. Accessed 22 August 2002.

MS FT 35   Harney, A., 'Shiseido in marketing agreement', *Financial Times*, 11 June 1998. Available at: http://search.ft.com/search/article. html?id=980611007930. Accessed 23 August 2002.

MS FT 36   Harverson, P., 'Don't mention the wall', *Financial Times*, 22 June 1997. Available at: http://search.ft.com/search/article.html?id= 970622000368. Accessed 23 August 2002.

MS FT 37   Harvey, F., 'Mobile marketing meets its moment of mayhem', *Financial Times*, 15 November 2000. Available at: http://search.ft. com/search/article.html?id=001115001425. Accessed 23 August 2002.

MS FT 38   Hatfield, S., 'A model of its kind', *Financial Times*, 17 August 1997. Available at: http://search.ft.com/search/article.html?id= 970817000530. Accessed 22 August 2002.

MS FT 39   Hutton, B., 'Winning word-of-mouth approval', *Financial Times*, 7 September 1997. Available at: http://search.ft.com/search/ article.html?id=970907000622. Accessed 23 August 2002.

MS FT 40   'Internet advertising', *Financial Times*, 26 June 1999. Available at: http://search.ft.com/search/article.html?id=990626005525. Accessed 23 August 2002.

MS FT 41   Jack, A., 'Natexis: the birth of a name', *Financial Times*, 9 February 1997. Available at: http://search.ft.com/search/article.html?id= 970209000106. Accessed 23 August 2002.

MS FT 42   Jacob, R., 'Hong Kong shows a friendlier face', *Financial Times*, 17 May 2001. Available at: http://search.ft.com/search/article.html?id= 010517001485. Accessed 23 August 2002.

MS FT 43   Jenkins, P., 'Riding on the back of the bug', *Financial Times*, 4 December 1999. Available at: http://search.ft.com/search/article.html?id= 991204005551. Accessed 23 August 2002.

MS FT 44   Jones, A., 'Brewing group left in limbo as fate is decided', *Financial Times*, 24 May 2001. Available at: http://search.ft.com/search/ article.html?id=970914001043. Accessed 22 August 2002.

MS FT 45   Jones, A., 'Guidelines relaxed on marketing in schools', *Financial Times*, 18 October 2001. Available at: http://search.ft.com/search/ article.html?id=011018001738. Accessed 23 August 2002.

MS FT 46   Jones, H., 'The ad agency that finally grew up', *Financial Times*, 28 September 1997. Available at: http://search.ft.com/search/ article.html?id=970928001153. Accessed 23 August 2002.

MS FT 47   Jones, H., 'Cafe society: branding', *Financial Times*, 6 July 1997. Available at: http://search.ft.com/search/article.html?id=970706000361. Accessed 22 August 2002.

MS FT 48   Jones, H., 'Guinness benefits from rebellion against bland beer', *Financial Times*, 14 September 1997. Available at: http://search.ft.com/ search/article.html?id=970914001043. Accessed 23 August 2002.

MS FT 49   Kitcatt, P., 'Direct marketing', *Financial Times*, 6 November 2001. Available at: http://search.ft.com/search/article.html?id= 011106001310. Accessed 23 August 2002.

MS FT 50   Lancaster, G., 'Brands with attitude', *Financial Times*, 1 May 2001. Available at: http://search.ft.com/search/article.html?id= 010501001947. Accessed 22 August 2002.

MS FT 51   Liu, B., 'Advertising campaign aims to restore Coke's fizz', *Financial Times*, 20 April 2001. Available at: http://search.ft.com/search/article.html?id=010420002066. Accessed 22 August 2002.

MS FT 52   'Marketing and holidays', *Financial Times*, 12 June 2001. Available at: http://search.ft.com/search/article.html?id=010612000384. Accessed 23 August 2002.

MS FT 53   'Marketing practice suspended', *Financial Times*, 23 February 1998. Available at: http://search.ft.com/search/article.html?id=980223004467. Accessed 23 August 2002.

MS FT 54   Matthews, V., 'Bringing up baby – on enfant cuisine', *Financial Times*, 11 May 1997. Available at: http://search.ft.com/search/article.html?id=970511000144. Accessed 22 August 2002.

MS FT 55   Matthews, V., 'The era of relationship marketing', *Financial Times*, 16 November 1997. Available at: http://search.ft.com/search/article.html?id=971116001789. Accessed 23 August 2002.

MS FT 56   Matthews, V., 'Lego builds an image for the future', *Financial Times*, 1 October 1998. Available at: http://search.ft.com/search/article.html?id=981001009300. Accessed 23 August 2002.

MS FT 57   Matthews, V., 'What Tesco will never rule out', *Financial Times*, 1 December 1998. Available at: http://search.ft.com/search/article.html?id=981201001081. Accessed 23 August 2002.

MS FT 58   McGookin, S., 'Self-regulation key to net ads', *Financial Times*, 15 June 1997. Available at: http://search.ft.com/search/article.html?id=970615000388. Accessed 23 August 2002.

MS FT 59   'Mixed response to internet advertising', *Financial Times*, 5 March 1998. Available at: http://search.ft.com/search/article.html?id=980305005021. Accessed 23 August 2002.

MS FT 60   Newman, C., 'A legend in world advertising', *Financial Times*, 22 July 1999. Available at: http://search.ft.com/search/article.html?id=990722014825. Accessed 22 August 2002.

MS FT 61   O'Connor, A., 'Genesis of BBC's "original" title', *Financial Times*, 3 August 2000. Available at: http://search.ft.com/search/article.html?id=000803000209. Accessed 23 August 2002.

MS FT 62   O'Connor, A., 'Radio advertising', *Financial Times*, 24 April 2001. Available at: http://search.ft.com/search/article.html?id=010424001125. Accessed 23 August 2002.

MS FT 63   Pilling, D., 'Direct promotion of brands gives power to the patients', *Financial Times*, 30 April 2001. Available at: http://search.ft.com/search/article.html?id=010430000867. Accessed 22 August 2002.

MS FT 64   Pilling, D., 'Relentless rise in role of reps and big launches', *Financial Times*, 30 April 2001. Available at: http://search.ft.com/search/article.html?id=010430000869. Accessed 23 August 2002.

MS FT 65   'Pizza gaining popularity with teenagers', *Financial Times*, 4 June 1998. Available at: http://search.ft.com/search/article.html?id=980604008197. Accessed 23 August 2002.

MS FT 66   'Radio wins 5.4% of display advertising market', *Financial Times*, 3 February 1999. Available at: http://search.ft.com/search/article.html?id=990203000450. Accessed 23 August 2002.

MS FT 67 'Rebel evades brand police at party to launch PwC', *Financial Times*, 1 July 1998. Available at: http://search.ft.com/search/article. html?id=980701007896. Accessed 23 August 2002.

MS FT 68 Robinson, G., 'Joint Asian marketing plan', *Financial Times*, 18 February 1999. Available at: http://search.ft.com/search/article. html?id=990218000244. Accessed 22 August 2002.

MS FT 69 Rogers, D., 'Break free from the bonds of traditional advertising', *Financial Times*, 5 June 2001. Available at: http://search.ft.com/ search/article.html?id=010605000802. Accessed 22 August 2002.

MS FT 70 Smith, A., 'Accountancy firm makes big-screen debut', *Financial Times*, 21 September 1997. Available at: http://search.ft.com/ search/article.html?id=970921000756. Accessed 22 August 2002.

MS FT 71 Smith, A., 'Advertising under fire', *Financial Times*, 11 February 1997. Available at: http://search.ft.com/search/article.html?id= 970211000097. Accessed 22 August 2002.

MS FT 72 Smith, A., 'Baby boomers get the message', *Financial Times*, 25 May 1997. Available at: http://search.ft.com/search/article.html?id= 970525000104. Accessed 22 August 2002.

MS FT 73 Smith, A., 'Companies fail in annual reports', *Financial Times*, 2 February 1997. Available at: http://search.ft.com/search/article.html?id= 970202000083. Accessed 22 August 2002.

MS FT 74 Smith, A., 'How pride can lead to consumer prejudice', *Financial Times*, 24 August 1997. Available at: http://search.ft.com/search/ article.html?id=970824000491. Accessed 23 August 2002.

MS FT 75 Smith, A., 'Mass market awaits rebirth', *Financial Times*, 13 April 1997. Available at: http://search.ft.com/search/article.html?id= 970413000125. Accessed 23 August 2002.

MS FT 76 Smith, A., 'Ogilvy's one-stop shop', *Financial Times*, 29 June 1997. Available at: http://search.ft.com/search/article.html?id= 970629000386. Accessed 23 August 2002.

MS FT 77 Smith, A., 'One company, two products', *Financial Times*, 29 June 1997. Available at: http://search.ft.com/search/article.html?id= 970629000381. Accessed 23 August 2002.

MS FT 78 Smith, A., 'A challenge from chocolate with an ethical flavour', *Financial Times*, 17 September 1998. Available at: http://search.ft. com/search/article.html?id=980917008662. Accessed 22 August 2002.

MS FT 79 Smith, A., 'Doubts over shopping data', *Financial Times*, 12 March 1998. Available at: http://search.ft.com/search/article.html?id= 980312006181. Accessed 22 August 2002.

MS FT 80 Smith, A., 'Haagen-Dazs to push sorbets', *Financial Times*, 4 June 1998. Available at: http://search.ft.com/search/article.html?id= 980604008199. Accessed 23 August 2002.

MS FT 81 Smith, A., 'Having a party with your Polaroid camera', *Financial Times*, 25 May 1998. Available at: http://search.ft.com/search/article. html?id=980525008018. Accessed 23 August 2002.

MS FT 82 Smith, A., 'Music to lighten the load of the weary shopper', *Financial Times*, 7 May 1998. Available at: http://search.ft.com/search/ article.html?id=980507006934. Accessed 23 August 2002.

MS FT 83   Smith, A., 'A shopping trolleyful of triggers', *Financial Times*, 3 March 1998. Available at: http://search.ft.com/search/article.html?id= 980303004973. Accessed 22 August 2002.

MS FT 84   Smith, A., 'Trevor and Frank join forces', *Financial Times*, 2 April 1998. Available at: http://search.ft.com/search/article.html?id= 980402006931. Accessed 23 August 2002.

MS FT 85   Solomons, M., 'Advertising via text messages', *Financial Times*, 29 May 2001. Available at: http://search.ft.com/search/article.html?id= 010529010151. Accessed 22 August 2002.

MS FT 86   'The strategic advantages of direct selling', *Financial Times*, 26 October 1998. Available at: http://search.ft.com/search/article. html?id=981026008140. Accessed 22 August 2002.

MS FT 87   Tomkins, R., 'Sold to the person on hold', *Financial Times*, 21 September 1997. Available at: http://search.ft.com/search/article. html?id=970921000752. Accessed 21 August 2002.

MS FT 88   Tomkins, R., 'The resurrection of a salesman', *Financial Times*, 16 October 1999. Available at: http://search.ft.com/search/article. html?id=991016006101. Accessed 23 August 2002.

MS FT 89   Tomkins, R., 'Small room, big audience', *Financial Times*, 8 June 1999. Available at: http://search.ft.com/search/article.html?id= 990608014212. Accessed 23 August 2002.

MS FT 90   Tomkins, R., 'The end for old economy brands?' *Financial Times*, 19 July 2000. Available at: http://search.ft.com/search/article.html?id= 000719004154. Accessed 23 August 2002.

MS FT 91   Tomkins, R., 'Labelled as the devil of the consumer society', *Financial Times*, 25 April 2001, p. 13.

MS FT 92   Tyson, L., 'Banks pursue women', *Financial Times*, 28 September 1997. Available at: http://search.ft.com/search/article.html?id= 970928001155. Accessed 21 August 2002.

MS FT 93   Westell, D., 'Heinz must amend marketing', *Financial Times*, 2 August 2000. Available at: http://search.ft.com/search/article.html?id= 000802000090. Accessed 21 August 2002.

MS FT 94   Willman, J., 'Hilton owners in $10m ad link-up', *Financial Times*, 1 October 1998. Available at: http://search.ft.com/search/article. html?id=981001009301. Accessed 23 August 2002.

MS FT 95   Willman, J., 'Lolly to cash in on World Cup', *Financial Times*, 30 April 1998. Available at: http://search.ft.com/search/article.html?id= 980430007057. Accessed 23 August 2002.

MS FT 96   Willman, J., 'Sweet taste test for salty Pretzel', *Financial Times*, 7 May 1998. Available at: http://search.ft.com/search/article.html?id= 980507006936. Accessed 3 August 2002.

MS FT 97   Willman, J., 'Unilever plans internet marketing', *Financial Times*, 1 July 1998. Available at: http://search.ft.com/search/article.html?id= 980701007837. Accessed 23 August 2002.

MS FT 98   Wolffe, R., 'A comfort zone built on branding', *Financial Times*, 27 February 1997. Available at: http://search.ft.com/search/ article.html?id=970227000062. Accessed 23 August 2002.

Table A.1 Metaphoric expressions in marketing and sales corpus per publication

Lemma	Lexeme	Total	Publication			
			BW	EC	FO	FT
CAMPAIGN	campaign/campaigner, to campaign	152	39	18	22	73
LAUNCH	launch, to launch, pre-/post-launch	127	36	26	12	53
TARGET	target, to target	89	28	18	11	32
PLAY	play/player, to out/play, playful	36	13	3	16	4
BATTLE	battle/-field/-ground, to battle, embattled	28	10	4	11	3
WAR	war/warfare/warrior, warlike/warring	26	15	4	6	1
FIGHT	fight/-er, to fight	24	7	1	8	5
GAME	gambler/game, to gamble	21	8	4	9	3
SURVIVAL	survival/survivor, to survive	21	10	4	3	4
BET	bet, to bet	18	7	4	6	1
JUMP	jump, to jump	18	11	0	4	3
ARMS	arms (weapons)/armour/army, to arm	16	3	4	6	3
GOAL	goal	16	8	1	4	3
KILLER	killer/killing, to kill	15	3	3	8	1
FAST	fast	14	6	3	2	3
FAIRNESS	fairness, un/fair	13	1	4	7	1
BLITZ	blitz, to blitz	12	7	2	2	1
RUN	run/runner, to run, runaway	10	1	2	5	2
RACE	race, to race, racy	9	5	1	1	2
SPEED	speed, to speed, speedy	9	5	3	1	0
CATCH	catch, to catch	8	5	1	1	1
FIERCE	fierce	8	4	0	1	3
THROW	throw, to throw	8	0	2	5	1
BOMB	bomb/-shell, to bomb/bombard	7	2	2	1	2

Table A.1 Continued

Lemma	Lexeme	Total	Publication			
			BW	EC	FO	FT
SCORE	score, to score	7	3	1	1	2
SHOOT	shootout/shot/-gun, to shoot	7	2	2	2	1
TIRE	to tire, tired/tireless/tiresome	7	1	2	3	1
TRENCH	trench, to en/retrench	7	4	0	3	0
FIELD	field, to field	5	2	0	2	1
FRONT	front	5	1	1	0	3
STAKES	stakes	5	1	3	1	0
ASSAULT	assault, to assault	4	2	1	1	0
BRUISE	bruise, to bruise	4	2	1	1	0
CHAMPION	champion, to champion	4	0	3	0	1
CHIP	chip	4	2	1	0	1
HEAD-TO-HEAD	head-to-head	4	1	1	1	1
PUNCH	punch, to punch	4	2	0	2	0
RIP	rip-off, to rip off	4	0	0	1	3
TRUMP	trump, to trump	4	2	0	2	0
VETERAN	veteran	4	1	1	2	0
ATTACK	attack, to attack	3	1	1	0	1
CARD	card	3	1	1	1	0
ENEMY	enemy, inimical	3	0	1	1	1
GUARD	to guard	3	1	1	0	1
KICK	kick-off, to kick off	3	2	0	0	1
LUCK	luck, lucky	3	0	0	2	1
PACK	pack	3	1	1	1	0
TURF	turf	3	0	2	1	0
BALL	ball	2	1	0	1	0

BANKROLL	bankroll, to bankroll	2	1	1	0	0
BLOOD	blood, to bleed, bloody	2	1	0	1	0
CASUALTY	casualty	2	0	1	0	1
COMBAT	combat, to combat, combative	2	1	0	1	0
GAMBIT	gambit	2	2	0	0	0
HAND	hand	2	1	1	0	0
MANOEUVRE	manoeuvre, to manoeuvre	2	1	0	1	0
SURRENDER	surrender, to surrender	2	0	1	1	0
TROOPS	troops	2	1	1	0	0
VICTORY	victory, victorious	2	0	0	2	0
WEAPON	weapon/-ry	2	1	0	1	0
BACKFIRE	to backfire	1	0	0	0	1
BRUTALITY	brutality, brutal	1	0	0	1	0
CHEAT	cheat, to cheat	1	0	0	1	0
CONQUEROR	conqueror/conquest, to conquer	1	0	1	0	0
CUT-THROAT	cut-throat	1	0	1	0	0
DEFEAT	defeat, to defeat	1	1	0	0	0
ENDGAME	endgame	1	1	0	0	0
JACKPOT	jackpot	1	0	0	1	0
LEAGUE	league	1	0	0	0	1
OPENING	opening	1	1	0	0	0
PAWN	pawn	1	1	0	0	0
POKER	poker, to poker, pokerfaced	1	0	0	1	0
TIME-OUT	time-out	1	1	0	0	0
Totals		**845**	**281**	**145**	**192**	**227**
		100%	**33.25%**	**17.16%**	**22.72%**	**26.86%**

Note: No relevant metaphoric occurrences of ace, to beleaguer, blank, breathless, casino, checkmate, chess, coach/to coach, to deal, die/to dice, to double down, draw/to draw, to dribble, foul/to foul/foul, full house, grand slam, joker, lottery, match, pass/to pass, piker, pole position, raffle/to raffle, red/yellow card, roulette, to shuffle, soldier/soldierly, volley, winning/losing streak.

Table A.2 Metaphoric expressions in marketing and sales corpus per word class

Lemma	Lexeme	Total	Word class		
			Noun (56.18%*)	Verb (29.90%*)	Adjective/adverb (13.92%*)
CAMPAIGN	campaign/campaigner, to campaign	152	99NN, 51NNS/1NNS	1VBZ	–
LAUNCH	launch, to launch, pre-/post-launch	127	33NN, 5NNS	20VB, 21VBD, 15VBG, 27VBN, 4VBZ	2JJ
TARGET	target, to target	89	27NN, 11NNS	15VB, 13VBG, 19VBN, 4VBZ	–
PLAY	play/player, to out/play, playful	36	4NN/1NN, 14NNS	8VB, 5VBG, 3VBN, 1VBZ	0
BATTLE	battle/-field/-ground, to battle, embattled	28	18NN, 1NNS/0/3NN	1VB, 2VBG, 1VBZ	2JJ
WAR	war/warfare/warrior, warlike/warring	26	11NN, 10NNS/2NN/1NN, 1NNS	–	1JJ
FIGHT	fight/-er, to fight	24	7NN/1NNS	3VB, 10VBG, 2VBN, 1VBZ	–
GAME	gambler/game, to gamble	21	17NN, 3NNS/0	1VBG	–
SURVIVAL	survival/survivor, to survive	21	4NN/1NNS	12VB, 2VBG, 2VBN	–
BET	bet, to bet	18	10NN	2VB, 6VBG	–
JUMP	jump, to jump	18	1NN	8VB, 5VBD, 3VBG, 1VBN	–
ARMS	arms (weapons)/armour/army, to arm	16	3NNS/0/2NN, 2NNS	1VBG, 8VBN	–

GOAL	goal	16	12NN, 4NNS	—	—
KILLER	killer/killing, to kill	15	5NN/1NN	3VB, 3VBG, 2VBD, 1VBN	—
FAST	fast	14	—	—	3JJ, 11RB
FAIRNESS	fairness, un/fair	13	1NN	—	12JJ
BLITZ	blitz, to blitz	12	7NN, 1NNS	1VB, 1VBD, 2VBN	—
RUN	run/runner, to run, runaway	10	2NN, 1NNS/1NNS	1VB, 2VBG, 1VN	2JJ
RACE	race, to race, racy	9	7NN	1VBN, 1VBZ	0
SPEED	speed, to speed, speedy	9	3NN	5VB, 1VBG	0
CATCH	catch, to catch	8	1NN	4VB, 1VBD, 2VBG	—
FIERCE	fierce	8	—	—	7JJ, 1RB
THROW	throw, to throw	8	1NN	3VB, 2VBG, 2VBN	—
BOMB	bomb/-shell, to bomb/bombard	7	1NN/0	1VB, 1VBG/3VBN, 1VBZ	—
SCORE	score, to score	7	1NNS	2VB, 2VBD, 1VBN, 1VBZ	—
SHOOT	shootout/shot/-gun, to shoot	7	0/4NN, 1NNS/0	1VB, 1VBN	—
TIRE	to tire, tired/tireless/tiresome	7	—	2VB	1JJ/1JJ/3JJ
TRENCH	trench, to en/retrench	7	1NN	5VBN/1VBG	—
FIELD	field, to field	5	4NN	1VBD	—
FRONT	front	5	5NN	—	—
STAKES	stakes	5	5NNS	—	—
ASSAULT	assault, to assault	4	3NN	1VBG	—
BRUISE	bruise, to bruise	4	1NNS	3VBG	—
CHAMPION	champion, to champion	4	1NN	1VB, 1VBG, 1VBN	—
CHIP	chip	4	3NN, 1NNS	—	—
HEAD-TO-HEAD	head-to-head	4	—	—	1JJ, 3RB
PUNCH	punch, to punch	4	4NN	0	—
RIP	rip-off, to rip off	4	1NN	2VB, 1VBN	—
TRUMP	trump, to trump	4	2NN	2VB	—

Table A.2 Continued

Lemma	Lexeme	Total	Word class		
			Noun (56.18%*)	Verb (29.90%*)	Adjective/adverb (13.92%*)
VETERAN	veteran	4	2NN, 2NNS	–	–
ATTACK	attack, to attack	3	1NN, 1NNS	1VBD	–
CARD	card	3	1NN, 2NNS	–	–
ENEMY	enemy, inimical	3	1NN, 2NNS	–	0
GUARD	to guard	3	–	1VB, 2VBN	–
KICK	kick-off, to kick off	3	1NN	1VB, 1VBD	–
LUCK	luck, lucky	3	0	–	3JJ
PACK	pack	3	3NN	–	–
TURF	turf	3	3NN	–	–
BALL	ball	2	2NN	–	–
BANKROLL	bankroll, to bankroll	2	0	1VB, 1VBG	–
BLOOD	blood, to bleed, bloody	2	1NN	0	1JJ
CASUALTY	casualty	2	1NN, 1NNS	–	–
COMBAT	combat, to combat, combative	2	2NN	0	0
GAMBIT	gambit	2	2NN	–	–
HAND	hand	2	1NN, 1NNS	–	–
MANOEUVRE	manoeuvre, to manoeuvre	2	2NN	0	–
SURRENDER	surrender, to surrender	2	0	1VB, 1VBN	–
TROOPS	troops	2	2NNS	–	–
VICTORY	victory, victorious	2	2NN	–	0
WEAPON	weapon/-ry	2	2NN/0	–	–

BACKFIRE	to backfire	1		—	1VB		—
BRUTALITY	brutality, brutal	1	0			1JJ	—
CHEAT	cheat, to cheat	1	1NN	—	0		—
CONQUEROR	conqueror/conquest, to conquer	1	0/1NN		0		—
CUT-THROAT	cut-throat	1	1NN			1JJ	—
DEFEAT	defeat, to defeat	1	0	—	1VBD		—
ENDGAME	endgame	1	1NN				—
JACKPOT	jackpot	1	1NN				—
LEAGUE	league	1	1NN				—
OPENING	opening	1	1NN				—
PAWN	pawn	1	1NNS				—
POKER	poker, to poker, pokerfaced	1	0		0	1RB	—
TIME-OUT	time-out	1	1NN	—			—
Totals		845	475		313	57	
		100%	56.21%		37.04%	6.75%	

Notes: No relevant metaphoric occurrences of ace, to beleaguer, blank, breathless, casino, checkmate, chess, coach/to coach, to deal, die/to dice, to double down, draw/to draw, to dribble, foul/to foul/foul, full house, grand slam, joker, lottery, match, pass/to pass, piker, pole position, raffle/to raffle, red/yellow card, roulette, to shuffle, soldier/soldierly, volley, winning/losing streak. Zero value (0) indicates that the corpus was not scanned for a particular lemma. A dash indicates that instances were looked for but not found in the corpus. Abbreviations are taken from the Bank of English tag set: NN = singular noun, NNS = plural noun; VB = verb base form, VBD = past tense, VBG = -ING form, VBN = past participle, VBZ = 3rd person singular present; JJ = adjective; RB = adverb. *percentage in lexical fields.

Table A.3 Alternative metaphoric expressions in marketing and sales corpus

Lemma	Lexeme	Total	Publication				Word class		
			BW	EC	FO	FT	Noun (55.88%*)	Verb (20.59%*)	Adjective/adverb (23.55%*)
WOOER	wooer, to woo	9	8	1	0	0	0	6VB, 1VBD, 2VBG	–
LOVE	love/lover, to love, lovable	8	2	2	3	1	2NN/ 1NNS	4VB, 1VBD	0
DESIRE	desire, to desire, desirable	6	2	0	0	4	2NN, 3NNS	1VBN	0
FRIEND	friend/friendship, friendly	5	0	1	0	4	3NNS/1NN	–	1JJ
FAMILY	family	4	0	3	0	1	4NN	–	–
HEART	heart	3	2	0	1	0	1NN, 2NNS	–	–
COURT	courtship, to court, courtly	2	1	0	1	0	0	1VB, 1VBG	0

EMBRACE	embrace, to embrace	2	0	0	1	1	0	2VB	–
AFFAIR	affair	1	0	1	0	0	1NN	–	–
AFFECTION	affection, affectionate	1	0	1	0	0	1NNS	–	0
FAITHFUL	faithful	1	0	1	0	0	–	–	1JJ
LUST	lust, to lust, lustful	1	1	0	0	0	1NN	0	0
MARRIAGE	marriage, to marry	1	1	0	0	0	0	1VB	–
SEX	sex, sexual/sexy	1	0	1	0	0	0	0	1JJ
WIFE	wife	1	0	0	0	1	1NN	–	–
Totals		**46**	**17**	**11**	**6**	**12**	**23**	**20**	**3**
		100%	36.96%	23.91%	13.04%	26.09%	50%	43.48%	6.52%

Notes: No relevant metaphoric occurrences of arms (body part), altar, bed/-fellow, bride/bridegroom/bridal, consummation/to consummate, dalliance/to dally, divorce/to divorce, fiancé(e), flirt/flirtation/to flirt/flirtatious/flirty, honeymoon, husband, infatuation/infatuated, kiss/to kiss, mate/to mate, nuptials/nuptial, passion/passionate, romance/romantic, spouse, suitor, wedding/to wed.
Zero value (0) indicates that instances were looked for but not found in the corpus. A dash indicates that the corpus was not scanned for a particular lemma. Abbreviations are taken from the Bank of English tag set: NN = singular noun, NNS = plural noun; VB = verb base form, VBD = past tense, VBG = -ING form, VBN = past participle, VBZ = 3rd person singular present; JJ = adjective; RB = adverb.
*percentage in lexical field.

Corpus B (Mergers and acquisitions)

(a) Business Week

MA BW 1   Barrett, A., Licking, E. and Carey, J., 'Addicted to mergers?', *Business Week*, 6 December 1999. Available at: http://www.businessweek. com/@@yyyCnIcQ0bJxkwcA/archives/1999/b3658148.arc.htm. Accessed 22 August 2002.

MA BW 2   Bremner, B., 'This hybrid is looking plenty tough', *Business Week*, 3 April 2000. Available at: http://www.businessweek.com/ @@5EQj4IcQzrJxkwcA/archives/2000/b3675168.arc.htm. Accessed 2 August 2002.

MA BW 3   Capell, K., 'Diageo hits the bottle', *Business Week*, 31 July 2000. Available at: http://www.businessweek.com/ @@th6*4YcQtbJxkwcA/archives/2000/b3692157.arc.htm. Accessed 22 August 2002.

MA BW 4   Capell, K. and Baker, S., 'Vodafone's power play', *Business Week*, 29 November 1999. Available at: http://www.businessweek.com/ @@Ye77nYcQvrJxkwcA/archives/1999/b3657017.arc.htm. Accessed 22 August 2002.

MA BW 5   Crockett, R. O., 'The single life may not agree with Sprint', *Business Week*, 31 July 2000. Available at: http://www.businessweek.com/ @@5EQj4IcQzrJxkwcA/archives/2000/b3692067.arc.htm. Accessed 22 August 2002.

MA BW 6   Edmondson, G., 'Spanish banks are scaling the Pyrenees', *Business Week*, 29 November 1999. Available at: http://www.businessweek. com/@@ulIJS4cQtLJxkwcA/archives/1999/b3657254.arc.htm. Accessed 22 August 2002.

MA BW 7   Elstrom, P., 'George Bell: the year of living painfully', *Business Week*, 3 April 2000. Available at: http://www.businessweek. com/@@G6D7PocQv7JxkwcA/archives/2000/b3675029.arc.htm. Accessed 22 August 2002.

MA BW 8   Fairlamb, D., 'Coming soon: Europe's first $1 trillion bank?', *Business Week*, 1 November 1999. Available at: http://www. businessweek.com/@@m9PKq4cQt7JxkwcA/archives/1999/ b3653219.arc.htm. Accessed 22 August 2002.

MA BW 9   Fairlamb, D., 'A Swedish surprise', *Business Week*, 11 September 2000. Available at: http://www.businessweek.com/ @@0VdUDYcQ1LJxkwcA/archives/2000/b3698224.arc.htm. Accessed 22 August 2002.

MA BW 10   Katz, I., 'Brazil's breweries: the more mergers the merrier?', *Business Week*, 27 March 2000. Available at: http://www.businessweek.com/ @@@OMz*IcQtrJxkwcA/archives/2000/b3674248.arc.htm. Accessed 22 August 2002.

MA BW 11   Lowry, T., 'AOL Time Warner: the thrill is gone', *Business Week*, 16 October 2000. Available at: http://www.businessweek.com/ @@@OMz*IcQtrJxkwcA/archives/2000/b3703138.arc.htm. Accessed 22 August 2002.

MA BW 12   Marcial, G. G., 'Goldman & Schwab?', *Business Week*, 2 October 2000. Available at: http://www.businessweek.com/

@@G6D7PocQv7JxkwcA/archives/2000/b3701156.arc.htm. Accessed 22 August 2002.

MA BW 13   Matlack, C., 'The raiders are coming! The raiders are coming!', *Business Week*, 24 April 2000, p. 20.

MA BW 14   Muller, J., 'DaimlerChrysler: your turn to drive, Mr. Holden', *Business Week*, 29 November 1999. Available at: http://www.businessweek.com/@@P6vzv4cQybJxkwcA/archives/1999/b3657203.arc.htm. Accessed 22 August 2002.

MA BW 15   Reed, S. and Matlack, C., 'The big grab', *Business Week*, 14 January 2000. Available at: http://www.businessweek.com/@@G6VTxocQ4LBxkwcA/2000/00_04/b3665092.htm. Accessed 27 August 2003.

MA BW 16   Shari, M., 'If you can't beat 'em . . .', *Business Week*, 7 February 2000, pp. 22–3.

MA BW 17   Siklos, R., 'The talented Ms. Redstone', *Business Week*, 3 April 2000. Available at: http://www.businessweek.com/@@yyyCnIcQ0bJxkwcA/archives/2000/b3675178.arc.htm. Accessed 22 August 2002.

MA BW 18   Siklos, R. and Grover, R., 'Bronfman and Diller: together forever?', *Business Week*, 18 September 2000. Available at: http://www.businessweek.com/@@th6*4YcQtbJxkwcA/archives/2000/b3669076.arc.htm. Accessed 22 August 2002.

MA BW 19   Siklos, R. and Yang, C., 'Welcome to the 21st century', *Business Week*, 24 January 2000. Available at: http://www.businessweek.com/@@@pYqI4cQz7JxkwcA/archives/2000/b3665001.arc.htm. Accessed 22 August 2002.

MA BW 20   Sparks, D., 'Those sexy consultants', *Business Week*, 21 February 2000. Available at: http://www.businessweek.com/@@72vCB4cQzbJxkwcA/archives/2000/b3669120.arc.htm. Accessed 22 August 2002.

MA BW 21   Thornton, E., 'Auto alliances in Japan: foreign buyers beware', *Business Week*, 27 March 2000. Available at: http://www.businessweek.com/@@AqsDnIcQ5rBxkwcA/2000/00_13/b3674233.htm. Accessed 14 September 2003.

MA BW 22   Thornton, E., 'It's open season at DLJ', *Business Week*, 23 October 2000. Available at: http://www.businessweek.com/@@@pYqI4cQz7JxkwcA/archives/2000/b3704218.arc.htm. Accessed 22 August 2002.

MA BW 23   Thornton, E., 'J. P. Morgan: dressed for a deal?', *Business Week*, 18 September 2000. Available at: http://www.businessweek.com/@@ZiAuR4cQ5bBxkwcA/2000/00_38/b3699254.htm. Accessed 14 September 2003.

MA BW 24   Tierney, C., Karnitschnig, M. and Muller, J., 'Defiant Daimler', *Business Week*, 18 September 2000. Available at: http://www.businessweek.com/@@49V*1YcQy7JxkwcA/archives/2000/b3693010.arc.htm. Accessed 2 August 2002.

MA BW 25   Timmons, H., 'Can the Wells Fargo wagon roll alone?', *Business Week*, 23 October 2000. Available at: http://www.businessweek.com/@@REXVBIcQs7JxkwcA/archives/2000/b3704216.arc.htm. Accessed 22 August 2002.

MA BW 26   Timmons, H., 'The chase to become a financial supermarket', *Business Week*, 25 September 2000. Available at: http://www.businessweek.com/@@@OMz*IcQtrJxkwcA/archives/2000/b3700063.arc.htm. Accessed 22 August 2002.

MA BW 27   Weiss, G., 'Tiger is licking its wounds', *Business Week*, 13 March 2000. Available at: http://www.businessweek.com/@@jSh7r4cQ07JxkwcA/archives/2000/b3672123.arc.htm. Accessed 22 August 2002.

MA BW 28   Willen, L., 'Go to the head of the class', *Business Week*, 3 April 2000. Available at: http://www.businessweek.com/@@ulIJS4cQtLJxkwcA/archives/2000/b3675159.arc.htm. Accessed 22 August 2002.

MA BW 29   Yang, C., 'Cutting AOL Time Warner down to size', *Business Week*, 18 September 2000. Available at: http://www.businessweek.com/@@yyyCnIcQ0bJxkwcA/archives/2000/b3699205.arc.htm. Accessed 22 August 2002.

(b) The Economist

MA EC 1   'Altogether', *The Economist*, 14 August 1999, p. 54.

MA EC 2   'Ambivalent', *The Economist*, 7 October 2000, pp. 93–4.

MA EC 3   'Andersen's android wars', *The Economist*, 12 August 2000, p. 72.

MA EC 4   'Barbarians at the gate', *The Economist*, 3 April 1999, pp. 55–6.

MA EC 5   'The battle for the last mile', *The Economist*, 1 May 1999, pp. 63–4.

MA EC 6   'Beating a retreat', *The Economist*, 16 September 2000, pp. 102–4.

MA EC 7   'Bid blockers', *The Economist*, 19 December 1998, pp. 108, 111.

MA EC 8   'BMW's British bruises', *The Economist*, 5 December 1998, pp. 78–9.

MA EC 9   'Building a new Boeing', *The Economist*, 12 August 2000, pp. 69–70.

MA EC 10   'Chase's morganatic marriage', *The Economist*, 16 September 2000, p. 24.

MA EC 11   'Clinched?', *The Economist*, 5 February 2000, pp. 65–6.

MA EC 12   'Crossing Rubicam', *The Economist*, 6 May 2000, pp. 67, 70.

MA EC 13   'The DaimlerChrysler emulsion', *The Economist*, 29 July 2000, pp. 69–70.

MA EC 14   'Devalued', *The Economist*, 7 October 2000, pp. 88, 93.

MA EC 15   'Drug-induced seizures', *The Economist*, 13 November 1999, p. 18.

MA EC 16   'Europe's merger morass', *The Economist*, 23 September 2000, pp. 85–6.

MA EC 17   'A fight to the wire', *The Economist*, 27 November 1999, pp. 75–6.

MA EC 18   'First among equals', *The Economist*, 26 August 2000, pp. 63–4.

MA EC 19   'Food fights', *The Economist*, 6 May 2000, p. 67.

MA EC 20   'Forced friendship in South Korea', *The Economist*, 8 August 1998, p. 66.

MA EC 21   'French fusion', *The Economist*, 4 September 1999, pp. 67–8.

MA EC 22   'Going for broke', *The Economist*, 16 September 2000, p. 88.

MA EC 23   'Goldman Sachs, traders', *The Economist*, 16 September 2000, p. 100.

MA EC 24   'Hard pounding', *The Economist*, 4 December 1999, pp. 74, 79.

MA EC 25   'Here we don't go again', *The Economist*, 29 July 2000, pp. 76–7.

MA EC 26   'Hold my hand', *The Economist*, 15 May 1999, pp. 81–2.

MA EC 27   'How mergers go wrong', *The Economist*, 22 July 2000. Available at: http://www.economist.com/editorial/justforyou/current/ld6656. htm. Accessed 28 August 2003.

MA EC 28   'Internet riders', *The Economist*, 28 November 1998, pp. 73–4.

MA EC 29   'Little big men', *The Economist*, 15 May 1999, p. 82.

MA EC 30   'Marital problems', *The Economist*, 14 October 2000, pp. 86, 91.

MA EC 31   'Merger à la française', *The Economist*, 18 September 1999, p. 83.

MA EC 32   'Merging, Japan-style', *The Economist*, 18 March 2000, pp. 84–5.

MA EC 33   'Neighbours from hell', *The Economist*, 4 December 1999, pp. 79–80.

MA EC 34   'The net gets real', *The Economist*, 15 January 2000, pp. 21–3.

MA EC 35   'New media, old message', *The Economist*, 7 October 2000, p. 24.

MA EC 36   'Oil's well that ends well', *The Economist*, 15 August 1998, pp. 49–50.

MA EC 37   'Old-world charm', *The Economist*, 12 June 1999, pp. 69–70.

MA EC 38   'One house, many windows', *The Economist*, 18 August 2000, pp. 68–9.

MA EC 39   'Pfizer's prize', *The Economist*, 12 February 2000, p. 73.

MA EC 40   'Reading the bans', *The Economist*, 19 December 1998, pp. 126, 129.

MA EC 41   'The record industry takes fright', *The Economist*, 29 January 2000, pp. 75–6.

MA EC 42   'Road rage', *The Economist*, 26 February 2000, p. 85.

MA EC 43   'Son of Netscape', *The Economist*, 12 August 2000, pp. 59–60.

MA EC 44   'Too friendly', *The Economist*, 13 November 1999, p. 78.

MA EC 45   'Two sharks in a fishbowl', *The Economist*, 11 September 1999, pp. 73–4.

MA EC 46   'Unconsummated lust', *The Economist*, 9 January 1999, p. 20.

MA EC 47   'Wall Street's old order changes', *The Economist*, 16 September 2000, pp. 99–102.

MA EC 48   'Water with your whisky?', *The Economist*, 17 June 2000, pp. 76, 81.

MA EC 49   'Wireless war', *The Economist*, 9 January 1999, pp. 59–60.

(c) Fortune

MA FO 1   Brown, E., 'Why the FTC needs to chill', *Fortune*, 14 April 1997. Available at: http://www.fortune.com/fortune/articles/0,5114, 378523,00.html. Accessed 9 December 2003.

MA FO 2   Chen, C. Y., 'Gorilla in the midst', *Fortune*, 14 August 2000. Available at: http://www.fortune.com/fortune/investing/articles/0,15114, 373533,0.html. Accessed 11 July 2003.

MA FO 3   Goldblatt, H. and Schwartz, N., 'Telecom in play', *Fortune*, 10 November 1997, pp. 57–60.

MA FO 4   Grant, L., 'Why FedEx is flying high', *Fortune*, 10 November 1997, pp. 86–9.

MA FO 5   Gunther, M., 'CBS is touched by an angel – Viacom', *Fortune*, 4 September 2000, p. 19.

MA FO 6   Guyon, J., 'The emperor and the investment bankers', *Fortune*, 1 May 2000. Available at: http://www.fortune.com/indexw.jhtml?channel= artcol.jhtml&doc_id=00001302. Accessed 23 August 2002.

MA FO 7   Kupfer, A., 'An exciting story about Nynex – really', *Fortune*, 18 March 1996, pp. 40–1.

MA FO 8   Loomis, C. J. and Kupfer, A., 'High noon for John Malone', *Fortune*, 13 January 1997, pp. 40–6.

MA FO 9   Mardesich, J., 'The merger and MP3s', *Fortune*, 12 January 2000. Available at: http://www.fortune.com/indexw.jhtml?channel= artcol.jhtml&doc_id=37353. Accessed 23 August 2002.

MA FO 10   Martin, J. and Goode, D., 'Surviving a head-on collison', *Fortune*, 14 April 1997. Available at: http://www.fortune.com/fortune/ articles/0,15114,380110,00.html. Accessed 9 December 2003.

MA FO 11   McLean, B., 'An urge to merge', *Fortune*, 13 January 1997, pp. 78–9.

MA FO 12   McLean, B., 'Washington Mutual's remarkable rise', *Fortune*, 8 December 1997. Available at: http://www.fortune.com/fortune/ articles/0,15114,376168,00.html. Accessed 9 December 2003.

MA FO 13   McLean, B., 'Sprained marriage', *Fortune*, 15 May 2000. Available at: http://www.fortune.com/indexw.jhtml?channel=artcol.jhtml&doc_ id=00001217. Accessed 23 August 2002.

MA FO 14   Mehta, S., 'Dial M for merger', *Fortune*, 28 July 2000. Available at: http://www.fortune.com/indexw.jhtml?channel=artcol. jhtml&doc_id=51185. Accessed 23 August 2002.

MA FO 15   Miller, K., 'How the merger boom will end', *Fortune*, 27 October 1997, pp. 127–8.

MA FO 16   Schlender, B., 'Killer chip', *Fortune*, 10 November 1997, pp. 50–5.

MA FO 17   Sellers, P., 'Don't mess with Darla', *Fortune*, 8 September 1997, pp. 30–6.

MA FO 18   Sellers, P., 'CEO deathmatch!', *Fortune*, 20 March 2000. Available at: http://www.fortune.com/indexw.jhtml?channel=artcol. jhtml&doc_id=00001528. Accessed 23 August 2002.

MA FO 19   Serwer, A., 'Health care stocks: the hidden growth stars', *Fortune*, 14 October 1996. Available at: http://ask.elibrary.com/login.asp. Accessed 23 August 2002.

MA FO 20   Stewart, T. A., 'Owens Corning: back from the dead', *Fortune*, 26 May 1997, pp. 78–82.

MA FO 21   Useem, J., 'Boeing vs. Boeing', *Fortune*, 2 October 2000, pp. 92–102.

MA FO 22   Warner, M., 'How Barry Sternlicht became the king of hotels', *Fortune*, 8 December 1997, pp. 14–16.

(d) Financial Times

MA FT 1   'All change?', *Financial Times*, 17 October 2000. Available at: http://search.ft.com/search/article.html?id=001017001281. Accessed 26 August 2002.

MA FT 2   Barker, T., 'Europe's online groups fail to click', *Financial Times*, 27 October 2000. Available at: http://search.ft.com/search/article. html?id=001027001160. Accessed 26 August 2002.

MA FT 3   'Bigger oil', *Financial Times*, 18 October 2000. Available at: http://search.ft.com/search/article.html?id=001018000667. Accessed 26 August 2002.

MA FT 4   Boland, V., 'Waiting time for groups with an eye on the LSE', *Financial Times*, 17 October 2000. Available at: http://search.ft.com/ search/article.html?id=001017001181. Accessed 26 August 2002.

MA FT 5 Boland, V. *et al.*, 'Deadline looms over OM's bid for LSE', *Financial Times*, 27 October 2000. Available at: http://search.ft.com/search/article.html?id=001027004036. Accessed 26 August 2002.

MA FT 6 'BPI may be open to offers for takeover', *Financial Times*, 30 March 2000. Available at: http://search.ft.com/search/article.html?id=000330000486. Accessed 26 August 2002.

MA FT 7 Burns, T. and Crawford, L., 'Iberdrola agrees to bid from Endesa', *Financial Times*, 18 October 2000. Available at: http://search.ft.com/search/article.html?id=001018000713. Accessed 26 August 2002.

MA FT 8 Burt, T. and Lambert, R., 'The Schrempp gambit', *Financial Times*, 30 October 2000. Available at: http://search.ft.com/search/article.html?id=001030000794. Accessed 26 August 2002.

MA FT 9 'Cadbury-Schweppes has a nibble at some salty snacks', *Financial Times*, 1 July 2000. Available at: http://search.ft.com/search/article.html?id=000701000286. Accessed 22 August 2002.

MA FT 10 Cameron, D., 'Citigroup record profits driven by markets and buoyant M&A', *Financial Times*, 17 October 2000. Available at: http://search.ft.com/search/article.html?id=001017004642. Accessed 26 August 2002.

MA FT 11 Cameron, D. and Hall, W., 'Bank Austria accepts €7bn offer', *Financial Times*, 28 September 2000. Available at: http://search.ft.com/search/article.html?id=000928001370. Accessed 26 August 2002.

MA FT 12 'Cantab confirms approaches', *Financial Times*, 1 November 2000. Available at: http://search.ft.com/search/article.html?id=001101007042. Accessed 26 August 2002.

MA FT 13 'Carl Icahn launches new $1.3bn assault on Nabisco', *Financial Times*, 1 November 2000. Available at: http://search.ft.com/search/article.html?id=000330012942. Accessed 26 August 2002.

MA FT 14 Catan, T., 'LatAm internet portal agrees merger', *Financial Times*, 31 October 2000. Available at: http://search.ft.com/search/article.html?id=001031000613. Accessed 26 August 2002.

MA FT 15 Clifford, Lisa, 'Avesta agrees merger terms without Outokumpu Steel', *Financial Times*, 28 September 2000. Available at: http://search.ft.com/search/article.html?id=000928004804. Accessed 26 August 2002.

MA FT 16 'Commerzbank still on look out for partner', *Financial Times*, 30 March 2000. Available at: http://search.ft.com/search/article.html?id=000330000489. Accessed 26 August 2002.

MA FT 17 Durgin, H., 'Chevron with Texaco may have edge on growth', *Financial Times*, 27 October 2000. Available at: http://search.ft.com/search/article.html?id=001027001112. Accessed 26 August 2002.

MA FT 18 Durgin, H., 'Merger realises size advantage', *Financial Times*, 17 October 2000. Available at: http://search.ft.com/search/article.html?id=001017011321. Accessed 26 August 2002.

MA FT 19 Edgecliff-Johnson, A., 'Honeywell takeover gets mixed reaction', *Financial Times*, 18 October 2000. Available at: http://search.ft.com/search/article.html?id=001021000999. Accessed 26 August 2002.

MA FT 20 George, N. and Taylor, A., 'Vattenfall rejects alliance with Southern Utilities', *Financial Times*, 29 September 2000. Available at:

http://search.ft.com/search/article.html?id=000929000256. Accessed 26 August 2002.

MA FT 21 Grimes, C., 'Primedia agrees to buy internet rival for $690 m', *Financial Times*, 31 October 2000. Available at: http://search.ft.com/search/article.html?id=001031001386. Accessed 26 August 2002.

MA FT 22 Grimes, C. and O'Connor, A., 'Unaggressive auction ends in elevation to global hot spot', *Financial Times*, 28 October 2000. Available at: http://search.ft.com/search/article.html?id=001028000795. Accessed 26 August 2002.

MA FT 23 Guerrera, F., 'British Biotech in drug deal with Swiss group', *Financial Times*, 18 October 2000. Available at: http://search.ft.com/search/article.html?id=001018000783. Accessed 26 August 2002.

MA FT 24 Harding, J. and Grimes, C., 'Bertelsmann and Napster form strategic alliance', *Financial Times*, 31 October 2000. Available at: http://search.ft.com/search/article.html?id=001031009789. Accessed 26 August 2002.

MA FT 25 Harding, J., Hargreaves, D. and Spiegel, P., 'Music groups are forced to change their tune', *Financial Times*, 29 September 2000. Available at: http://search.ft.com/search/article.html?id=000929000307. Accessed 26 August 2002.

MA FT 26 Harnischfeger, U., 'Tax reform puts a dampener on activity', *Financial Times*, 29 September 2000. Available at: http://search.ft.com/search/article.html?id=001023001093. Accessed 26 August 2002.

MA FT 27 Leahy, J., Ibison, D. and Merchant, K., 'JF fights to keep identity in bulge bracket', *Financial Times*, 18 October 2000. Available at: http://search.ft.com/search/article.html?id=001018001694. Accessed 26 August 2002.

MA FT 28 MacCarthy, C., 'Merger creates a national champion', *Financial Times*, 18 October 2000. Available at: http://search.ft.com/search/article.html?id=001031001463. Accessed 26 August 2002.

MA FT 29 Mackintosh, J., 'Abbey looks for European partner', *Financial Times*, 29 September 2000. Available at: http://search.ft.com/search/article.html?id=000929000228. Accessed 26 August 2002.

MA FT 30 Mackintosh, J., 'Harley sees predators lurking', *Financial Times*, 29 September 2000. Available at: http://search.ft.com/search/article.html?id=000929000082. Accessed 26 August 2002.

MA FT 31 Major, T., 'Careful unification of two cultures', *Financial Times*, 30 June 2000. Available at: http://search.ft.com/search/article.html?id=000630000368. Accessed 26 August 2002.

MA FT 32 Major, T. and Willman, J., 'German banks must prevent the blood from flowing', *Financial Times*, 30 June 2000, p. 22.

MA FT 33 Malkani, G. and Pretzlik, C., 'Suitors run careful eye over group's uncertain attractions', *Financial Times*, 27 October 2000. Available at: http://search.ft.com/search/article.html?id=001027001081. Accessed 26 August 2002.

MA FT 34 'Merger speculation in Italy's banking sector', *Financial Times*, 26 January 1998. Available at: http://search.ft.com/search/article.html?id=980126002094. Accessed 26 August 2002.

MA FT 35 Michaels, A., 'AIG shows interest in acquisitions', *Financial Times*, 27 October 2000. Available at: http://search.ft.com/search/article.html?id=001027001175. Accessed 26 August 2002.

MA FT 36 Nakamoto, M. and Waters, R., 'AOL and DoCoMo in PC/internet deal', *Financial Times*, 28 September 2000. Available at: http://search.ft.com/search/article.html?id=000928001387. Accessed 26 August 2002.

MA FT 37 Newing, R., 'Competitors form new alliances', *Financial Times*, 18 October 2000. Available at: http://search.ft.com/search/article.html?id=001018000918. Accessed 26 August 2002.

MA FT 38 'Not every marriage is made in heaven', *Financial Times*, 1 April 2000. Available at: http://search.ft.com/search/article.html?id=000401000349. Accessed 26 August 2002.

MA FT 39 Odell, M., 'Iberia eyes deal for home rival', *Financial Times*, 31 October 2000. Available at: http://search.ft.com/search/article.html?id=001031001303. Accessed 26 August 2002.

MA FT 40 Pilling, D., 'SB and Glaxo continue strong growth', *Financial Times*, 23 October 2000. Available at: http://search.ft.com/search/article.html?id=001101001667. Accessed 26 August 2002.

MA FT 41 Pretzlik, C., 'Foreign institutions gobble up the goodies', *Financial Times*, 23 October 2000. Available at: http://search.ft.com/search/article.html?id=001023001091. Accessed 26 August 2002.

MA FT 42 Pretzlik, C., 'Talent war', *Financial Times*, 30 June 2000. Available at: http://search.ft.com/search/article.html?id=000630000367. Accessed 21 August 2002.

MA FT 43 Pruzan, J., 'Mulling the rush that never came', *Financial Times*, 30 June 2002. Available at: http://search.ft.com/search/article.html?id=000630000374. Accessed 26 August 2002.

MA FT 44 Puranam, P., Singh, H. and Zollo, M., 'Bringing some discipline to M&A mania', *Financial Times*, 30 October 2000. Available at: http://search.ft.com/search/article.html?id=001030003725. Accessed 26 August 2002.

MA FT 45 Ratner, J., 'Global ambitions fuel a takeover boom', *Financial Times*, 30 June 2000. Available at: http://search.ft.com/search/article.html?id=000630000371. Accessed 26 August 2002.

MA FT 46 Ratner, J., 'KKR and Sasol reach end in Condea bid', *Financial Times*, 30 October 2000. Available at: http://search.ft.com/search/article.html?id=001030000828. Accessed 26 August 2002.

MA FT 47 Roberts, D., 'BT still talking to AT&T on business services tie-up', *Financial Times*, 18 October 2000. Available at: http://search.ft.com/search/article.html?id=001018005151. Accessed 26 August 2002.

MA FT 48 'Schroder backs telecoms merger', *Financial Times*, 19 May 1999. Available at: http://search.ft.com/search/article.html?id=990519015250. Accessed 26 August 2002.

MA FT 49 'Self-help', *Financial Times*, 1 Nov. 2000. Available at: http://search.ft.com/search/article.html?id=001101001567. Accessed 26 August 2002.

MA FT 50 Siagol, L., 'BPI bought stake in Macfarlane', *Financial Times*, 30 October 2000. Available at: http://search.ft.com/search/article.html?id=001030000873. Accessed 26 August 2002.

MA FT 51   Siagol, L., 'Nomura emerges with surprise bid for Carlton's Technicolor', *Financial Times*, 1 July 2000. Available at: http://search.ft.com/search/article.html?id=000701000305. Accessed 26 August 2002.

MA FT 52   Silverman, G., 'Team entering a new era', *Financial Times*, 30 June 2000. Available at: http://search.ft.com/search/article.html?id=000630000372. Accessed 26 August 2002.

MA FT 53   'Struggling to stay on target', *Financial Times*, 31 March 2000. Available at: http://search.ft.com/search/article.html?id=000331005103. Accessed 26 August 2002.

MA FT 54   Swann, C., 'The weak will become prey: hostile takeovers', *Financial Times*, 30 June 2000, p. IV.

MA FT 55   Taylor, A., 'Big activity on acquisition front', *Financial Times*, 29 September 2000. Available at: http://search.ft.com/search/article.html?id=000929000416. Accessed 26 August 2002.

MA FT 56   Tett, G., 'Evolution likely, not revolution', *Financial Times*, 30 June 2000. Available at: http://search.ft.com/search/article.html?id=000630000383. Accessed 26 August 2002.

MA FT 57   Tomkins, R., 'Dotcoms devoured', *Financial Times*, 23 October 2000. Available at: http://search.ft.com/search/article.html?id=001023000180. Accessed 14 September 2003.

MA FT 58   'Toy Biz proposes merger with Marvel', *Financial Times*, 8 October 1997. Available at: http://search.ft.com/search/article.html?id=971008002456. Accessed 26 August 2002.

MA FT 59   Tricks, H., 'Cemex buys Southdown for $2.8 bn', *Financial Times*, 30 September 2000. Available at: http://search.ft.com/search/article.html?id=000930001088. Accessed 26 August 2002.

MA FT 60   'Vaccine companies approach Peptide', *Financial Times*, 30 March 2000. Available at: http://search.ft.com/search/article.html?id=000330000454. Accessed 26 August 2002.

MA FT 61   'VAW favourite to win Stade stake', *Financial Times*, 23 October 2000. Available at: http://search.ft.com/search/article.html?id=001023001067. Accessed 26 August 2002.

MA FT 62   Ward, A., 'Dating agency trio plans to make beautiful music', *Financial Times*, 1 July 2000. Available at: http://search.ft.com/search/article.html?id=000701000304. Accessed 26 August 2002.

MA FT 63   'When culture masks communication', *Financial Times*, 23 October 2000. Available at: http://search.ft.com/search/article.html?id=001023000928. Accessed 26 August 2002.

MA FT 64   Wiggins, J., 'Comerica to buy Imperial Bancorp for $1.3 bn in stock', *Financial Times*, 1 November 2000. Available at: http://search.ft.com/search/article.html?id=001101009072. Accessed 26 August 2002.

Table A.4 Metaphoric expressions in mergers and acquisitions corpus per publication

Lemma	Lexeme	Total	Publication			
			BW	EC	FO	FT
TARGET	target, to target	91	24	10	5	52
HOSTILITY	hostility, hostile	71	14	27	5	25
BATTLE	battle/-field/-ground, to battle, embattled	49	25	12	7	5
WAR	war/warfare/warrior, warlike/warring	36	16	5	8	7
DEFENCE	defence, to defend, defensive	34	9	13	0	12
MARRIAGE	marriage, to marry	34	10	16	3	5
FIGHT	fight/-er, to fight	30	5	10	10	5
RELATIONSHIP	relationship	20	7	5	3	5
PREDATOR	predator, predatory	18	4	9	0	5
RAID	raid/raider, to raid	18	12	1	3	2
SURVIVAL	survival/survivor, to survive	17	4	6	3	4
VULNERABILITY	vulnerability, vulnerable	14	4	7	0	3
ATTACK	attack, to attack	12	5	3	2	2
VICTORY	victory, victorious	12	2	5	4	1
SUITOR	suitor	11	6	2	0	3
SHOOT	shootout/shot/-gun, to shoot	10	4	1	5	0
COURT	court/-ship, to court, courtly	9	1	3	3	2
DIGESTION	in/digestion, to digest, digestible	9	2	1	2	4
FIERCE	fierce	9	1	3	4	1
GOBBLE	to gobble (up)	8	1	4	2	1
TROOPS	troops	8	6	0	2	0
BED	bed/-fellow	7	0	6	0	1
DEFEAT	defeat, to defeat	7	2	4	0	1
KILLER	killer/killing, to kill	7	1	1	5	0
SWALLOW	to swallow	7	3	2	2	0

Table A.4 Continued

Lemma	Lexeme	Total	Publication			
			BW	EC	FO	FT
PREY	prey, to prey (up)on	7	2	1	1	3
ARMS	arms (body part)	6	1	4	1	0
ARMS	arms (weapons)/armour/army, to arm	6	0	3	3	0
BRUISE	bruise, to bruise	6	3	1	2	0
AFFAIR	affair	5	2	3	0	0
ASSAULT	assault, to assault	5	1	0	0	4
BLOOD	blood, to bleed, bloody	5	0	2	0	3
DESIRE	desire, to desire, desirable	5	0	1	1	3
ENEMY	enemy, inimical	5	0	2	1	2
LOVE	love/lover, to love, lovable	5	1	2	2	0
SEX	sex, sexual/sexy	5	2	1	2	0
APPETITE	appetite/-izer	4	1	1	1	1
BRUTALITY	brutality, brutal	4	2	1	0	1
COMBAT	combat, to combat, combative	4	2	0	1	1
VETERAN	veteran	4	2	0	2	0
VICTIM	victim	4	0	2	1	1
WOOER	wooer, to woo	4	2	0	2	0
ALTAR	altar	3	1	2	0	0
DIVORCE	divorce	3	1	2	0	0
FLIRT	flirt/-ation, to flirt, flirtatious/flirty	3	0	3	0	0
FRONT	front	3	0	0	3	0
GREED	greed, greedy	3	0	3	0	0
KISS	kiss, to kiss	3	0	0	3	0
MATE	mate, to mate	3	1	2	0	0
BELEAGUER	to beleaguer	2	0	1	1	0

		686 100%	202 29.45%	203 29.59%	109 15.89%	172 25.07%
CONSUMMATION	consummation, to consummate	2	1	1	0	0
DALLIANCE	dalliance, to dally	2	0	2	0	0
HUNGER	hunger, to hunger, hungry	2	0	0	1	1
LUST	lust, to lust, lustful	2	1	1	0	0
MANOEUVRE	manoeuvre, to manoeuvre	2	1	0	1	0
NUPTIALS	nuptials, nuptial	2	0	1	0	1
SURRENDER	surrender, to surrender	2	0	1	0	1
WEDDING	wedding, to wed	2	1	1	0	0
AFFECTION	affection, affectionate	1	0	1	0	0
BITE	bite, to bite	1	0	0	0	1
BOMB	bomb/-shell, to bomb/bombard	1	1	0	0	0
CASUALTY	casualty	1	0	0	1	0
CONQUEROR	conqueror/conquest, to conquer	1	0	0	0	1
DEVOUR	to devour	1	0	0	0	1
FOOD	feeder/food, to feed	1	1	0	0	0
GULP	gulp, to gulp	1	1	0	0	0
JUICY	juicy	1	0	1	0	0
NIBBLE	nibble, to nibble	1	0	0	0	1
PALATABLE	un/palatable	1	1	0	0	0
ROMANCE	romance, romantic	1	0	1	0	0
SOLDIER	soldier, soldierly	1	1	0	0	0
SPIT	to spit out	1	1	0	0	0
WEAPON	weapon/-ry	1	0	0	1	0
Totals		686 100%	202 29.45%	203 29.59%	109 15.89%	172 25.07%

Note: No relevant metaphoric occurrences of *to backfire, bride/-groom/bridal, chew, course, delicious, diet/to diet/dietary, dinner/to dine, dish, eat/(un)eatable, (in)edible, embrace/to embrace, faithful, feast/to feast, fiancé(e), glutton/-y/gluttonous, to gorge, helping, honeymoon, husband, infatuation/infatuated, maiden (n.), meal, morsel, nourishment/to nourish, passion/passionate, rape/to rape, ravenous, (in)satiable, spouse, starvation/to starve, taste/tasting/to taste/tasty, wife.*

Table A.5 Metaphoric expressions in mergers and acquisitions corpus per word class

Lemma	Lexeme	Total	Noun (52.43%*)	Word class Verb (26.70%*)	Adjective/adverb (20.87%*)
TARGET	target, to target	91	56NN, 25NNS	1VB, 2VBG, 5VBN, 2VBZ	–
HOSTILITY	hostility, hostile	71	8NN, 1NNS	–	62JJ
BATTLE	battle/-field/-ground, to battle, embattled	49	38NN, 7NNS/1NN/2NN	1VBG	0
WAR	war/warfare/warrior, warlike/warring	36	23NN, 10NNS/2NN/1NN	–	0/0
DEFENCE	defence/defender, to defend, defensive	34	10NN, 4NNS/0, 1NNS	4VB, 1VBD, 4VBG, 1VBN	9JJ
MARRIAGE	marriage, to marry	34	27NN, 3NNS	2VB, 1VBD, 1VBG	
FIGHT	fight/-er, to fight	30	12NN, 2NNS/0NN	5VB, 2VBD, 7VBG, 1VBN, 1VBZ	
RELATIONSHIP	relationship	20	14NN, 6NNS	–	–
PREDATOR	predator, predatory	18	7NN, 10NNS	–	1JJ
RAID	raid/raider, to raid	18	2NN, 1NNS/4NN, 10NNS	1VBG	–
SURVIVAL	survival/survivor, to survive	17	2NN/5NN	7VB, 1VBG, 1VBN, 1VBZ	–
VULNERABILITY	vulnerability, vulnerable	14	0	–	14JJ
ATTACK	attack, to attack	12	2NN, 1NNS	3VB, 2VBD, 2VBG, 2VBN	–
VICTORY	victory, victorious	12	11NN, 1NNS	–	0
SUITOR	suitor	11	8NN, 3NNS	–	–

Keyword	Gloss	Freq			
SHOOT	shot/-gun/shootout, to shoot	10	2NN/3NN/1NN	2VB, 2VBZ	–
COURT	court/-ship, to court, courtly	9	2NN/2NN, 3NNS	0	2JJ
DIGESTION	in/digestion, to digest, digestible	9	1NN	2VB, 5VBG, 1VBN	0
FIERCE	fierce	9	–	–	6JJ, 3RB
GOBBLE	to gobble (up)	8	–	3VB, 1VBD, 2VBG, 2VBN	–
TROOPS	troops	8	8NNS	–	–
BED	bed/-fellow	7	6NN/1NNS	–	–
DEFEAT	defeat, to defeat	7	3NN	1VB, 1VBG, 2VBN	–
KILLER	killer/killing, to kill	7	2NN/0	4VB, 1VBG	–
PREY	prey, to prey (up)on	7	7NN	0	–
SWALLOW	to swallow	7	–	3VB, 1VBD, 3VBN	–
ARMS	arms (body part)	6	1NN, 5NNS	–	–
ARMS	arms (weapons)/armour/-y, to arm	6	4NN	1VBG, 1VBN	–
BRUISE	bruise, to bruise	6	1NNS	4VBG, 1VBN	–
AFFAIR	affair	5	1NN, 4NNS	–	–
ASSAULT	assault, to assault	5	5NN	0	–
BLOOD	blood, to bleed, bloody	5	5NN	0	0
DESIRE	desire, to desire, desirable	5	3NN	0	2JJ
ENEMY	enemy, inimical	5	4NN, 1NNS	–	0
LOVE	love/lover, to love, lovable	5	5NN	–	0
SEX	sex, sexual/sexy	5	1NN	–	4JJ/0
APPETITE	appetite/-izer, appetizing	4	3NN, 1NNS	–	0

Table A.5 Continued

Lemma	Lexeme	Total	Word class		
			Noun (52.43%*)	Verb (26.70%*)	Adjective/adverb (20.87%*)
BRUTALITY	brutality, brutal	4	0	–	4JJ
COMBAT	combat, to combat, combative	4	1NN	2VB	1JJ
VETERAN	veteran	4	1NN, 3NNS	–	–
VICTIM	victim	4	2NN, 2NNS	–	–
WOOER	wooer, to woo	4	0	3VB, 1VBN	–
ALTAR	altar	3	3NN	0	–
DIVORCE	divorce, to divorce	3	3NN	–	–
FLIRT	flirt/-ation, to flirt, flirtatious/flirty	3	2NN	1VBG	0/0
FRONT	front	3	1NN, 2NNS	–	–
GREED	greed, greedy	3	2NN	–	1RB
KISS	kiss, to kiss	3	3NNS	0	–
MATE	mate, to mate	3	2NN	1VBG	–
BELEAGUER	to beleaguer	2	–	2VBN	–
CONSUMMATION	consummation, to consummate	2	0	1VB, 1VBN	–
DALLIANCE	dalliance, to dally	2	1NN	1VBG	–
HUNGER	hunger, to hunger, hungry	2	0	0	2JJ
LUST	lust, to lust, lustful	2	1NN	1VBZ	0
MANOEUVRE	manoeuvre, to manoeuvre	2	1NN	1VBG	–

Lexical field	Lemma(s)	n	NN/NNS	VB	JJ
NUPTIALS	nuptials, nuptial	2	2NNS	—	0
SURRENDER	surrender, to surrender	2	1NN	1VBD	—
WEDDING	wedding, to wed	2	1NNS	1VBN	0
AFFECTION	affection, affectionate	1	1NNS	—	—
BITE	bite, to bite	1	1NN	0	—
BOMB	bomb/-shell, to bomb/bombard	1	0/1NN	0	—
CASUALTY	casualty	1	1NNS	—	—
CONQUEROR	conqueror/conquest, to conquer	1	0/1NN	0	—
DEVOUR	to devour	1	—	1VBN	—
FOOD	food/feeder, to feed	1	0	1VB	—
GULP	gulp, to gulp	1	1NN	0	—
JUICY	juicy	1	—	—	1JJ
NIBBLE	nibble, to nibble	1	1NN	0	—
PALATABLE	un/palatable	1	—	—	0/1JJ
ROMANCE	romance, romantic	1	1NN	—	0
SOLDIER	soldier, soldierly	1	1NNS	—	0
SPIT	to spit out	1	—	1VBG	—
WEAPON	weapon/-ry	1	1NN/0	—	—
Totals		**686** **100%**	**449** **65.45%**	**124** **18.08%**	**113** **16.47%**

Notes: No relevant metaphoric occurrences of to backfire, bride/-groom/bridal, to chew, course, delicious, diet/to diet/dietary, dinner/to dine, dish, eat/(un)eatable, (in)edible, embrace/to embrace, faithful, feast/to feast, fiancé(e), glutton/-y/gluttonous, to gorge, helping, honeymoon, husband, infatuation/infatuated, maiden (n.), meal, morsel, nourishment/to nourish, passion/passionate, rape/to rape, ravenous, (in)satiable, spouse, starvation/to starve, taste/tasting/to taste/tasty, wife.

Zero value (0) indicates that instances were looked for but not found in the corpus. A dash indicates that the corpus was not scanned for a particular lemma. Abbreviations are taken from the Bank of English tag set: NN = singular noun, NNS = plural noun; VB = verb base form, VBD = past tense, VBG = -ING form, VBN = past participle, VBZ = 3rd person singular present; JJ = adjective; RB = adverb.

*percentage in lexical fields.

Table A.6 Additional metaphoric expressions in mergers and acquisitions corpus

Lemma	Lexeme	Total	Publication				Word class		
			BW	EC	FO	FT	Noun (59.65%*)	Verb (14.03%*)	Adjective/adverb (26.31%*)
EMPIRE	empire/emperor/empress, imperial/imperious	21	9	8	4	0	14NN, 4NNS/1NN/0	–	0/2JJ
CHIEF	chief/chieftain	13	4	1	8	0	9NN, 3NNS/1NNS	–	–
TERRITORY	territory, territorial	8	1	1	4	2	6NN, 2NNS	–	0
COUP	coup	7	1	3	2	1	7NN	–	–
KING	king/kingdom	7	2	0	5	0	7NN/0	–	–
COURT	court/courtier, courtly	5	1	0	4	0	3NN/0	–	2JJ
MOGUL	mogul	4	1	2	1	0	3NN, 1NNS	–	–
ARISTOCRACY	aristocracy, aristocratic	3	0	3	0	0	0	–	3JJ
BOUNDARY	boundary	3	1	1	1	0	2NN, 1NNs	–	–
QUEEN	queen	3	0	0	3	0	3NN	–	–

RULE	rule/ruler, to rule	3	2	0	1	0	0	2VB, 1VBN	–
HEIR	heir/heiress apparent	2	0	1	0	1	2NN/0	–	–
CROWN	crown, to crown	1	0	1	0	0	1NN	0	0
PRINCE	prince/princess, princely	1	0	0	1	0	1NN/0	–	0
REALM	realm	1	0	0	1	0	1NN	–	–
REGALIA	regalia, regal	1	0	0	1	0	0	–	1RB
THRONE	throne, to enthrone/dethrone	1	0	0	1	0	1NN	0	–
Totals		**84** 100%	**22** 26.19%	**21** 25%	**37** 44.05%	**4** 4.76%	**73** 86.9%	**3** 3.57%	**8** 9.52%

Notes: No relevant metaphoric occurrences of abdication/to abdicate, border/to border/cross-border, caesar/caesarian (adj.), colony/to colonize, czar, highness, lady, lord, majesty/majestic, monarch/monarchic, reign/to reign, royal, sceptre, sovereign/sovereignty, sycophant/sycophantic, tribe/tribal, tyranny/tyrant/tyrannical, usurper/to usurp.

Zero value (0) indicates that instances were looked for but not found in the corpus. A dash indicates that the corpus was not scanned for a particular lemma. Abbreviations are taken from the Bank of English tag set: NN = singular noun, NNS = plural noun; VB = verb base form, VBD = past tense, VBG = -ING form, VBN = past participle, VBZ = 3rd person singular present; JJ = adjective; RB = adverb.

*percentage in lexical field (not reproduced)

Table A.7 Alternative metaphoric expressions in mergers and acquisitions corpus

Lemma	Lexeme	Total	Publication				Word class		
			BW	EC	FO	FT	Noun (50.77%*)	Verb (41.54%*)	Adjective/adverb (7.69%*)
DANCE	dance/dancer, to dance	4	1	1	2	0	3NN/0	1VBG	–
STEP	step, to step	4	1	0	2	1	3NN	1VBG	–
ROUND	round, to round	3	2	0	0	1	3NN	0	–
BEAT	beat	1	0	0	1	0	1NN	–	–
BOOGIE	boogie, to boogie	1	0	0	1	0	0	1VB	–
FOLLOW	to follow	1	0	0	0	1	–	1VBD	–
HARMONY	harmony, harmonize, harmonious	1	0	1	0	0	0	1VB	0
LEAD	lead, to lead	1	0	0	0	1	1NN	0	–
RUMBA	rumba, to rumba	1	0	0	1	0	0	1VB	–
SWING	swing, to swing	1	0	0	1	0	0	1VBG	–
SWIRL	swirl, to swirl	1	1	0	0	0	0	1VBG	–
TURN	turn, to turn	1	0	0	1	0	1NN	0	–
Totals		**20** 100%	**5** 25%	**2** 10%	**9** 45%	**4** 20%	**12** 60%	**8** 40%	**0** 0%

Notes: No relevant metaphoric occurrences of ball/ballroom, ballet, cheek-to-cheek, choreographer/choreography/to choreograph, circle/to circle/circular, figure, foxtrot/to foxtrot, pirouette/to pirouette, polka/to polka, promenade/to promenade, rhythm/rhythmic, rock('n'roll)/to rock, samba/to samba, spin/to spin, to sway, to swivel, synchronicity/synchronize/synchronous, tango/to tango, tempo, twirl/to twirl, twist/to twist, verve, waltz/to waltz.

Zero value (0) indicates that instances were looked for but not found in the corpus. A dash indicates that the corpus was not scanned for a particular lemma. Abbreviations are taken from the Bank of English tag set: NN = singular noun, NNS = plural noun, VB = verb base form, VBD = past tense, VBG = -ING form, VBN = past participle, VBZ = 3rd person singular present; JJ = adjective; RB = adverb.

*percentage in lexical field.

Notes

1 Introduction: masculinized metaphors

1. Proof of how deeply the notion of man-as-warrior is ingrained in patriarchal society is the fact that even the various groups that can be associated loosely under the umbrella term 'men's movement' (especially the so-called 'mythopoetics') criticize militarism but still embrace the warrior archetype to construct masculinity (Bly, 1991; Keen, 1991; Lorentzen, 1998).
2. In 1998, 11.1 per cent of all seats on US boards were held by women (Brancato and Patterson, 2001), with female CEOs accounting for less than 1 per cent (Lavelle, 2001). In the UK in 2001, 10 per cent of all board members of the FTSE 100 companies were female, with just one of those companies being headed by a woman managing director (Daily Telegraph, 2001).
3. However, Eubanks (2000) also notes that women, while using the WAR metaphor as much as men, tend to focus on its attenuated strategy rather than on its confrontation aspect (p. 163).

2 Theory: a critical cognitive framework for metaphor research

1. The example shows that it is not always the competition that is conceptualized as the enemy, but that prospects can also be the object of aggression (see section 4.2).
2. Inverted commas indicate that the example features as a quotation in the article it is taken from.
3. The input space of TAKEOVER is obviously the more complex one since it is itself constituted by a metaphor.
4. Halliday and Hasan (1985, p. 29) sub-divide the ideational into 'experiential meaning' and 'logical meaning'.
5. The objection of an unidentified 'spokesman' to the WAR metaphor ('Cyber Wars', 1996, para. 30) is not taken up at all by the other participants.
6. To break down the definition further, social practices are 'relatively stabilized form[s] of social activity' (Chiapello and Fairclough, 2002, p. 193).
7. The primary and secondary discourse of marketing merge in the hybrid genre of the advertorial.
8. Examples have been taken from the spoken part of the British National Corpus.
9. A somewhat different account of the socio-cultural function of metaphor is by Goatly (1997), who integrates Sperber and Wilson's (1986) relevance theory into CDA (in particular, Fairclough, 1989).
10. Such a purpose can, for example, be found in the example of *jail bait* provided by Turner and Fauconnier (1995, paras. 37–42). Used to denote an under-age girl whom an older man finds sexually attractive, this metaphoric

blend is achieved by drawing on particular social models highlighting particular features (ibid., para. 42). Thus, *jail bait* as a concept is constructed from a male perspective which presupposes an intention on part of the girl, thereby shifting the blame for sexual exploitation away from the perpetrator.

11. This view is similar to Kövecses' (2000, pp. 183–6) notion of 'body-based constructionism'. However, while Kövecses' focus is on the perceived physical constraints on cultural models, the argument is here reversed by stressing the socio-cultural influences on originally embodied concepts.

12. As the emphasis in this book is on how dynamic cognitive models such as metaphors interact with their socio-cultural environment in the form of discourse, metaphor is viewed not so much as a social schema but as, strictly speaking, a social representation (Moscovici, 2000).

13. An earlier formulation of this idea can be found in Richards (1936/2001): 'The processes of metaphor in language . . . are superimposed upon a perceived world that is itself a product of earlier or unwitting metaphor' (p. 73).

14. Clausewitz (1952, p. 178) regards the relationship between the fight and strategy aspects of war as one of sequence rather than blending when he traces the development of war from medieval fistfights to armed conflicts between states.

15. Although quite a few metaphoric expressions are triggered by the topic of the text in which they occur (for example, *Opel takes unusual marketing route* [MS FT 4], or *Cadbury-Schweppes has a nibble at some salty snacks* [MA FT 9]), those cases will not be dealt with in this context.

16. On a general note, Gramsci (2000) reasons that if

> every language contains the elements of a conception of the world and of a culture, [then] from anyone's language one can access . . . his conception of the world. (p. 326)

17. One form of such subordinated masculinities is, for example, represented by gay men. The fact that both non-hegemonic masculinities and femininity are subordinated in patriarchal societies betrays the structural link between homophobia and misogyny.

18. Private communication with Peter Döge (Institute for Application-orientated Innovation and Future Research, Berlin), 30 June 2000.

19. But see Augoustinos and Walker (1995, pp. 45–7) for a discussion of circumstances favouring data-driven categorization.

20. Note that 'cluster' here does not refer to Lakoff's (1987, pp. 74–6) use of the term as combining models with different degrees of prototypicality into one cluster model.

21. Seen as such, syncopation is blending theory's rephrasing of Lakoff and Johnson's (1980) highlighting and hiding function of metaphor, with part–whole compression closely resembling synechdoche.

22. The demand that CDA should incorporate the study of the cognitive determinants of discourse has not been met with universal approval. Chouliaraki and Fairclough (1999), albeit supporting the idea that 'social life [is] produced in thought' (p. 28), claim that, since cognitive phenomena cannot be studied directly, any account would necessarily be mediated. Yet, while

researchers should be aware of the fact that all research on cognitive models is represented in the form of new cognitive models – just as all writing on ideology is itself ideologically vested – this fact should not be taken to *preclude* any further research.

3 Method: quantitative and qualitative analyses of metaphor

1. This relatively high number can be traced back to the magazine's love of the MATING metaphor: A stunning 43.48 per cent of its occurrences appears in *The Economist* (see Tables A.4 and 5.2 on pp. 120 and 209).
2. This information was kindly provided by Heike Brodersen, International Sales, Fortune Europe.
3. Information on circulation and reader profile was kindly made available by Sarah Griffiths, Advertising FT newspaper, UK edition.
4. A short note on terminology seems helpful here: contrary to Crystal's use of the term *lemma* ('Lemma', 2003), the term is here employed to mean a head-word (for example, *prey*) that can be split up into several lexemes, including phrasal ones (for example, *prey, to prey [up]on*). These lexemes in turn comprise various word forms (for example, *preying, preys, preyed*) (see also Lipka, 1992, pp. 73–4).
5. Boundaries between active and inactive metaphoric expressions are very much blurred in any synchronic language system and, consequently, some inconsistencies have to be admitted. Thus the fields include *campaign, launch* and *target* but not *slogan*, which should diachronically be seen as being derived from the WAR metaphor as well: etymologically, the unit comprises the Gaelic *sluagh* 'army' and *ghairm* 'cry', denoting a war cry of the old Highland clans (Ammer, 1999, p. 225; Wilkinson, 1993, p. 44), with this military sense persisting until 1879 ('Slogan', 1999). As a technical term in marketing, it can be found seven times in the corpus.
6. Kittay's (1987, p. 9) concern whether 'metaphor can be given a computable realization' has occupied researchers into artificial intelligence (AI) for quite some time. An anthology covering recent developments in the by now quite substantial area of metaphor and AI is Barnden and Lee (2001). Interest in computational models of metaphor seems to be growing, constituting perhaps another indication of the shift towards a more natural science-orientated paradigm in metaphor research, as problematized in Chapter 2. Still, AI research should perhaps not forget totally about Lakoff's (1993) caveat that image schemas are by definition not amenable to algorithmic processes (p. 249), and Eubanks' (2000) additional reservation that rule-governed computational models cannot account for the social dimension of metaphor (p. 132). On a more practical note, despite the headway it has made, AI research has yet to produce and market any off-the-shelf software for metaphor researchers.
7. Data from the Bank of English sample, sub-corpus of media texts.
8. There is one marked instance of *shotgun marriage* in the Bank of English; however, this is itself an example of a metaphor from mergers and acquisitions discourse. The respective concordance line runs as follows: 'mind,

amongst them the idea of a "shotgun marriage" between companies if . . .'.
Note also that the marked metaphoric expression is hedged by means of
quotation marks.

4 Business media on marketing: metaphors of war, sports and games

1. While *launch* also has nautical collocations, corpus research has shown that its most frequent usage is with abstract nouns involving military plans (Stubbs, 2001, p. 307).
2. Bryson (1990, p. 174) identifies football as a key sport, in which 81 per cent of Australian males and 61 per cent of Australian women over 16 years of age declare themselves to be interested. Similarly, Messner (1992, p. 8) lists football, basketball and baseball as being among 'the U.S. "major sports"'.
3. Although of no synchronic relevance, it should still be noted that the term *match* is a first hint at the cognitive model relating romance and aggression (see Chapter 5). Having its origins in the Indo-European root **mag-*, 'to knead, to fit together', it later came to mean 'spouse' (compare the expression *a perfect match*). The notion of counterparts was subsequently transferred to the semantic domain of contest (Malszecki, 1995, p. 300).
4. While it could be argued that *shot, to shoot* is already a metaphor in a sports context, its inclusion in the ball game glossaries consulted (First Base Sports, 2001; Sydney Storm, 1998) suggests that it is lexicalized up to the point where it can be considered a technical – if not 'dead' – metaphor.
5. For the conceptual relations between war and chess, see also Ritchie (2003). In addition, Green (1982, p. 342) quotes chess champion Bobby Fisher characterizing his game as 'limited warfare'. Beyond that, chess not only provides a link between games and war but also between games and sports, as it is officially classified as a sports discipline.
6. Because of cross-classification of the lemmas *play, game, shoot, field* and *ball*, the number of tokens for the three domains totals 918, thus exceeding the number of 845 metaphoric expressions given in Tables A.1 and A.2 (see pp. 191 and 194).
7. It comes as no surprise that authors writing for the *Financial Times* should betray a very pronounced tendency to use highly conventionalized metaphoric expressions. Because of the particular conditions of high-pressure newspaper production, the three most frequent expressions account for a stunning 70 per cent of all metaphoric expressions searched for in that publication.
8. However, users of the metaphor seem to be aware of it being a metaphor, as evidenced by visual representations such as the one in Greene (2002), which consists of a collage showing a Microsoft top executive aiming at targets with a bow and arrow.
9. See Reardon (1985, p. 48) for the allegedly 'feminine' nature of guerrilla warfare.
10. Please note that the numbers in both lines and columns have been added, whereas percentages have been calculated across lines only. Because of cross-classifications of the lemmas *play, game, shoot, field* and *ball*, figures in Table

4.5 differ from those in Table A.2 in three cases: the total number of nominal metaphoric expressions, the total number of verbal metaphoric expressions and, consequently, the overall number of metaphoric expressions in the corpus.

11. This view is corroborated quantitatively by the BNC yielding 38 instances of the collocation *state of war* compared to 138 tokens of *to wage war*.

12. See Koller and Mautner (forthcoming) for a discussion of this 'loss in semiotic richness'.

13. This US flavour of the GAMES metaphor is corroborated by Köves' (2002) comparative study on metaphors for life among US and Hungarian informants. One possible explanation the author gives is the importance of card games in the quintessentially US Frontier experience.

14. The expression *red chip* for a Hong Kong state company is in fact an analogical extension of *blue chip*, which, of course, derives from casino terminology and denotes a big company guaranteeing crisis-proof investment. As a novel extension, *red chip* is more recognizable as a metaphoric expression than the rather entrenched *blue chip*.

15. The phenomenon that one metaphoric expression or scenario can unconsciously trigger another has elsewhere been dubbed 'parapraxis' (Cameron, 2002).

16. In doing so, the writer is in line with advocates of Relationship Marketing (Searls, 1997; Sheth and Parvatiyar, 2000).

17. The term *trenches* can, moreover, feature as a metaphoric expression in the realm of football, as observed by Howe (1988, pp. 95–6).

18. For evidence of the ORGANISM metaphor in the neighbouring field of economics, see Charteris-Black and Ennis, 2001. For its extension to COMPANIES ARE ORGANISMS, see Morgan (1997, pp. 33–71).

19. This instance of the MACHINE metaphor could well be motivated by the article being about a company producing loudspeakers. However, while the fact that both persons quoted are engineers may explain the creative metaphor extension, it does not weaken it.

20. In this context, another (indirect) conceptual link between the domains of war and sports is conveyed by Messner's (1992) empirical observation that male athletes tend 'to experience their own bodies as machines' (p. 151).

21. This view of the ambiguity of the GAMES metaphor is by no means universal. Hunt and Menon (1995), for example, rather understand it as

> emphasizing and promoting either sportsmanship or gamesmanship norms which have starkly different ethical frameworks. Sportsmanship emphasizes fairness and civility over victory and outcomes . . . In contrast, gamesmanship emphasizes victory through Machiavellian maneuvering.
> (pp. 87–8)

22. Eubanks refers in particular to Ries and Trout's (1986) *Marketing Warfare*. Similar works include Cohen, 1986; Durö and Sandström, 1988; Michaelson, 1987; and Rogers, 1987; as well as a related video series ('Great Marketing Wars', 1983), making for a 1980s fad in the field of marketing handbooks. For a critique of this kind of handbook, see Winsor (1996). By contrast, a defence of the WAR metaphor in marketing is Michaelson (1989). In any case,

the WAR metaphor in marketing discourse has obviously outlived both short-term fashion and critique.

23. The two schemata mesh in the term *arms race* (Chilton and Lakoff, 1995, pp. 48–50). For a feminist critique of the notion, see Strange (1989).

24. American football is a case in point, being masculinized to a degree where it functions as one of the 'flag carriers of hegemonic masculinity' (Bryson, 1990, p. 174). In his discussion on WAR and SPORTS metaphors in US political discourse, Howe (1988) similarly notes that football, in contrast to basketball or baseball, was traditionally played only by men, which may have contributed to its success as a metaphor in the comparably masculinized sphere of politics (p. 92). As very much the same holds true for the sphere of business, it should come as no surprise that it is the FOOTBALL metaphor that is spelt out so explicitly in the *Fortune* sample (FO, lines 13–14).

25. One of these links is constituted by the fact that stardom is not only granted to sports champions but was also extended to – mostly male – CEOs during the heady days of the Internet boom in the latter half of the 1990s.

26. While men may, of course, lack first-hand experience of war or even competitive sports, the two spheres continue to define masculinity and hence exert an influence on male identity construction (Bryson, 1990, p. 173). This is not to say, however, that men embrace WAR and SPORTS metaphors unanimously. For a male reader voicing criticism of metaphoric expressions of sport in the *Financial Times*, see Finney (1998).

27. This notion is strongly reminiscent of Habermas's (1981) concept of money and power substituting language (vol. 1, p. 458; vol. 2, p. 232).

28. Against the backdrop of finite game theory, Hunt and Menon (1995) rather see the GAMES metaphor as holding potential for notions of teamwork and co-operation.

5 Business media on mergers and acquisitions: metaphors of evolutionary struggle

1. Both *embattled* and *infatuated*, although formally past participles, count as adjectives, as they either have no infinitive form (*to infatuate) or are used in their (attributive) participle form in the overwhelming majority of cases (In the BoE, the exclusive word form of *embattled* is the participle, with 121 out of 122 tokens being attributive, whereas the BNC records one third-person-singular token as opposed to 114 participle tokens, 113 of which show attributive function).

2. The numbers in both lines and columns have been added, whereas percentages have been calculated across lines only.

3. A related case is the etymologically metaphoric expression *vagina*, a translation of the Latin word for *sheath* (Wilkinson, 1993, p. 39).

4. If company A (the *black knight*) threatens to take over company B against the will of the latter's board, a third company C may act as a *white knight* by agreeing to a friendly takeover with company B (that is, one involving the consent of B's board). (Hirsch, 1986, p. 830, offers a different definition of a *black knight*, namely company C making another hostile bid.) A *grey knight*, by contrast, is defined as

a second, unsolicited bidder in a corporate takeover who enters the scene in order to take advantage of any problems between the first bidder and the target company. (Investopedia, 1999–2002, n. par.)

Finally, a *yellow knight* denotes a company A trying to attempt a takeover of company B but ultimately finding itself in merger negotiations instead. Gendered fairy tale vocabulary is also represented by the term *sleeping beauty*, to denote a company that is a valuable takeover target but has not yet been approached.

5. Relevant metaphoric expressions deriving from *(to) follow* and *(to) lead* are restricted to the sense of 'physically following/leading in a dance'.

6. See also the MATRIMONY–ROYALTY/ARISTOCRACY–MILITARISM cluster that Pieper and Hughes (1997) identify in media discourse on M&A. Given the democratic history of the USA, it is an astonishing finding that the EMPIRE metaphor and its monarchic overtones are most popular with US publications. This phenomenon can probably best be accounted for by the fact that the EMPIRE metaphor lends an exotic flavour to US texts, and therefore functions as an attention-getter.

7. The authors there refer to ARGUMENT IS WAR. However, they later revised the notion of ARGUMENT IS DANCE as a completely novel metaphor, regarding it rather as an extension of the existing conceptual metaphor THINKING IS MOVING (Lakoff, 2002; Lakoff and Johnson, 1999, pp. 236–8).

8. This article (MA FT 44) accounts for no less than a third of the 91 occurrences of *target*. Again, it can be seen that conventionalized language is most prominent in the *Financial Times*, the one newspaper in the corpus: almost half of the 172 tokens this publication contributes are spread over the two most frequent types.

9. A related point concerns authors of popular management handbooks (for example, Michaelson, 1987; Rogers, 1987), who also refer to literal wars and historic military leaders to account for business practices. Paradoxically, as Köves (2002) has shown, the metaphor LIFE IS WAR is not used among members of the US army – after all, for them, life *is* war.

10. Of the 62 tokens of *hostile* in the present corpus, 16 collocate with *bid* and 6 with *takeover*. The respective numbers for the BoE are 38 and 23 out of 751.

11. An exception is the one occurrence of *nibble*, which, however, can be regarded as topic-triggered, appearing as it does in an article about Cadbury-Schweppes acquiring a snacks brand (MA FT 9).

12. In fact there is no pattern at all. The 24 *Business Week* articles with single-gender authorship (50 per cent each for women and men) yield 25 metaphoric expressions of mating. Of these, 60 per cent were produced by women and 40 per cent by men. This slight over-representation of women as users of the MATING metaphor is countered by the findings for *Fortune* magazine. Here, the 21 articles written by only men or only women (each again accounting for roughly 50 per cent) contain 12 relevant tokens, two-thirds of which can be traced back to male authors. Finally, the *Financial Times* sub-corpus includes 44 texts written either by only women (a quarter) or by only men (three-quarters). The texts show 13 metaphoric expressions of MATING, of which 23.08 per cent are contributed by women and 76.92 per

cent by men, thus representing a percentage proportionate to authorship figures.

13. On the metaphor MARKETS ARE FOOD, see also Searls Group (1999, para. 44).

14. The following people kindly shared their thoughts about, and evidence of, this sub-meaning of *sexy*: Esther Kim Choi elaborated on the term's semantic components, while Robin Turner provided late-1970s evidence from scientific and media discourse as well as discussing DESIRE as a source domain. Alan Wallington provided the above *Wall Street Journal* quote from the OED, and Kevin Wiliarty offered further evidence of the term in a mid-1980s academic setting as well as the quote on the hidden presence of the [+EROTIC] component (Koller, 2003).

15. Although the collocations *hostile bid* and *hostile takeover* function as technical terms in M&A discourse, they are not the only means of denoting an acquisition (attempt) without the approval of the target company's board of directors. The expression *unfriendly takeover/bid* may be less frequent than both *hostile takeover* and its antonym, *friendly takeover/bid*, yet it can be attested twice in the present corpus (MA EC 21, MA FT 54) and once in the BoE. (Numbers for *hostile takeover/bid* are 40 in the corpus at hand [see Tables A.4 and A.5 on pp. 209 and 212], 53 in the BoE and two in the BNC, while *friendly takeover/bid* features four times in the present corpus, but does not appear in either the BoE or the BNC.) Thus journalists may be constrained in their choice of terms, but not exclusively so.

16. For a tongue-in-cheek explanation of the literal roots of these terms, see *The Economist* (2000b).

17. An example of *predator* being more than just phonetically related to *prey* is the terms' co-occurrence in *the group turned from predator to prey* (MA FT 33).

18. Usage of this device by *The Economist* authors is not restricted to the sample at hand, as shown by the following quotation: 'Mergers, like marriages, can be legally defined and therefore readily counted. Alliances are more like love affairs' (MA EC 26).

19. The 'personal chemistry' between Citibank and Travelers CEOs John Reed and Sandi Weill that the writer refers to was also the topic of a *Business Week* cover story (Silverman and Spiro, 1999). A picture of the two men was placed next to the headline 'Is this marriage working?' on both the cover and inside the magazine (US edition). The article not only elaborates that 'Weill courted Reed' (1999, para. 24) but in a supplementary interview, Sandi Weill also uses the MATING metaphor several times, mentioning that he has 'no problem being a partner with John' (*Business Week*, 1999, para. 1) as well as talking about 'first [getting] married and [finding] what each other is about [*sic*]' (ibid., para. 9). The metaphor here highlights how homo-social settings can acquire homo-erotic overtones when the generally male CEOs come to stand metonymically for their companies.

20. Another way of inserting a component [+BRUTAL] into the EVOLUTIONARY STRUGGLE metaphor is focusing on and augmenting certain aspects of DOCTORING and GARDENING metaphors. Doing so yields metaphoric expressions such as *mergers . . . make it easier to cut fat and trim costs* (MA EC 15) or *bosses should swallow their pride and prune their empires* (MA EC 29), which are not so much about care and affection as aggression and violence, thus subtly supporting the FIGHTING metaphor.

21. The author's pejorative attitude towards mergers is in fact backed by figures. Among the ten biggest mergers in 2000, one brought about zero change in the newly created company's share price after twelve months, two recorded modest single-digit growth rates, and only one merger resulted in a share price increase of a quarter. On the other hand, the share price of the remaining six new companies had fallen by an average of 50.17 per cent one year after the merger (Dettmer *et al.*, 2002, p. 89).

22. Alternatively, the schema could also be seen as encompassing the other constituents of the model.

23. Because of globalized business activities, the boundaries between literal and metaphoric territories can sometimes be blurred; for example, if two CEOs, *having carved up Spain and Latin America between them . . . are now making the whole Continent their battleground* (MA BW 6), or if *investment banks have . . . turned Germany into the new battleground* (MA FT 41).

24. Apart from that, it is another example of the latent homo-eroticism present in homo-social settings (see n. 19).

25. For exceptions, see the *Fortune* sample and MA EC 29 ('the current merger madness [as] "the rush to find a partner . . . at a school dance after the big boys have picked the best ones"'). Hirsch and Andrews (1983, p. 154) furthermore define *hot pursuit* as 'a warfare image referring to an aggressive hostile acquirer', while the gloss they give for *pursuit* is 'a courtship image referring to a strenuous wooing'. Unfortunately, the authors again fail to provide any empirical evidence.

26. The relevant theoretical literature includes Cuomo, 1996; Elshtain and Tobias, 1990; Enloe, 1983; Goldstein, 2001; Hey *et al.*, 1999; Isaksson, 1988; Russell, 1989; Schmölzer, 1996; Skjelsbæk, 1997; Vickers, 1993. For a discussion of some central works, see Hedinger, 1999.

27. The German original runs as follows: 'Der Krieg der wirklichen Welt ist . . . kein solches Äußerstes, was seine *Spannung* in einer einzigen *Entladung löst*, sondern er ist das Wirken von Kräften, die . . . jetzt hinreichend *aufschwellen*, um den Widerstand zu überwinden, den die Trägheit und die Friktion ihr entgegenstellen, ein anderes Mal aber zu schwach sind, um eine Wirkung zu äußern; so ist er gewissermaßen ein *Pulsieren* der Gewaltsamkeit, mehr oder weniger heftig, folglich mehr oder weniger schnell die *Spannungen lösend* und die *Kräfte erschöpfend*; mit anderen Worten: mehr oder weniger schnell *ans Ziel führend*'.

28. See Emanatian's (1999) data on the Chagga language, and Wolf's (1996) study on metaphors for sex in rural areas in Malawi. See also Hiraga's (1991) study on metaphors for women in Japanese, and Maalej's (2001) data, in which the WOMAN IS FOOD metaphor is realized in 15 out of 17 languages and language varieties.

29. In this context, Hunt and Menon's (1995, p. 87) critique of the MARRIAGE metaphor in Relationship Marketing – that is, that its focus on monogamous couples is inappropriate for a network economy – could also be applied to M&A discourse. See MA EC 26 for the metaphoric use of *promiscuous*.

30. In the first half of 2002, the worldwide value of mergers collapsed to $633 billion, while the number of announced hostile takeovers stood at a record low of ten (Herden and Butollo, 2002, pp. 40–1).

6 Conclusion: gender-neutral metaphors

1. This is underscored by the fact that there are a total of eight occurrences of *peace, peaceful* in the two corpora taken together – two of which are negations – as opposed to a combined number of 54 tokens of *war*, a single instance of *truce* and none of either *armistice* or *ceasefire*. It seems as if there is tacit consent to avoid the model of peace altogether.
2. For *aggressive* as a positively evaluated term, see Mautner (2000).
3. For anecdotal evidence of combat fatigue in businessmen, see Gude-Hohensinner (2002), and Der Hovanesian and Conlin (2002).
4. A case in point is the expression 'Baby Bells' for the companies resulting from the 1984 split-up of AT&T for anti-trust reasons. A creative extension of that metaphor is the term 'Baby Bills', which came into being during the late 1990s anti-trust investigation involving Microsoft.
5. The metaphor GENERALS ARE SHEPHERDS must necessarily be all the more striking against the background of Christian iconography and its depiction of Jesus, conceptualized in Christian religion as the epitome of pacifism, as the good shepherd.

Bibliography

Abric, J.-C. (1984) 'A theoretical and experimental approach to the study of social representation', in R. M. Farr and S. Moscovici (eds), *Social Representations* (Cambridge University Press), pp. 169–83.

Akioye, A. A. (1994) 'The rhetorical construction of radical Africanism at the United Nations: Metaphoric cluster as strategy', *Discourse & Society*, vol. 5, no. 1, pp. 7–31.

'Aktionsart' (2002) *Lexikon der Sprachwissenschaft*, 3rd edn, Hadumod Bußmann (ed.) (Stuttgart: Kröner).

Althusser, L. (1970/1971) 'Ideology and ideological state apparatuses', *Lenin and Philosophy and Other Essays*, pt 2, trans. B. Brewster (New York: Monthly Review Press). Rpt in *From Marx to Mao*, D. J. Romagnolo (ed.). Available at: http://www.marx2mao.org/Other/LPOE70ii.html#s5. 2002. Accessed 11 August 2003.

Ammer, C. (1999) *Fighting Words: From War, Rebellion, and Other Combative Capers*, 2nd edn (Chicago: NTC Publishing).

'Aspect' (2003) *A Dictionary of Linguistics and Phonetics*, 5th edn, D. Crystal (ed.) (Malden, Mass.: Blackwell).

'Aspekt' (2002) *Lexikon der Sprachwissenschaft*, 3rd edn, Hadumod Bußmann (ed.) (Stuttgart: Kröner).

Augoustinos, M. and Walker, I. (1995) *Social Cognition: An Integrated Introduction* (London: Sage).

Austin, J. L. (1962/1999) *How to Do Things with Words* (Oxford University Press). Rpt in A. Jaworski and N. Coupland (eds), *The Discourse Reader* (London: Routledge), pp. 63–75.

Bakhtin, M. (1986) *Speech Genres and Other Late Essays*, C. Emerson and M. Holquist (eds), trans. V. W. McGee (Austin, Tx: University of Texas Press).

Ballroomdancers.com (1997) *Glossary of Ballroom Dancing Terms*. Available at: http://www.ballroomdancers.com/Learning_Center/Glossary/. Accessed 11 August 2003.

Barnden, J. A. and Lee, M. G. (eds) (2001) *Metaphor and Artificial Intelligence*, Special issue of *Metaphor and Symbol*, vol. 16, nos 1–2.

Bastien, D. T. (1989/2000) 'Communication, conflict, and learning in mergers and acquisitions', in A. H. Van de Ven, H. L. Angle and M. S. Poole (eds), *Research on the Management of Innovation: The Minnesota Studies* (New York: Harper & Row). Rpt Oxford University Press, 2000, pp. 367–96.

Beaugrande, R. de (1997) *New Foundations for a Science of Text and Discourse: Cognition, Communication, and the Freedom of Access to Knowledge and Society*. Advances in Discourse Processes, 61 (Norwood, NJ: Ablex).

Beigbeder, F. (2000) *99 Francs* (Paris: Grasset).

Beneke, J. (1988) 'Metaphorik in Fachtexten', in R. Artz (ed.), *Textlinguistik und Fachsprache: AILA-Symposion Hildesheim* (Hildesheim: Olms), pp. 197–213.

Bianco, A., Symonds, W. and Byrnes, N. (2002) 'The rise and fall of Dennis Koslowski', *Business Week*, 23 December, pp. 48–56.

Black, M. (1962) *Models and Metaphors: Studies in Language and Philosophy* (Ithaca, NY: Cornell University Press).

Black, M. (1977/1993) 'More about metaphor', *Dialectica*, vol. 31, nos 3–4, pp. 43–57. Rpt in A. Ortony (ed.) *Metaphor and Thought*, 2nd edn (Cambridge University Press), pp. 19–41.

Bly, R. (1991) *Iron John: A Book about Men* (Reading, Mass.: Addison-Wesley).

Boers, F. (1999) 'When a bodily source domain becomes prominent: the joy of counting metaphors in the socio-economic domain', in R. W. Gibbs and G. Steen (eds), *Metaphor in Cognitive Linguistics*, Current Issues in Linguistic Theory Series 175 (Amsterdam: Benjamins), pp. 47–56.

Boers, F. (2000) 'Enhancing metaphoric awareness in specialised reading', *English for Specific Purposes*, vol. 19, pp. 137–47.

Boudette, N. E. (2000) 'Amid a rash of corporate weddings, AOL Europe still plays the field', *Wall Street Journal Europe*, 8 February 2000, p. 4.

Bourdieu, P. (1991) *Language and Symbolic Power*, trans. G. Raymond and M. Adamson (Cambridge, Mass.: Harvard University Press).

Boyd, J. (1995) 'An Indiana utility defends against a hostile takeover: a case study in the rhetoric of war', Speech Communication Association Convention, San Antonio.

Brancato, C. K. and Patterson, D. J. (2001) 'Diversity in the boardroom?' Available at: http://www.managementfirst.com/articles/boardroom.htm. Accessed 22 January 2002.

Broussine, M. and Vince, R. (1996) 'Working with metaphor towards organisational change', in C. Oswick and D. Grant (eds), *Organisation Development: Metaphorical Explorations* (London: Pitman), pp. 57–72.

Browne, M. N. and Quinn, J. K. (1999) 'Dominant economic metaphors and the postmodern subversion of the subject', in M. Woodmannsee and M. Osteen (eds), *The New Economic Criticism* (London: Routledge), pp. 131–49.

Bryson, L. (1990) 'Challenges to male hegemony in sport', in M. A. Messner and D. F. Sabo (eds), *Sport, Men and the Gender Order: Critical Feminist Perspectives* (Champaign, Ill.: Human Kinetics Books), pp. 173–84.

'BT – brand as friend' (no date) Available at: http://ww.worldwide.bt.com/brand_as_friend. Accessed 27 May 2000.

Burke, W. W. (1992) 'Metaphors to consult by', *Group & Organization Management*, vol. 17, no. 3, pp. 255–9.

Business Week (1999) 'Weill: "I have no problem being a partner with John"', 7 June. Available at: http://www.businessweek.com/1999/99_23/b3632007.htm. Accessed 12 August 2003.

Business Week (2002a) 'BW Media Kit: Business Week International Europe edition'. Available at: http://mediakit.businessweek.com/m-intnl-eu.html. Accessed 14 November 2002.

Business Week (2002b) 'BW Media Kit: Circulation growth'. Available at: http://mediakit.businessweek.com/a-abcg.html. Accessed 14 November 2002.

Business Week (2002c) 'BW Media Kit: Our mission'. Available at: http://mediakit.businessweek.com/mkh-edall.html. Accessed 11 August 2003.

Business Women's Network (2002) 'Women and diversity WOW! Facts 2002'. Available at: http://ewowfacts.com/pdfs/chapters/29.pdf. Accessed 11 August 2003.

Cameron, L. (1999) 'Operationalising "metaphor" for applied linguistic research', in L. Cameron and G. Low (eds), *Researching and Applying Metaphor* (Cambridge University Press), pp. 3–28.

Cameron, L. (2002) 'Metaphor-led discourse analysis', Conference on Metaphor in Language and Thought, Pontifical Catholic University of São Paulo, São Paulo, 21–25 October.

Cameron, L. and Low, G. (1999) 'Metaphor', *Language Teaching*, vol. 32, pp. 77–96.

'Campaign' (1995a) *Collins Cobuild English Dictionary* (London: HarperCollins).

'Campaign' (1995b) *The Concise Oxford Dictionary*, 9th edn (Oxford: Clarendon Press).

'Campaign' (1995c) *Longman Dictionary of Contemporary English*, 3rd edn (Munich: Langenscheidt-Longman).

CBS (no date) *Auto Racing Glossary*. Available at: http://cbs.sportsline.com/u/ racing/auto/glossary/t_glossary.htm. Accessed 19 September 2002.

CBS (no date) *Horse Racing Glossary*. Available at: http://www.sportsline.com/ horseracing/index.html. Accessed 11 August 2003.

Chapkis, W. (1988) 'Sexuality and militarism', in E. Isaksson (ed.), *Women and the Military System* (New York: St. Martin's Press), pp. 106–13.

Charteris-Black, J. and Ennis, T. (2001) 'A comparative study of metaphor in Spanish and English financial reporting', *English for Specific Purposes*, vol. 20, pp. 249–66.

Chiapello, E. and Fairclough, N. (2002) 'Understanding the new management ideology: a transdisciplinary contribution from Critical Discourse Analysis and New Sociology of Capitalism', *Discourse & Society*, vol. 13, no. 2, pp. 185–208.

Chilton, P. (1987) 'Metaphor, euphemism and the militarization of language', *Current Research on Peace and Violence*, vol. 1, no. 1, pp. 7–19.

Chilton, P. and Ilyin, M. (1993) 'Metaphor in political discourse: the case of the "common European house"', *Discourse & Society*, vol. 4, no. 1, 7–31.

Chilton, P. and Lakoff, G. (1995) 'Foreign policy by metaphor', in C. Schäffner and A. L. Wenden (eds), *Language and Peace* (Aldershot: Dartmouth), pp. 37–59.

Chouliaraki, L. and Fairclough, N. (1999) *Discourse in Late Modernity* (Edinburgh: Edinburgh University Press).

Clausewitz, C. von (1952) *Vom Kriege* (First published 1832), Intro. W. Hahlweg, 16th edn (Bonn: Ferdinand Dümmler).

Clausner, T. and Croft, W. (1997) 'Productivity and schematicity in metaphors', *Cognitive Science*, vol. 21, no. 3, pp. 247–82.

Cleary, C. and Packard, T. (1992) 'The use of metaphors in organizational assessment and change', *Group & Organization Management*, vol. 17, no. 3, pp. 229–41.

Cohen, W. A. (1986) *Winning on the Marketing Front: The Corporate Manager's Game Plan* (New York: John Wiley).

Cohn, C. (1987) 'Sex and death in the rational world of defense intellectuals', *Signs*, vol. 12, no. 4, pp. 687–718. Rpt in D. E. H. Russell (ed.), *Exposing Nuclear Phallacies* (New York: Pergamon Press, 1989), pp. 127–59. Rpt as 'A feminist spy in the house of death: unravelling the language of strategic analysis', in E. Isaksson (ed.), *Women and the Military System* (New York: St. Martin's Press, 1988), pp. 288–317. Rpt as '"Clean bombs" and clean language', in J. B.

Elshtain and S. Tobias (eds), *Women, Militarism and War* (Savage, Md.: Rowman & Littlefield, 1990), pp. 33–55.

Cole, P. and Morgan, J. L. (1975) *Speech Acts.* Syntax and Semantics, vol. 3 (New York: Academic Press).

Connell, R. W. (1987) *Gender and Power: Society, the Person and Sexual Politics* (Stanford, Calif.: Stanford University Press).

Connell, R. W. (1995) *Masculinities* (Berkeley, Calif. and Los Angeles: University of California Press).

Connell, R. W. (1998) 'Masculinities and globalization', *Men and Masculinities*, vol. 1, no. 1, pp. 3–23.

Coulson, S. and Oakley, T. (2000) 'Blending basics', *Cognitive Linguistics*, vol. 11, no. 3–4, pp. 175–96.

'Courtship' (1995a) *Collins Cobuild English Dictionary* (London: HarperCollins).

'Courtship' (1995b) *The Concise Oxford Dictionary*, 9th edn (Oxford: Clarendon Press).

'Courtship' (1995c) *Longman Dictionary of Contemporary English*, 3rd edn (Munich: Langenscheidt-Longman).

Cox, R. W. (1993) 'Gramsci, hegemony and international relations: an essay in method', in S. Gill (ed.), *Gramsci, Historical Materialism and International Relations* (Cambridge University Press), pp. 49–66.

Cuomo, C. J. (1996) 'War is not just an event: reflections on the significance of everyday violence', *Hypatia*, vol. 11, no. 4, pp. 30–45.

'Cyber Wars' (1996) Transcript Available at: http://www.pbs.org/newshour/bb/cyberspace/july-dec96/net_wars_9-20.html, 20 September 1996. Accessed 11 August 2003.

Daily Telegraph (2001) 'Regiment of women on the march', 15 January. Available at: http://www.telegraph.co.uk/money/main.jhtml?xml=%2Fmoney%2F2001%2F01%2F15%2Fcbgirl15.xml. Accessed 12 August 2003.

Deignan, A. (1997) 'Metaphors of desire', in K. Harvey and C. Shalom (eds), *Language and Desire: Encoding Sex, Romance and Intimacy* (London: Routledge), pp. 21–42.

Deignan, A. (1999) 'Corpus-based research into metaphor', in L. Cameron and G. Low (eds), *Researching and Applying Metaphor* (Cambridge University Press), pp. 177–99.

Der Hovanesian, M. and Conlin, M. (2002) 'Wall Street's broken spirit', *Business Week*, 2 September, pp. 58–9.

Desmond, J. (1997) 'Marketing and the war machine', *Marketing Intelligence and Planning*, vol. 15, no. 7, pp. 338–51.

Dettmer, M., Fleischhauer, J., Jung, A. and Reiermann, C. (2002) 'Gier ohne Grenzen', *Der Spiegel*, vol. 28, pp. 84–99.

Duchesneau, D. (1997) 'Guerilla SQA', Tenth Intenational Software Quality Week, San Francisco, 27–30 May.

Durö, R. and Sandström, B. (1988) *The Basic Principles of Marketing Warfare* (Chichester: John Wiley).

Eco, U. (1994) *L'isola del giorno prima* (Milan: Bompiani).

Eco, U. (1995) *Gesammelte Streichholzbriefe*, trans. B. Kroeber (Munich: Deutscher Taschenbuch Verlag).

Economist, The (1997) 'The big one?', 31 March, p. 90.

Economist, The (1999) 'On a wing and a hotel room', 9 January, p. 64.

Economist, The (2000a) 'Shotgun courtship' 24 June, p. 105.

Economist, The (2000b) 'You beasts', 23 November, p. 12.

Economist, The (2001) 'Risky business', 14 September. Available at: http://www.economist.com/PrinterFriendly.cfm?story_ID=368245. Accessed 12 August 2003.

Economist, The (2002) 'Advertising information'. Available at: http://ads.economist.com. Accessed 11 August 2003.

Economist, The (2003) 'French twist?' 12 July, p. 58.

Economist, The (no date) 'About us: about *The Economist*'. Available at: http://www.economist.com/help/DisplayHelp.cfm?folder=663377#About_The _Economist. Accessed 11 August 2003.

Economist, The (no date) 'Style guide: metaphors'. Available at: http://www.economist.com/research/styleGuide/index.cfm?page=673913. Accessed 11 August 2003.

Einstürzende Neubauten, *Tabula Rasa*, trans. M. Partridge (Berlin: Mute, 1993).

Elman, J. L., Bades, E. A., Johnson, M. H., Karmiloff-Swith, A., Parisi, D. and Plunkett, K. (1996) *Rethinking Innateness: A Connectionist Perspective on Development* (Cambridge, Mass.: MIT Press).

Elshtain, J. B. and Tobias, S. (eds) (1990) *Women, Militarism and War* (Savage, Md.: Rowman & Littlefield).

Emanatian, M. (1999) 'Congruence by degree: on the relation between metaphor and cultural models', in R. W. Gibbs and G. Steen (eds) *Metaphor in Cognitive Linguistics*, Current Issues in Linguistic Theory Series, 175 (Amsterdam: Benjamins), pp. 205–18.

Emanatian, M. (2000) 'Metaphor clustering in discourse', Conceptual Structure, Discourse, and Language Conference, Santa Barbara, Calif., 13 May.

Emmanuel, F. (2000) *La question humaine* (Paris: Editions Stock).

Engberg, J. (2003) 'Von der Kultur hin zur Kompetenz – Überlegungen zu einer Neuorientierung in der Fachsprachenforschung', Linguistics Circle, Vienna University of Economics and Business Administration, Vienna, 13 January.

Enloe, C. (1983) *Does Khaki Become You? The Militarization of Women's Lives* (London: Pandora).

Eubanks, P. (2000) *A War of Words in the Discourse of Trade: The Rhetorical Constitution of Metaphor* (Carbondale, Ill.: Southern Illinois University Press).

Fairclough, N. (1989) *Language and Power* (London: Longman).

Fairclough, N. (1992) 'Discourse and text: linguistic and intertextual analysis within discourse analysis', *Discourse & Society*, vol. 3, no. 2, pp. 193–217. Rpt in A. Jaworski and N. Coupland (eds), *The Discourse Reader*. (London: Routledge, 1999), pp. 183–211.

Fairclough, N. (1995a) *Critical Discourse Analysis* (London: Longman).

Fairclough, N. (1995b) *Media Discourse* (London: Edward Arnold).

Fairclough, N. (1996) 'Technologisation of discourse', in C. R. Caldas-Coulthard and M. Coulthard (eds), *Texts and Practices: Readings in Critical Discourse Analysis* (London: Routledge), pp. 71–83.

Fauconnier, G. and Turner, M. (2002) *The Way We Think: Conceptual Blending and the Mind's Hidden Complexities* (New York: Basic Books).

Finney, D. (1998) Letter, *Financial Times*, 24 July. Available at: http://globalarchive.ft.com/search/articles.html?print=true&id=980724003025. Accessed 2 April 2001.

First Base Sports (2001) *Sports Glossaries*. Available at: http://www.firstbasesports. com/glossary.html. Accessed 12 August 2003.

Fiske, S. T. and Taylor S. E. (1991) *Social Cognition*, 2nd edn (New York: McGraw-Hill).

Fleischmann, S. (2001) 'Language and medicine', in D. Schiffrin, D. Tannen and H. E. Hamilton (eds), *The Handbook of Discourse Analysis* (Malden, Mass.: Blackwell), pp. 470–502.

Foucault, M. (1972) 'The discourse on language', trans. Rupert Sawyer, in M. Foucault, trans. A. M. Sheridan Smith, *The Archaeology of Knowledge and the Discourse on Language* (London: Tavistock), pp. 215–37.

Fowler, R. (1985) 'Power', in T. A. van Dijk (ed.) *Discourse Analysis in Society. Handbook of Discourse Analysis*, vol. 4 (London: Academic Press), pp. 61–82.

Fowler, R. (1987) 'Notes on critical linguistics', in R. Steele and T. Threadgold (eds), *Language Topics: Essays in Honour of Michael Halliday* (Amsterdam: Benjamins). Rpt as 'On Critical Linguistics', in C. R. Caldas-Coulthard and M. Coulthard (eds), *Texts and Practices: Readings in Critical Discourse Analysis* (London: Routledge, 1996), pp. 3–14.

'Gambling Glossary' (no date) Available at: http://www.winyourwager.com/ gambling_glossary.html. Accessed 12 August 2003.

Gibbs, R. W., Bogdanovich, J. M., Sykes, J. R. and Barr, D. J. (1997) 'Metaphor in idiom comprehension', *Journal of Memory and Language*, vol. 37, pp. 141–54.

Gibbs, R. W. and Steen, G. (2002) 'Finding metaphor in language and thought: metaphor in language as use', Conference on Metaphor in Language and Thought, Pontifical Catholic University of São Paulo, São Paulo, 21–25 October.

'Glutton' (1995) *Longman Dictionary of Contemporary English*, 3rd edn (Munich: Langenscheidt-Longman).

Goatly, A. (1997) *The Language of Metaphors* (London: Routledge).

Goldstein, J. S. (2001) *War and Gender* (Cambridge University Press).

Grady, J. (1997) 'Foundations of Meaning: Primary Metaphors and Primary Scenes', Dissertation, University of California at Berkeley.

Grady, J. E., Oakley, T. and Coulson, S. (1999) 'Blending and metaphor', in R. W. Gibbs and G. Steen (eds), *Metaphor in Cognitive Linguistics*, Current Issues in Linguistics Series, 175 (Amsterdam: Benjamins), pp. 101–24. Available at: http://www.wam.umd.edu/~mturn/WWW/blendaphor.html. Accessed 12 August 2003.

Gramsci, A. (2000) *The Gramsci Reader: Selected Writings 1916–1935*, ed. D. Forgacs, trans. Q. Hoare and G. Nowell-Smith (New York: New York University Press).

'Great Marketing Wars' (1983) 3 vols, Videocassette (Englewood Cliffs, NJ: Prentice-Hall Media).

Green, J. (comp.) (1982) *A Dictionary of Contemporary Quotations* (London: Pan).

Greene, J. (2002) 'Beyond the office', *Business Week*, 16 September, pp. 58–60.

Greenwald, J. and Moody, J. (1995) 'Hands across the cable', *Time Magazine*, 2 October, p. 34.

Gude-Hohensinner, H. (2002) 'Wenn das Ego Amok läuft', *Der Standard*, 12/13 October, p. K1.

Habermas, J. (1981) *Theorie des kommunikativen Handelns*, 2 vols (Frankfurt am Main: Suhrkamp).

Haddad, C. and Foust, D. (2002) 'WorldCom's sorry legacy', *Business Week*, 8 July, pp. 40–2.

Halliday, M. A. K. (1978) *Language as Social Semiotic: The Social Interpretation of Language and Meaning* (London: Edward Arnold).

Halliday, M. A. K. (1994) *An Introduction to Functional Grammar*, 2nd edn (London: Edward Arnold).

Halliday, M. A. K. and Hasan, R. (1985) *Language, Context, and Text: Aspects of Language in a Social Semiotic Perspective* (Geelong, Australia: Deakin University).

Hedinger, S. (1999) 'Sechs Frauen über Krieg und Frieden: Die Bedeutung von "gender" im Wandel', Dissertation, University of St Gallen.

Heilbrunn, J. (1989) 'Make love, not war', *Marketing News*, 30 January, pp. 4, 18.

Heiss, M. (1994) 'Die Organismusmetapher in der Managementwissenschaft', M.A. thesis, University of Innsbruck.

Henderson, W. (1994) 'Metaphor and economics', in R. E. Backhouse (ed.), *New Directions in Economic Methodology* (London: Routledge), pp. 343–67.

Henderson, W. (2000) 'Metaphor, economics and ESP: some comments', *English for Specific Purposes*, vol. 19, pp. 167–73.

Henry, D. (2002) 'Mergers: why most big deals don't pay off', *Business Week*, 14 October, pp. 72–7.

Herden, R. W. and Butollo, M. (2002) 'Proseminar mergers and acquisitions', Unpublished material, Vienna University of Economics and Business Administration, Vienna.

Herrera, H. and White, M. (2002) 'Business is war or the language of takeovers', in M. Fornés Guardia, J. M. Molina Valero and L. Pérez Hernández (eds), *Pragmática y Análisis del Discurso. Panorama Actual de la Lingüística Aplicada: Conocimiento, Procesamiento y Uso del Lenguaje*, vol. 1 (Rioja: Universidade de la Rioja), pp. 231–9.

Hey, B., Huber, C. and Schmidlechner, K., in co-operation with Koordinationsstelle für Frauenforschung und Frauenstudien (eds) (1999) *Krieg, Geschlecht und Gewalt*, Grazer Gender Studies Series, 5 (Graz: Leykam).

Hickok, R. (1999–2002) *Tennis Glossary*. Available at: http://www.hickoksports.com/glossary/gtennis.shtml. Accessed 12 August 2003.

Hines, C. (1999) 'Rebaking the pie: The WOMAN AS DESSERT metaphor', in M. Bucholtz, A. C. Liang and L. A. Sutton (eds), *Reinventing Identities: The Gendered Self in Discourse* (Oxford University Press), pp. 145–62.

Hiraga, M. (1991) 'Metaphors Japanese women live by', Working papers on Language, Gender and Sexism, vol. 1, AILA Commission on Language and Gender, pp. 38–57.

Hirsch, P. M. (1986) 'From ambushes to golden parachutes: corporate takeovers as an instance of cultural framing and institutional integration', *American Journal of Sociology*, vol. 91, no. 4, pp. 800–37.

Hirsch, P. M. and Andrews, J. A. Y. (1983) 'Ambushes, shootouts, and Knights of the Round Table: the language of corporate takeovers', in L. R. Pondy *et al.* (eds), *Organizational Symbolism*, Monographs in Organizational Behavior and Industrial Relations, 1 (Greenwich, Conn.: JAI Press), pp. 145–55.

Hodge, R. and Kress, G. (1993) *Language as Ideology*, 2nd edn (London: Routledge).

Hodge, R., Kress, G. and Jones, G. (1979) 'The ideology of middle management', in R. Fowler *et al.*, *Language and Control* (London: Routledge & Kegan Paul), pp. 81–93.

Howe, N. (1988) 'Metaphor in contemporary American political discourse', *Metaphor and Symbolic Activity*, vol. 3, no. 2, pp. 87–104.

Hunt, S. D. and Menon, A. (1995) 'Metaphors and competitive advantage: evaluating the use of metaphors in theories of competitive strategy', *Journal of Business Research*, vol. 33, pp. 81–90.

Investopedia (1999–2002) 'Dictionary'. Available at: http://www.investopedia.com/dictionary. Accessed 12 August 2003.

Isaksson, E. (ed.) (1988) *Women and the Military System* (New York: St. Martin's Press).

Jacobs, G. (1999) *Pre-formulating the News: An Analysis of the Metapragmatics of Press Releases*. (Amsterdam: John Benjamins).

Jäkel, O. (1997) *Metaphern in abstrakten Diskursdomänen*, Duisburg Papers on Research in Language and Culture Series, 30 (Frankfurt am Main: Peter Lang).

Jansen, S. C. and Sabo, D. F. (1994) 'The sport/war metaphor: hegemonic masculinity, the Persian Gulf War, and the New World Order', *Sociology of Sport Journal*, vol. 11, no. 1, pp. 1–17.

Johnson, C. (1999) 'Constructional grounding: the role of interpretational overlap in lexical and constructional acquisition', Dissertation, University of California at Berkeley.

Johnson, L. (2001) *Performing Penthesilea*, Unpublished manuscript, Director Marion Dimali, Theater Drachengasse, Vienna.

Johnson, S. (1997) 'Theorizing language and masculinity: a feminist perspective', in S. Johnson and U. H. Meinhof (eds), *Language and Masculinity* (Oxford: Basil Blackwell), pp. 8–26.

Jones, L. (1994) *A Glossary of Poker Terms*. Available at: http://www.conjelco.com/pokglossary.html. Accessed 12 August 2003.

Kanzen, J. (2000–2002) *Lotto Lottery Glossary*. Available at: http://www.ildado.com/lottery_glossary.html. Accessed 12 August 2003.

Karvy Consultants Stock Market Glossary (2003) 'Stag'. Available at: http://www.karvy.com/market/glosss.htm (no date). Accessed 12 August 2003.

Katschnig-Fasch, E. (1999) 'Zur Genese der Gewalt der Helden. Gedanken zur Wirksamkeit symbolischer Geschlechterkonstruktionen', in B. Hey, C. Huber and K. Schmidlechner, in co-operation with Koordinationsstelle für Frauenforschung und Frauenstudien (eds), *Krieg: Geschlecht und Gewalt*, Grazer Gender Studies, Series 5 (Graz: Leykam), pp. 64–77.

Katzenbach, J. R. and Santamaria, J. A. (1999) 'Firing up the front line', *Harvard Business Review*, May–June, pp. 106–17.

Keen, S. (1991) *Fire in the Belly: On Being a Man* (New York: Bantam).

Kidd, B. (1990) 'The men's cultural centre: sports and the dynamics of woman's oppression/men's repression', in M. A. Messner and D. F. Sabo (eds), *Sport, Men and the Gender Order: Critical Feminist Perspectives* (Champaign, Ill.: Human Kinetics Books), pp. 31–43.

Kilbane, M. (no date) 'Fighting the war of the millennium: strategies for year 2000 project managers'. Available at: http://www.year2000.com/archive/NFfighting.html. Accessed 12 August 2003.

Kittay, E. F. (1987) *Metaphor: Its Cognitive Force and Linguistic Structure* (Oxford: Clarendon Press).

Klein, P. (1993) 'IPALCO's bid for PSI fueling speculation', *Indianapolis Star*, 17 March, p. A01.

Koller, V. (2003) 'Summary: "sexy"', E-mail to the CogLing mailing list, 3 February 2003. Available at: http://listserv.linguistlist.org/cgi-bin/wa?A2= ind0302&L=cogling&P=R227. Accessed 11 September 2003.

Koller, V. (2004) 'Businesswomen and war metaphors: "Possessive, jealous and pugnacious"?', *Journal of Sociolinguistics*, vol. 8, no. 1, pp. 3–23.

Koller, V. (Forthcoming) 'Brothers in arms: contradictory metaphoric constructions in contemporary marketing discourse', in M. S. Zanotto, L. Cameron and M. Cavalcanti (eds), *Metaphor in Applied Linguistics: Research Perspectives* (Amsterdam: Benjamins).

Koller, V. and Mautner, G. (2004) 'Computer applications in Critical Discourse Analysis', in C. Coffin, A. Hewings and K. O'Halloran (eds), *Applying English Grammar* (Milton Keynes: Open University), pp. 216–28.

Kövecses, Z. (1986) *Metaphors of Anger, Pride, and Love: A Lexical Approach to the Structure of Concepts* (Amsterdam: John Benjamins).

Kövecses, Z. (2000) *Metaphor and Emotion: Language, Culture, and Body in Human Feeling* (Cambridge University Press).

Kövecses, Z. (2002) *Metaphor: A Practical Introduction* (Oxford University Press).

Köves, N. (2002) 'Metaphors of life in the US, Hungary and the US army', First Viennese Metaphor and Cognitive Linguistics Workshop, Vienna University/Vienna University of Economics and Business Administration, Vienna, 10–11 December.

Krantz, M. (1996) 'A marriage is blessed', *Time Magazine*, 29 July, p. 62.

Kraus, K. (1926/1964) *Die letzten Tage der Menschheit*, 2 vols (Munich: Deutscher Taschenbuch Verlag).

Kress, G. (1985) 'Ideological structures in discourse', in T. A. van Dijk (ed.), *Discourse Analysis in Society*, Handbook of Discourse Analysis, vol. 2 (London: Academic Press), pp. 27–42.

Kress, G. (1989) *Linguistic Processes in Sociocultural Practice*, 2nd edn (Oxford University Press).

Küster, R. (1978) *Militärmetaphorik im Zeitungskommentar*, Göppinger Arbeiten zur Germanistik, 246 (Göppingen: Kümmerle).

Kunda, Z. (1999) *Social Cognition: Making Sense of People* (Cambridge, Mass.: MIT Press).

Kyratzis, S. (1997) 'Metaphorically speaking: sex, politics and the Greeks', Dissertation, Lancaster University.

Lakoff, G. (1987) *Women, Fire, and Dangerous Things: What Categories Reveal about the Mind* (Chicago: University of Chicago Press).

Lakoff, G. (1992) 'Metaphor and war: the metaphor system used to justify war in the Gulf', in M. Pütz (ed.), *Thirty Years of Linguistic Evolution: Studies in Honour of René Dirven on the Occasion of his Sixtieth Birthday* (Amsterdam: Benjamins), pp. 463–81.

Lakoff, G. (1993) 'The contemporary theory of metaphor', in A. Ortony (ed.), *Metaphor and Thought*, 2nd edn (Cambridge University Press), pp. 202–51. Available at: http://www.ac.wwu.edu/~market/semiotic/lkof_met.html. Accessed 12 August 2003.

Lakoff, G. (1994) *Conceptual Metaphor Homepage*, Linguistics Dept, University of California at Berkeley. Available at: http://cogsci.berkeley.edu. Accessed 12 August 2003.

Lakoff, G. (2002) 'Schematicity of metaphor', E-mail to the CogLing mailing list, 24 November. Available at: http://listserv.linguistlist.org/cgi-bin/wa?A2=ind0211&L=cogling&D=1&F=&S=&P=7395. Accessed 12 August 2003.

Lakoff, G. and Johnson, M. (1980) *Metaphors We Live By* (Chicago: University of Chicago Press).

Lakoff, G. and Johnson, M. (1999) *Philosophy in the Flesh: The Embodied Mind and Its Challenge to Western Thought* (New York: Basic Books).

Lakoff, G. and Kövecses, Z. (1983) *The Cognitive Model of Anger Inherent in American English*, Berkeley Cognitive Science Report, 10, Berkeley Cognitive Science Program, Institute of Cognitive Studies, University of California at Berkeley.

Lakoff, G. and Turner, M. (1989) *More than Cool Reason* (Chicago: University of Chicago Press).

Larsen, P. T. (2003) 'MGM withdraws bid for Vivendi assets', *Financial Times*, 29 July. Available at: http://search.ft.com/search/article.html?id=030729006203. Accessed 16 September 2003.

'Launch' (1995) *Longman Dictionary of Contemporary English*, 3rd edn (Munich: Langenscheidt-Longman).

Lavelle, L. (2001) 'For female CEOs, it's stingy at the top', *Business Week*, 23 April. Available at: http://www.businessweek.com/magazine/content/01_17/b372916.htm. Accessed 10 February 2003.

'Lemma' (2003) *A Dictionary of Linguistics and Phonetics*. D. Crystal (ed.), 5th edn (Malden, Mass.: Blackwell).

Lipka, L. (1992) *An Outline of English Lexicology*, Forschung & Studium Anglistik, 3 (Tübingen: Max Niemeyer).

Lorentzen, J. (1998) Review of *The Politics of Manhood: Profeminist Men Respond to the Mythopoetic Men's Movement*, M. Kimmel (ed.), *Men and Masculinities*, vol. 1, no. 1, pp. 112–15.

Lotter, W. (2000) 'Elefanten im Galopp', *brand eins*, November, pp. 83–9.

Low, G. (1988) 'On teaching metaphor', *Applied Linguistics*, vol. 9, no. 2, pp. 125–47.

Low, G. (1999) 'Validating metaphor research projects', in L. Cameron and G. Low (eds), *Researching and Applying Metaphor* (Cambridge University Press), pp. 48–65.

Maalej, Z. (2001) 'Of animals, foods, objects, plants and others, or, how women are conceptualised and evaluated: a cross-cultural perspective', Conference on Researching and Applying Metaphor IV, University of Manouba, Tunis, 5–7 April.

Malszecki, G. M. (1995) ' "He shoots! He scores!": metaphors of war in sport and the political linguistics of virility', Dissertation, York University, North York, Ontario.

Mautner, G. (2000) 'Market-driven education: the discourse of mission statements and deans' messages on business schools' Internet web pages', British Association for Applied Linguistics Annual Meeting, Cambridge University, Cambridge, 8 September.

McNeilly, M. R. (1996) *Sun Tzu and the Art of Business: Six Strategic Principles for Managers* (Oxford University Press).

Merry, S. (2000) Letter, *The Economist*, 24 June, p. 4.

Messner, M. A. (1992) *Power at Play: Sports and the Problem of Masculinity* (Boston, Mass.: Beacon Press).

Michaelson, G. A. (1987) *Winning the Marketing War: A Field Manual for Business Leaders* (Lanham, Md.: Abt Books).

Michaelson, G. A. (1989) 'It's not "anything goes" in warfare – or in marketing', *Marketing News*, vol. 23, no. 7, pp. 4, 10.

Montgomery, M., Tolson, A. and Garton, G. (1989) 'Media discourse in the 1987 general election: ideology, scripts and metaphors', *English Language Research*, vol. 3, pp. 173–204.

'Mood' (2003) *A Dictionary of Linguistics and Phonetics*, D. Crystal (ed.), 5th edn (Malden, Mass.: Blackwell).

Morgan, G. (1997) *Images of Organization*, 2nd edn (Thousand Oaks, Calif.: Sage).

Morgan, P. and Bales, S. (2002) 'Competition, cooperation, and connection: how these metaphors affect child advocacy', *Kids Count E-Zine*, vol. 11. Available at: http://www.frameworksinstitute.org/products/issue11framing.shtml. Accessed 12 August 2003.

Moscovici, S. (2000) *Social Representations: Explorations in Social Psychology* (Cambridge: Polity Press).

Narayanan, S. (1997) 'Embodiment in language understanding: sensory-motor representations for metaphoric reasoning about event descriptions', Dissertation, University of California at Berkeley.

Nelson, J. A. (1995) 'Gender, metaphor and the definition of economics', *Economics and Philosophy*, vol. 8, pp. 103–25. Rpt in J. Humphries (ed.), *Gender and Economics*, International Library of Critical Writings in Economics, Series 45 (Aldershot: Edward Elgar), pp. 19–41.

Opitz, C. (1992) 'Von Frauen im Krieg zum Krieg gegen Frauen', *L'Homme*, vol. 3, no. 1, pp. 31–45.

Park, A. and Burrows, P. (2001) 'Dell, the conqueror', *Business Week*, 24 September. Available at: http://www.businessweek.com/@@SfuB34YQSOZxkwcA/magazine/content/01_39/b3750039.htm. Accessed 12 August 2003.

Perez, L. (1997) '21 ways to wage war: how to achieve decisive victories in sales and marketing'. Available at: http://home.earthlink.net/~humdev/21ways.htm. Accessed 12 August 2003.

Perpinan, M. S. (1990) 'The militarization of societies and it's [sic] impact on women', International Peace Research Association 25th Anniversary Conference, Groningen.

Pieper, C. and Hughes, K. (1997) 'Media on media: the framing of the Time-Warner/Turner–CNN merger'. Available at: http://www.americanreview.net/medstud1.htm. Accessed 15 September 2000.

Pietilä, H. (1990) 'Patriarchy is a state of war', International Peace Research Association 25th Anniversary Conference, Groningen.

Potter, J. and Wetherell, M. (1987) *Discourse and Social Psychology: Beyond Attitudes and Behaviour* (London: Sage).

Prince, V. and Ferrari, S. (1996) 'A textual clues approach for generating metaphors as explanations by an intelligent tutoring system', in S. Botley *et al.* (eds), *Proceedings of Teaching and Language Corpora 1996* (Lancaster: University Centre for Computer Corpus Research on Language), pp. 217–32.

Quinn, N. (1991) 'The cultural basis of metaphor', in J. W. Fernandez (ed.), *Beyond Metaphor: The Theory of Tropes in Anthropology* (Stanford, Calif.: Stanford University Press), pp. 56–93.

Raghavan, V. V. (1990) 'An approach to competitive modelling using the military metaphor and comprehensive situation mapping', Dissertation, Kent State University.

Read, S. J., Cesa, I. L., Jones, D. K. and Collins, N. L. (1990) 'When is the Federal budget like a baby? Metaphor in political rhetoric', *Metaphor and Symbolic Activity*, vol. 5, no. 3, pp. 125–49.

Reardon, B. A. (1985/1996) *Sexism and the War System* (New York: Teachers College Press). Rpt Syracuse: Syracuse University Press.

Richards, I. A. (1936/2001) *The Philosophy of Rhetoric*, in J. Constable (ed.) (London: Routledge).

Ries, A. and Trout, J. (1986) *Marketing Warfare* (New York: Penguin).

Ritchie, D. (2003) ' "ARGUMENT IS WAR" – or is it a game of chess? Multiple meanings in the analysis of implicit metaphors', *Metaphor and Symbol*, vol. 18, no. 2, pp. 125–46.

Robson, W. (1996) 'Changing the name of the game: how changing the metaphor for business could alter IS management priorities', UK AIS Conference on the Future for Information Systems, Cranfield, 10–12 April.

Rogers, D. J. (1987) *Waging Business Warfare* (New York: Zebra).

Rorty, R. (1979) *Philosophy and the Mirror of Nature* (Princeton, NJ: Princeton University Press).

Rosch, E. (1975) 'Cognitive representations of semantic categories', *Journal of Experimental Psychology*, vol. 104, pp. 192–233.

Rosch, E. (1978) 'Principles of categorization', in E. Rosch and B. Lloyd (eds), *Cognition and Categorization* (Hillsdale, NJ: Lawrence Erlbaum), pp. 27–48.

Rosenbush, S. (2003) 'Verizon's gutsy bet', *Business Week*, 4 August. Available at: http://www.businessweek.com/@@QbDm*oQQx7NxkwcA/magazine/content/03_31/b3844001_mz001.htm. Accessed 16 September 2003.

Rumpf, M. (1992) 'Staatliches Gewaltmonopol, nationale Souveränität und Krieg', *L'Homme*, vol. 3, no. 1, pp. 7–30.

Russell, D. E. H. (ed.) (1989) *Exposing Nuclear Phallacies* (New York: Pergamon).

Sabo, D. F. and Jansen, S. C. (1998) 'Prometheus unbound: constructions of masculinity in the sports media', in L. A. Wenner (ed.), *Media Sport* (London: Routledge), pp. 202–17.

Saylor, J. H. (1992) *TQM Field Manual* (New York: McGraw-Hill).

Schmölzer, H. (1996) *Der Krieg ist männlich. Ist der Friede weiblich?* (Vienna: Verlag für Gesellschaftskritik).

Schott, R. M. (1996) 'Gender and "postmodern war" ', *Hypatia*, vol. 11, no. 4, pp. 19–29.

Searle, J. R. (1979/1983) 'Metaphor', in A. Ortony (ed.), *Metaphor and Thought*, 2nd edn (Cambridge University Press), pp. 83–111.

Searls, D. (1997) 'Make money, not war'. Available at: http://www.searls.com/metaphor1.html. Accessed 12 August 2003.

Searls, D. and Weinberger, D. (2000) 'Markets are conversations', in R. Levine *et al.*, *The Cluetrain Manifesto: The End of Business as Usual* (London: ft.com), pp. 73–111.

Searls Group (1999) 'What we think'. Available at: http://www.searls.com/tsg/think.html. Accessed 12 August 2003.

Seidel, J. (1991) 'Method and madness in the application of computer technology to qualitative data analysis', in N. Fielding and R. M. Lee (eds), *Using Computers in Qualitative Research* (London: Sage), pp. 107–16.

Sheth, J. N. and Parvatiyar, A. (eds) (2000) *Handbook of Relationship Marketing* (Beverly Hills, Calif.: Sage).

Silverman, D. (1993) *Interpreting Qualitative Data* (London: Sage).

Silverman, G. and Spiro, L. N. (1999) 'Is this marriage working?', *Business Week*, 7 June. Available at: http://www.businessweek.com/1999/99_23/b3632001.htm. Accessed 12 August 2003.

Skjelsbæk, I. (1997) *Gendered Battlefields: A Gender Analysis of Peace and Conflict*, International Peace Research Institute Oslo, Report 6. Available at: www.prio.no/publications/reports/battlefields/battlefields.asp. Accessed 12 August 2003.

Sloan, A. (1995) 'Big boys with their bigger toys', *Newsweek*, 11 September, p. 35.

'Slogan' (1999) *Oxford English Dictionary*, CD-ROM (Oxford University Press).

Smith, D. C. (1997) 'De-militarizing language'. Available at: http://www.peacemagazine.org/9707/language.htm. Accessed 31 May 2000.

Sommer, E. and Weiss, D. (1996) *Metaphors Dictionary* (Detroit, Mich.: Visible Ink Press).

Sperber, D. and Wilson, D. (1986) *Relevance: Communication and Cognition* (Cambridge University Press).

Sprung, A. (2002) Letter, *Business Week*, 18 November. p. 10.

Steen, G. (1999) 'Metaphor and discourse: towards a linguistic checklist for metaphor analysis', in L. Cameron and G. Low (eds), *Researching and Applying Metaphor* (Cambridge University Press), pp. 81–104.

Stires, D. (2003) 'Ready to get swallowed', *Fortune*, 21 July. Available at: http://www.fortune.com/fortune/investing/articles/0,15114,463009,00.html. Accessed 16 September 2003.

Strange, P. (1989) 'It'll make a man of you: a feminist view of the arms race', in D. E. H. Russell (ed.), *Exposing Nuclear Phallacies* (New York: Pergamon Press), pp. 104–26.

Stubbs, M. (2001) 'Computer-assisted text and corpus analysis: lexical cohesion and communicative competence', in D. Schiffrin, D. Tannen and H. E. Hamilton (eds), *The Handbook of Discourse Analysis* (Malden, Mass.: Blackwell), pp. 304–20.

Sun Tzu (1910) *The Art of War*, trans. L. Giles, 1910. Available at: http://www.kimsoft.com/polwar02.htm. Accessed 12 August 2003.

Sydney Storm (1998) *Baseball Glossary*. Available at: http://www.storm.aapt.com.au/glossary.htm. Accessed 12 August 2003.

Talmy, L. (1988) 'Force dynamics in language and cognition', *Cognitive Science*, vol. 12, pp. 49–100.

Tannen, D. (1994) *Talking from 9 to 5* (London: Virago).

'Target' (1995) *Collins Cobuild English Dictionary* (London: HarperCollins).

Time Inc. *Fortune®* (1998) *Fortune Subscriber Portrait 1997* (Time Inc.).

Turner, M. and Fauconnier, G. (1995) 'Conceptual integration and formal expression', *Metaphor and Symbolic Activity*, vol. 10, no. 3, pp. 183–203. Available at: http://philosophy.uoregon.edu/metaphor/turner.htm. Accessed 12 August 2003.

US Department of Defense (1988) *Dictionary of Military Terms* (New York: Arco). Available at: http://www.dtic.mil/doctrine/jel/doddict/. Accessed 12 August 2003.

van Dijk, T. A. (1985) 'Introduction: levels and dimensions of Discourse Analysis', in T. A. van Dijk (ed.), *Dimensions of Discourse, Handbook of Discourse Analysis*, vol. 2 (London: Academic Press), pp. 1–11.

van Dijk, T. A. (1993) 'Principles of critical discourse analysis', *Discourse & Society*, vol. 4, no. 2, pp. 249–83.

van Dijk, T. A. (1995) 'Discourse analysis as ideology analysis', in C. Schäffner and A. L. Wenden (eds), *Language and Peace* (Aldershot: Dartmouth), pp. 17–33.

van Dijk, T. A. (1996) 'Discourse, power and access', in C. R. Caldas-Coulthard and M. Coulthard (eds), *Texts and Practices: Readings in Critical Discourse Analysis* (London: Routledge), pp. 84–104.

van Dijk, T. A. (1997) 'Discourse as interaction in society', *Discourse as Social Interaction, Discourse Studies*, vol. 2 (London: Sage), pp. 1–37.

van Dijk, T. A. (1998) 'Opinions and ideologies in the press', in A. Bell and P. Garrett (eds), *Approaches to Media Discourse* (Oxford: Blackwell), pp. 21–63.

van Dijk, T. A. (2001) 'Critical Discourse Analysis', in D. Schiffrin, D. Tannen and H. E. Hamilton (eds), *The Handbook of Discourse Analysis* (Malden, Mass.: Blackwell), pp. 352–71.

Vickers, J. (1993) *Women and War* (London: Zed Books).

Walters-York, L. M. (1996) 'Metaphor in accounting discourse', *Accounting, Auditing & Accountability Journal*, vol. 9, no. 5, pp. 45–70.

White, M. (1997) 'The use of metaphor in reporting financial market transactions', in A. Barcelona (ed.), *Cognitive Linguistics in the Study of English Language and Literature in English*, Cuadernos de Filología Inglesa, vol. 6, no. 2 (Murcia: Servicio de Publicaciones, Universidad de Murcia), pp. 233–45.

White, M. (1998) 'A cognitive linguistic view of the use of metaphor in headlines, leads and new stories', in A. D. Rothwell, A. J. Moya Guijarro and J. I. A. Hernández (eds), *Patterns in Discourse and Text* (Cuenca: Ediciones de la Universidad de Castilla-La Mancha), pp. 31–61.

White, M. and H. Herrera (2003) 'Metaphor and ideology in the press coverage of telecom corporate consolidations', in R. Dirven, R. Frank and M. Pütz (eds), *Cognitive Models in Language and Thought: Ideology, Metaphors and Meanings* (Berlin: Mouton de Gruyter), pp. 277–323.

Whitehead, S. M. (2003) *Men and Masculinities* (Cambridge: Polity Press).

Wilkinson, P. R. (1993) *Thesaurus of Traditional English Metaphors* (London: Routledge).

Wilson, F. (1992) 'Language, technology, gender, and power', *Human Relations*, vol. 45, no. 9, pp. 883–904.

Winsor, R. D. (1996) 'Military perspectives of organizations', *Journal of Organizational Change Management*, vol. 9, no. 4, pp. 34–42.

Wolf, A. (1996) 'Essensmetaphern im Kontext von Aids und Hexerei in Malawi', in A. Wolf and M. Stürzer (eds), *Die gesellschaftliche Konstruktion von Befindlichkeit: Ein Sammelband zur Medizinethnologie* (Berlin: Verlag für Wissenschaft und Bildung), pp. 205–21.

Wörsching, M. (1999) 'Metaphors of hegemonic masculinity – an analysis of sport and advertising in the German news magazine *Der Spiegel*, *Journal of European Area Studies*, vol. 7, no. 2, pp. 177–95.

Index

Entries in SMALL CAPITALS indicate conceptual metaphors, while page numbers in **bold** type refer to a central occurrence of the entry.

243